Śrī Rāya Rāmānanda Saṁvāda

The Conversation between
Śrī Caitanya Mahāprabhu & Śrī Rāmānanda Rāya

BOOKS BY ŚRĪ ŚRĪMAD BHAKTIVEDĀNTA NĀRĀYAṆA GOSVĀMĪ MAHĀRĀJA

Arcana-dīpikā
Beyond Nīrvāṇa
Śrī Bhakti-rasāmṛta-sindhu-bindu
Śrī Bhajana-rahasya
Bhakti-rasāyana
Bhakti-tattva-viveka
Śrī Brahma-saṁhitā
Controlled by Love
Dāmodara-līlā-mādhurī
The Essence of Bhagavad-gītā
Five Essential Essays
Going Beyond Vaikuṇṭha
Guru-devatātmā
Happiness in a Fools's Paradise
Jaiva-dharma
Śrī Manaḥ-śikṣā
Pinnacle of Devotion
Rāga-vartma-candrikā
Śrī Prabandhāvalī
Secret Truths of the Bhāgavatam
Secrets of the Undiscovered Self
Śiva-tattva
Śrī Camatkāra-candrikā
Śrī Dāmodarāṣṭakam
Śrī Gauḍīya Gīti-guccha
Śrī Gīta-govinda
Śrī Gopī-gīta
Śrī Harināma Mahā-mantra
Śrī Navadvīpa-dhāma
Śrī Prema-sampuṭa
Śrī Saṅkalpa-kalpadrumaḥ
Śrī Śikṣāṣṭaka
Śrī Upadeśāmṛta
Śrī Vraja-maṇḍala Parikramā
Śrīla Bhakti Prajñāna Keśava Gosvāmī – His Life and Teachings
Śrīmad Bhagavad-gītā
The Butter Thief
The Essence of All Advice
The Nectar of Govinda-līlā
The Origin of Ratha-yātrā
The Way of Love
Letters From America
My Śikṣā-guru and Priya-bandhu
Veṇu-gīta
Rays of The Harmonist (periodical)

For further information, free downloads of all titles,
world tour lectures, and more, please visit:

www.purebhakti.com

ISBN 978-1-935428-16-9
First printing: 2,000 copies

Printed at:- Samrat offset Pvt. Ltd.

śrī śrī guru-gaurāṅga jayataḥ

Śrī Rāya Rāmānanda Saṁvāda

The Conversation between
Śrī Caitanya Mahāprabhu & Śrī Rāmānanda Rāya

Chapter Eight of
Śrī Caitanya-caritāmṛta, Madhya-līlā
by
ŚRĪLA KṚṢṆADĀSA KAVIRĀJA GOSVĀMĪ

Commentary by
ŚRĪ ŚRĪMAD
BHAKTIVEDĀNTA NĀRĀYAṆA GOSVĀMĪ MAHĀRĀJA

VRINDAVAN, UTTAR PRADESH, INDIA

Dedicated to my Holy Master

śrī gauḍīya-vedānta-ācārya-kesarī nitya-līlā-praviṣṭa
oṁ viṣṇupāda aṣṭottara-śata śrī

Śrīmad Bhakti Prajñāna
Keśava Gosvāmī Mahārāja

the best amongst the tenth generation
of descendants in the bhāgavata-paramparā
from Śrī Kṛṣṇa Caitanya Mahāprabhu,
and the founder of the Śrī Gauḍīya Vedānta Samiti
and its branches throughout the world.

Acknowledgements

Translation:
Śrīpada B. V. Dāmodara Mahārāja

Fidelity and Sanskrit check:
Śrīpada B. V. Viṣṇu-daivata Mahārāja

Editors:
Vicitri dāsī, Prabhā dāsī

Assistant editor:
Vaijayantī-mālā dāsī

Proofreaders:
Jānakī dāsī, Śānti dāsī, Sulatā dāsī, and Śyāmarāṇī dāsī

Translation assistance:
Śrīpada B. V. Mādhava Mahārāja, Śrīpada B. V. Tīrtha Mahārāja,
Śyāmasundara Brahmacārī, Viṣṇu dāsa, Dhīra-kṛṣṇa dāsa,
Rāmacandra dāsa, and Vraja-sundarī dāsī

Layout & Design:
Kṛṣṇa-karuṇya dāsa

Front cover drawing:
Vāsudeva dāsa

Contents

Introduction

[to the first Hindi edition]

It is a matter of great joy that today, by the causeless mercy and inspiration of my most revered spiritual master, *oṁ viṣṇupāda aṣṭottara-śata śrī* Śrīmad Bhakti Prajñāna Keśava Gosvāmī Mahārāja, this commentary known as *Sajjana-toṣaṇī* on *Śrī Rāya Rāmānanda Saṁvāda* is being presented as a separate book for the faithful readers.

Śrī Rāya Rāmānanda Saṁvāda (the conversation between Śrī Caitanya Mahāprabhu and Śrī Rāya Rāmānanda) is one of the most shining treasures within the *Śrī Caitanya-caritāmṛta,* written by Śrīla Kṛṣṇadāsa Kavirāja. Indeed, it is like the Kaustubha-maṇi, the most brilliant jewel adorning the neck of Śrī Kṛṣṇa Himself. *Śrī Caitanya-caritāmṛta* is a most unprecedented, gem-like literature containing the *siddhānta* (transcendental conclusions) of pure devotion. With regards to this, the most respected Śrīla Narottama dāsa Ṭhākura has written the following:

kṛṣṇadāsa kavirāja, rasika bhakata-mājha,
jeṅho kailā caitanya-carita
gaura-govinda-līlā, śunite galaye śilā,
tāhāte nā haila mora cita

Prārthanā (2)

"Śrīla Kṛṣṇadāsa Kavirāja is an exceptionally high-class devotional poet. He is also *bhāvuka,* one who is immersed in experiencing the more elevated expressions of divine love. He has composed the unprecedented sacred texts, *Śrī Caitanya-caritāmṛta,* which describes the pastimes of Śrī Gaurāṅga, and *Śrī Govinda-līlāmṛta,* which depicts the pastimes of Śrī Govinda. Both of these books, being crown jewels of transcendental literature, are the best of all contributions."

Śrīmad-Bhāgavatam, the king of devotional literature and the essence of all Vedānta, is considered to be the birthplace of *śuddha-bhakti* (pure devotion) and it was revealed to Bhagavān Śrī Kṛṣṇa-dvaipāyana Vedavyāsa during his devotional trance. Similarly, the two above-mentioned books by Śrīla Kṛṣṇadāsa Kavirāja Gosvāmī are also acknowledged as the very essence of Veda, Vedānta, the Purāṇas, and all historical records.

Full of humility, Śrīla Kṛṣṇadāsa Kavirāja writes in *Śrī Caitanya-caritāmṛta*:

ei grantha lekhāya more 'madana-mohana'
āmāra likhana yena śukera paṭhana

sei likhi, madana-gopāla ye likhāya
kāṣṭhera puttalī yena kuhake nācāya

Śrī Caitanya-caritāmṛta, Ādi-līlā (8.78–79)

"Śrī Madana-mohana is directly writing this book through me. My writing is just like a parrot who repeats what it has learned from another. I am writing what Śrī Madana-gopāla is Himself dictating to me. I am simply a wooden puppet, dancing or writing according to His desire."

Regarding the creation of that scripture, Śrīla Kavirāja Gosvāmī states therein:

caitanya-līlā-ratna-sāra, svarūpera bhāṇḍāra,
teṅho thuilā raghunāthera kaṇṭhe
tāṅhā kichu ye śuniluṅ, tāhā ihāṅ vistāriluṅ,
bhakta-gaṇe diluṅ ei bheṭe

Śrī Caitanya-caritāmṛta, Madhya-līlā (2.84)

"For sixteen years Śrīla Raghunātha dāsa Gosvāmī, one of the six Gosvāmīs of Vṛndāvana, stayed directly at the lotus feet of Śrī Śacīnandana Gaurāṅga Mahāprabhu in Śrīdhāma Jagannātha Purī. That which he witnessed and heard directly by his transcendental eyes and ears, and that which he heard from his close association with Śrī Svarūpa Dāmodara Gosvāmī (who is an internal associate of the Lord), is the foundation for this *Śrī Caitanya-caritāmṛta*."

Śrīla Kṛṣṇadāsa Kavirāja Gosvāmī

author of *Śrī Caitanya-caritāmṛta.*

Commenting on this section of *Śrī Caitanya-caritāmṛta*, Śrīla Bhaktivinoda Ṭhākura writes in his *Amṛta-pravāha-bhāṣya*: "Śrīla Svarūpa Dāmodara Gosvāmī is one of the most intimate associates of Śrī Caitanya Mahāprabhu. He has described the final pastimes of Śrīman Mahāprabhu in his notebook, or *kaḍacā*, in the form of condensed anecdotes, or *sūtras*. Śrī Raghunātha dāsa Gosvāmī memorized all those notes. Śrīla Kṛṣṇadāsa Kavirāja Gosvāmī, heard those notes directly from him, and expanded upon them in composing his *Śrī Caitanya-caritāmṛta*. In this regard the author wrote elsewhere:

svarūpa gosāñi kaḍacāya ye līlā likhila
raghunātha-dāsa-mukhe ye saba śunila

sei saba līlā kahi saṅkṣepa kariyā
caitanya-kṛpāte likhi kṣudra-jīva hañā

Śrī Caitanya-caritāmṛta, Antya-līlā (3.269–270)

"I have heard from the mouth of Śrī Raghunātha dāsa Gosvāmī all about the pastimes of Śrī Caitanya Mahāprabhu that Svarūpa Dāmodara Gosvāmī recorded in his notebook. I have briefly described those pastimes. Whatever I have written is by the mercy of Śrī Caitanya Mahāprabhu, since I am an insignificant living being."

Śrī Kavirāja Gosvāmī took birth in the West Bengal village of Jhāmaṭapūra, which is near the well-known Naihāṭī railway station. He did not mention anywhere the name of his mother or father, his previous childhood name, or his status in terms of his caste (*varṇa*) and social position (*āśrama*). Based upon indications in his own writings and the literatures of others, we surmise that he was present in the world from 1452 until 1538.

In regard to the identity of his caste, there is difference of opinion among various learned persons. The Vaiṣṇava society awarded Śrīla Kavirāja Gosvāmī the title "Kavirāja," or "king of poets," for his significant contribution of poetic Sanskrit – *Śrī Govinda-līlāmṛta*. In Bengal, ayurvedic doctors are also called Kavirāja. For this reason, some people assume that he was also a doctor by caste.

Śrīla Kavirāja Gosvāmī perfectly exemplified the verse *tṛṇād api sunīcena* (*Śikṣāṣṭaka* 3). In other words, He possessed all the qualities of a humble Vaiṣṇava. He himself writes in *Śrī Caitanya-caritāmṛta*:

jagāi mādhāi haite muñi se pāpiṣṭha
purīṣera kīṭa haite muñi se laghiṣṭha

mora nāma śune yei, tāra puṇya kṣaya
mora nāma laya yei, tāra pāpa haya

Śrī Caitanya-caritāmṛta, Ādi-līlā (5.205–206)

"I am more wicked than Jagāi and Mādhāi and even lower than a worm in stool. Anyone who hears my name loses the results of his pious activities, and anyone who takes my name incurs sin."

The respected author identifies Śrī Ragunātha dāsa Gosvāmī, the eternal associate of Śrī Caitanya Mahāprabhu, as his spiritual master.

śrī-govinda, śrī-caitanya, śrī-nityānanda
śrī-advaita, śrī-bhakta, āra śrī-śrotṛ-vṛnda

śrī-svarūpa, śrī-rūpa, śrī-sanātana
śrī-raghunātha-dāsa śrī-guru, śrī-jīva-caraṇa

iṅhā-sabāra caraṇa-kṛpā ya lekhāya āmāre
āra eka haya—teṅho ati-kṛpā kare

Śrī Caitanya-caritāmṛta, Antya-līlā (20.96–98)

"I have written this book by the mercy of the lotus feet of Śrī Govinda-deva, Śrī Caitanya Mahāprabhu, Lord Nityānanda, Advaita Ācārya, other devotees, and the readers of this book, as well as Svarūpa Dāmodara Gosvāmī, Śrī Rūpa Gosvāmī, Śrī Sanātana Gosvāmī, Śrī Raghunātha dāsa Gosvāmī, who is my spiritual master, and Śrī Jīva Gosvāmī. A Supreme Personality has also favored me."

Śrīla Kavirāja Gosvāmī ends nearly every chapter of *Śrī Caitanya-caritāmṛta* by writing:

śrī-rūpa-raghunātha-pade yāra āśa
caitanya-caritāmṛta kahe kṛṣṇadāsa

"Always praying at the lotus feet of Śrī Rūpa and Śrī Raghunātha for their mercy, I, Kṛṣṇadāsa Kavirāja, recite this *Śrī Caitanya-caritāmṛta*."

Therein the author describes many jewels such as *Śrī Śikṣāṣṭaka*, spoken by Śrīman Mahāprabhu, *Śrī Rūpa-śikṣā* (Mahāprabhu's instructions to Śrī Rūpa Gosvāmī), *Śrī Sanātana-śikṣā* (Mahāprabhu's instructions to Śrī Sanātana Gosvāmī), *Śrī Rāya Rāmānanda Saṁvāda* (Mahāprabhu's discussions with Śrī Rāya Rāmānanda), and the questions and answers between Śrī Gopīnātha Ācārya and Sārvabhauma Bhaṭṭācārya. Each of these discussions gives the essence of all the scriptures. Each of them contains a perfect description of the conclusive truths concerning *sambandha* (one's relationship with Bhagavān), *abhidheya* (one's activities in that relationship), and *prayojana* (the ultimate goal of life).

In the conversation between Śrī Rāya Rāmānanda and Śrīman Mahāprabhu, the *prema* of Śrīmatī Rādhikā is established as the crest-jewel of all attainments. Later in the conversation, Śrī Rāya Rāmānanda describes the very elevated state of devotional love called *prema-vilasa-vivarta. Prema-vilāsa-vivarta* is a high level of *prema* experienced by Śrīmatī Rādhikā when, even at the time of separation from Śrī Kṛṣṇa, due the influence of *adhirūḍha-mahābhāva*, Śrīmatī Rādhikā feels that She is meeting with Him.

Upon hearing of this supremely exalted state, Śrīman Mahāprabhu accepted it as the soul's ultimate goal. Śrīman Mahāprabhu also accepted that following in the footsteps of the *sakhīs* of Vraja is the only method by which to attain this ultimate goal. By hearing with complete faith this conversation between Śrī Rāmānanda Rāya and Śrī Caitanya Mahāprabhu, one will achieve *prema-bhakti* to the lotus feet of Śrī Rādhā-Kṛṣṇa, and automatically, as a secondary result, one will also achieve complete knowledge of *kṛṣṇa-tattva, rādhā-tattva, prema-tattva*, and *rasa-tattva* – the fundamental truths regarding the Supreme Lord, Śrī Kṛṣṇa, His eternal consort Śrī Rādhā, the love They share, and the varieties of exchanges between Śrī Kṛṣṇa and His intimate associates.

Śrī Rāmānanda Rāya was the governor of the southern regions of the kingdom ruled by the heroic Orissan King Mahārāja Pratāparudra. Residing in Vidyānagara on the banks of the holy river Godāvarī, (present day Kobūra, Rājamundarī, in Andhra Pradesh) he performed his administrative duties.

On His journey to South India, Śrī Caitanya Mahāprabhu took *darśana* of Jiyaḍa-nṛsiṁha, after which He went to the bank of the Godāvarī for His early morning bath. Śrī Rāmānanda Rāya was also there taking bath, appearing like royalty and surrounded by many *brāhmaṇas* chanting Vedic *mantras*.

There they met, and were thoroughly struck by each other. Śrī Rāmānanda Rāya invited Śrī Caitanya Mahāprabhu to spend a few days in that place. On his insistence, Śrīman Mahāprabhu accepted the invitation and stayed on for several days at the house of a Vedic Vaiṣṇava *brāhmaṇa*.

Śrī Caitanya Mahāprabhu and Śrī Rāmānanda Rāya
met for the first time on the banks of the holy river Godāvarī.

On the day of their meeting, at dusk, Śrī Rāmānanda Rāya, wearing the dress of an ordinary person, returned to the bank of the river to meet Śrīman Mahāprabhu, who instructed him to present statements from various Vedic literatures on both the living entity's *sādhya* (ultimate goal) and *sādhana* (process by which the goal is attained).

Initially Rāmānanda Rāya suggested *varṇāśrama* as practiced by ordinary persons. Śrīman Mahāprabhu finally accepted *jñāna-śūnya śuddha-bhakti* as the goal.

Asked by Mahāprabhu to say more about *bhakti*, Śrī Rāmānanda Rāya first explained pure devotional attraction to Śrī Kṛṣṇa. He then successively described love for Kṛṣṇa in the mood of a servant (*dāsya-prema*), in the mood of a friend (*sakhya-prema*), and in the mood of a parent (*vātsalya-prema*), and finally he explained *kāntā-prema*, the love of a female beloved for Śrī Kṛṣṇa, as the essence of all ultimate attainments. On the platform of varieties of scriptural evidence, Rāmānanda Rāya also showed how *kāntā-prema* is the essence of all perfection.

Upon Śrīman Mahāprabhu's acceptance of *kāntā-prema* as the soul's ultimate goal, Śrīman Rāmānanda Rāya went on to describe the *prema* of Śrīmatī Rādhikā as the topmost. Hearing this, Śrīman Mahāprabhu became extremely pleased. He asked him to then describe the nature of Śrī Kṛṣṇa and Śrīmatī Rādhikā, and also the nature of *rasa-tattva* and *prema-tattva*. Using examples from scripture as a basis, Śrī Rāmānanda Rāya gave a most detailed, sequential account of these topics.

When Śrīman Mahāprabhu instructed him to explain these subjects more extensively, Śrī Rāmānanda Rāya sang a self-composed song extolling the state of *prema-vilāsa-vivarta*, which is comprised of the feelings of separation from Kṛṣṇa experienced in *adhirūḍha-bhāva*[1].

Finally, upon the request of Śrīman Mahāprabhu, Śrī Rāmānanda Rāya established the exclusive cultivation of devotional service under the guidance of the *sakhīs* of Vraja to be the one and only method of attaining the ultimate perfection of Śrī Rādhā-Kṛṣṇa's direct, loving service.

After many nights of continuously hearing and discussing topics about Śrī Rādhā and Kṛṣṇa, upon receiving the direct *darśana* of Śrīman Mahāprabhu's *mūla-tattva* (His own true identity as Śrī Kṛṣṇa covered by the sentiments and complexion of Śrī Rādhā) and His *sva-svarūpa* (His form as a *sannyāsī*), Śrī Rāmānanda Rāya fell unconscious.

With the supremely cooling touch of His lotus hands, Śrīman Mahāprabhu roused him, and after releasing him from His embrace, forbade him from revealing His form and identity to anyone.

Mahāprabhu ordered Śrī Rāmānanda Rāya to abandon his royal responsibilities and go to live in Śrī Jagannātha Purī. He told him that after visiting various holy places in South India, He would return there to Śrī Jagannātha Purī, and together they would dwell in complete happiness, hearing and chanting topics of Śrī Rādhā-Kṛṣṇa's pastimes for the rest of their lives.

---

1 *Adhirūḍha-bhāva* – the final limit of *mahābhāva*, which is the very essence of Kṛṣṇa's pleasure-giving potency. *Adhirūḍha-mahābhāva* is characterized by the feeling that each moment is like a day of Brahmā when one is separated from Kṛṣṇa, and the feeling that a day of Brahmā is like a moment when one is meeting Him.

Śrī Rāya Rāmānanda Saṁvāda Classes
Puruṣottama Month 2004, Śrī Jagannātha Purī.

Some years ago, I spent the month of Puruṣottama in Śrī Jagannātha Purī, discussing this conversation between Śrī Rāmānanda Rāya and Śrīman Mahāprabhu in depth. At the time, my dear daughter Savitā expertly took extensive notes. Later she gave those notes to my dear daughter Madhu Khandelval M.A., Ph.D. for editing. By adding Śrīla Bhaktivinoda Ṭhākura's *Amṛta-pravāha* commentary on *Śrī Caitanya-caritāmṛta* and Śrīla Bhaktisiddhānta Sarasvatī Ṭhākura Prabhupāda's *Anubhāṣya* commentary on the same, as well as a range of evidence from various books such as *Bhakti-rasāmṛta-sindhu*, *Śrī Ujjvala-nīlamaṇi*, *Vidagdha-mādhava*, and *Lalita-mādhava*, she produced a highly attractive and comprehensive manuscript. In completion, I made some further corrections and enhancements to the work. My hope is that the faithful readers will be benefited tremendously by reading and following this book.

I pray that Their Lordships Śrī Guru-Gaurāṅga-Gāndharvikā-Giridhārī may shower Their mercy upon everyone who contributed in various ways to the book's production.

Owing to the book's swift production, it will naturally contain some grammatical and typographical errors. If the kind readers would indicate these to me for correction, then the next edition will be improved. There is no need to say anything further about this.

Śrī Nandotsava
Kṛṣṇa Navamī
31 Śrāvaṇa, 520 Caitanyābda
17th August, 2006

Begging a particle of the mercy of
Śrī Hari, Guru, and Vaiṣṇavas,
Tridaṇḍi-bhikṣu
Śrī Bhaktivedānta Nārāyaṇa

oṁ viṣṇupāda paramahaṁsa parivrājakācārya

Śrī Śrīmad Bhaktivedānta Nārāyaṇa Gosvāmī Mahārāja

nitya-līlā-praviṣṭa oṁ viṣṇupāda
Śrī Śrīmad Bhaktivedānta Vāmana Gosvāmī Mahārāja

nitya-līlā-praviṣṭa oṁ viṣṇupāda

Śrī Śrīmad Bhaktivedānta Svāmī Mahārāja

nitya-līlā-praviṣṭa oṁ viṣṇupāda

Śrī Śrīmad Bhakti Prajñāna Keśava Gosvāmī Mahārāja

nitya-līlā-praviṣṭa oṁ viṣṇupāda

Śrī Śrīmad Bhaktisiddhānta Sarasvatī Prabhupāda

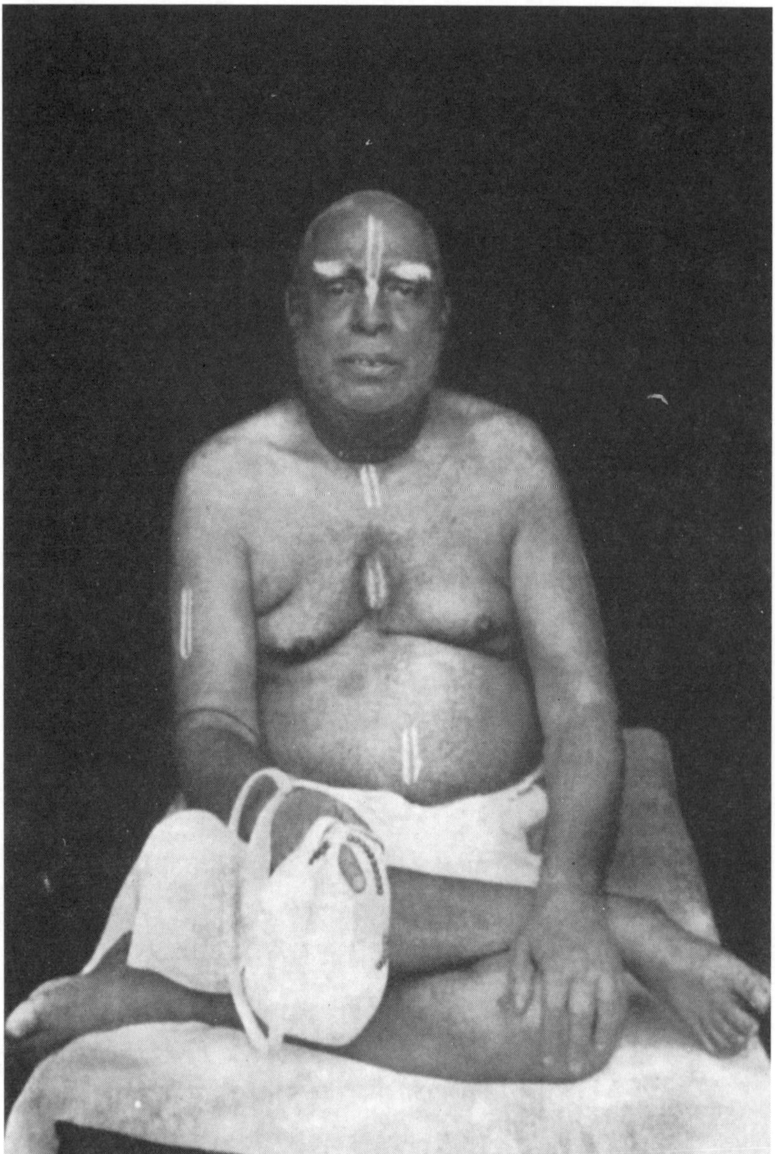

nitya-līlā-praviṣṭa oṁ viṣṇupāda

Śrīla Saccidānanda Bhaktivinoda Ṭhākura

Maṅgalācaraṇa

8.1

sañcārya rāmābhidha-bhakta-meghe
sva-bhakti-siddhānta-cayāmṛtāni
gaurābdhir etair amunā vitīrṇais
taj-jñatva-ratnālayatāṁ prayāti

Śrī Gaurāṅga Mahāprabhu is a boundless, nectarean ocean of the established conclusions of devotion (*bhakti-siddhāntas*), and His devotee Śrī Rāmānanda Rāya is the cloud whom He filled with these conclusions about devotion to Him. When Mahāprabhu experienced the rain of *bhakti-tattvas* that the Rāmānanda-cloud showered upon Him, He was transformed into an ocean of jewels.

Vivṛtti

śrī śrī guru-gauraṇgau jayataḥ

namaḥ oṁ viṣṇu-pādāya gaura-preṣṭhāya bhutale
śrī-śrīmad-bhakti-prajñāna-keśava iti nāmine

atimartya-caritrāya svāśritānāñ ca pāline
jīva-duḥke sadārttāya śrī-nāma-prema-dāyine

gaurāśraya-vigrahāya kṛṣṇa-kāmaika-cāriṇe
rūpānuga-pravarāya vinodeti svarūpiṇī

prabhupādāntaraṅgāya sarvasadguṇaśāline
māyāvāda-tamoghnāya vedāntārthavide namaḥ

namaḥ oṁ viṣṇu-pādāya kṛṣṇa-preṣṭhāya bhutale
śrīmate bhaktisiddhānta sarasvatīti nāmine

namo bhaktivinodāya saccidānanda-nāmine
gauraśakti-svarūpāya rūpānugavarāya te

yena vistārito gaura kṛpayā rasasāgaraḥ
viśākhikāsvarūpaṁ taṁ rāmānandamahaṁ bhaje

namo mahā-vadānyāya kṛṣṇa-prema-pradāya te
kṛṣṇāya kṛṣṇa-caitanya-nāmne gaura-tviṣe namaḥ

Millions and millions of times I reverently place my head at the lotus feet of my most venerable holy master *oṁ viṣṇupāda aṣṭottara-śata śrī* Śrīmad Bhakti Prajñāna Keśava Gosvāmī Mahārāja. Only by his causeless mercy and inspiration has a person as fallen as I am been able to to write this *vivṛtti*, or commentary, on the discussion between Śrī Rāmānanda Rāya and Śrī Caitanya Mahāprabhu. I also repeatedly offer my obeisances to the spotlessly pure, transcendental lotus feet of the universal preceptor, Śrīla Prabhupāda Śrī Śrīmad Bhaktisiddhānta Sarasvatī Ṭhākura, and to the lotus feet of Śrīla Saccidānanda Bhaktivinoda Ṭhākura, who is the Bhagīratha of Bhakti-Bhāgīrathī, the Ganges River of pure devotional service. [He is addressed thus because, just as Bhagīratha Mahārāja ushered the descent of the River Ganges to this world, Bhaktivinoda restored the flow of the Ganges River of pure devotional service, as inaugurated by Śrīman Mahāprabhu; thus Bhaktivinoda's feet bestow pure devotion.] Both these great personalities have manifested the very deep, confidential essence of the *Śrī Rāmānanda Rāya Saṁvāda*, through their respective commentaries on the *Śrī Caitanya-caritāmṛta*, namely *Anubhāṣya* and *Amṛta-pravāha*.

I surrender myself in turn at the lotus feet of Śrī Rāmānanda Rāya, who is Viśākhā Sakhī in the pastimes of Vraja and who expanded the ocean of *rasa* (transcendental mellows) by the mercy of Śrī Gaurāṅga Mahāprabhu. Finally, while holding in my heart Śrī Śacīnandana Gaurahari, who is Śrī Kṛṣṇa covered by the complexion and sentiments of Śrīmatī Rādhikā, I begin to write this *vivṛtti* (commentary) on *Śrī Rāmānanda Saṁvāda.*

Sañcārya – infusing. It is common knowledge that water evaporates from the ocean by the heat of the sun. The resultant vapor, having been purified of the ocean's salty nature, transforms into a cloud. When this cloud passes over a forest or collides into a mountain, the same water falls as rain and again returns to the ocean. Should that rain fall at the time of the Svāti constellation (*nakṣatra*), the oysters in the ocean, accepting this rain-water, produce pearls. The ocean, now filled with precious stones, becomes known as the abode of jewels (*ratnākara*).

With this metaphor, the author conveys that Śrī Caitanya Mahāprabhu is the ocean of the jewels of *bhakti-siddhānta*, and Śrī Rāya Rāmānanda is the rain-cloud filled with ambrosia. This Mahāprabhu, who is the unlimited ocean of the truths about *bhakti*, has covertly infused the heart of Śrī Rāmānanda Rāya with the vapor of the nectarean flow of mellows in servitorship – *dāsya*, friendship – *sakhya*, parenthood – *vātsalya*, and conjugal relationship – *mādhurya rasa*. This incomparable flow of nectar rained into the 'oysters' of Mahāprabhu's ears, where they transformed into the precious jewels of *siddhāntas* which the Lord drank. Thus He became the ocean laden with the jewels of *bhakti-siddhānta*.

This meaning emanates directly from Śrī Rāmānanda Rāya himself. Śrī Rāmānanda Rāya spoke the following essential statement:

eta tattva mora citte kaile prakāśana
brahmāke veda yena paḍāila nārāyaṇa

antaryāmī īśvarera ei rīti haye
bāhire nā kahe, vastu prakāśe hṛdaye

Śrī Caitanya-caritāmṛta, Madhya-līlā (8.263–264)

"You have manifested all these transcendental truths in my heart, just as Nārāyaṇa educated Lord Brahmā. The Supreme Lord dwelling within everyone's heart speaks not externally but from within, and in this way He gives instruction."

Rāmābhidha-bhakta-meghe. The crown jewel of *rasikas*, Śrī Rāmānanda Rāya, is the eternal associate of Śrī Gaurāṅga Mahāprabhu, who is the unfathomable ambrosial ocean of *bhakti-siddhānta*. This cloud-like devotee known as "Rāma" is supremely enchanting, desirable, alluring, and delectable. The choice of the adjective *bhakta* in this verse signifies that it is only in the hearts of devotees that the truths about devotion (*bhakti-tattva*) can manifest. No one else has the ability to bear the power that comes from these truths. Śrīman Rāmānanda Rāya is that devotee-cloud who can carry the weight of Śrī Caitanya Mahāprabhu's own *bhakti-siddhānta* and then distribute it to others as rainfall. After this shower of devotion was collected by the ocean of devotional sentiments in that devotee's heart, this rain of devotion bestowed an even more astonishing, indescribable taste for Mahāprabhu to experience.

Sva-bhakti-siddhānta-cayāmṛtāni – the nectarean collection of truths about the devotional service relating to Himself.

anarpita-carīṁ cirāt karuṇayāvatīrṇaḥ kalau
samarpayitum unnatojjvala-rasāṁ sva-bhakti-śriyam

Śrī Caitanya-caritāmṛta, Ādi-līlā (1.4)

"May the son of Śrīmatī Śacī-devī, Śrī Gaurahari, forever manifest spontaneously within the innermost core of your heart. Adorned with the radiant splendor of molten gold, He has descended (*avatīrṇaḥ*) in the Age of Kali by His causeless mercy to bestow upon the world that which has not been given for a long time – the beauty of His own brilliantly radiant *ujjvala-prema-rasa bhakti*, service in the highest mellow of amorous love."

In this verse, the word *sva-bhakti* refers to the supremely nectarean service performed in *svārasikī-upāsanā*[1] under the guidance of the *mañjarīs*. Only this is the *jīvas'* topmost goal. Before the advent of Śrīman Mahāprabhu no one had manifested this for the *sādhakas*.

1 *Svārasikī-upāsanā* – The pastimes of Śrī Kṛṣṇa performed in various places of Goloka Vṛndāvana are of many types; therefore, the worship that is performed through the limbs of *bhakti*, such as remembering, hearing, and chanting about those pastimes, which flow one after another, is called *svārasikī-upāsanā*.

In regard to the execution of this *mañjarī sevā*, Śrīmatī Rādhikā becomes the object of Her maidservant's permanent ecstatic emotion (*sthāyi-bhāva*) and Śrī Kṛṣṇa becomes the object of the maidservant's transitory emotion that nourishes the *sthāyi-bhāva*. This is then called the *sañcārī-bhāva*. In this service, the *mañjarīs* lovingly tend to Śrī Kṛṣṇa because He is the love of Rādhā's life and gives Her happiness. Thus, this *sva-bhakti-siddhānta*, sweet as nectar, is the philosophical understanding embodied in the followers of Śrī Rūpa Gosvāmī, who established the *rāgānuga-rūpānuga-siddhānta*[2]. This is the essence and the foundation of the ultimate expression of love.

Pure devotion, or *bhakti*, is always supremely relishable because it is joyful by nature. The possessor of this *bhakti*, which culminates in *mahābhāva*, is Śrīman Mahāprabhu Himself. The ocean of Śrī Caitanya Mahāprabhu contains no trace of saltiness. Rather, it is full of ambrosial devotional mellows (*rasa*). An ocean such as He has no deficiency, is complete in every respect, and is free from dangerous creatures such as sharks and crocodiles – meaning "fruitive action (*karma*), ritualistic worship (*upāsanā*), and empirical speculative knowledge (*jñāna*)." This ocean, filled with unending varieties of nectar, is most attractive to the heart. There are no huge, treacherous and deafening waves; instead there are gently billowing waves of meeting and separation (*saṁyoga* and *viyoga*), in which both Bhagavān and the devotee remain blissfully submerged.

Gaurābdhir etair amunā vitīrṇaiḥ. *Gaurābdhi* means the "Gaura-ocean." Śrī Kṛṣṇa who is *akhila-rasāmṛta-sindhu*, the complete ocean of nectarean flavors, is *gaurābdhi*, the golden ocean. The word *amunā* means "by him," as in the sense of "distributed to, or rained upon by the cloud named Rāmānanda." Thus, the import is that Śrīman Mahāprabhu impelled the Rāmānanda-cloud to rain the ambrosial conclusions of His own *bhakti* upon the ocean of His own self. These *siddhāntas* imperceptibly appeared in Rāmānanda Rāya's heart, and he in turn revealed them to Mahāprabhu. Then, Mahāprabhu again relished the mercy which He had

2 *Rāgānuga* – spontaneous devotional service which follows in the footsteps of the perfected souls. *Rūpānuga* – that *rāgānuga-bhakti* that specifically follows the moods of Śrīla Rūpa Gosvāmī.

imperceptibly bestowed upon Śrī Rāmānanda Rāya, and He accepted these jewels of devotion, or *bhakti-ratnas*.

In *Śrī Bhagavad-gītā* (18.55), Bhagavān Śrī Kṛṣṇa says, "*bhaktyā mām abhijānāti* – I am only understood by pure devotion." Therefore, for the welfare of the entire world, Mahāprabhu posed questions, and Rāmānanda Rāya answered Him.

Taj-jñatva-ratnālayatāṁ prayāti. The knowledge of this *bhakti-siddhānta* has been referred to here as a *ratna*, or precious jewel. When these devotional conclusions are soaked in *bhakti-rasa* and enter the ears of a single-pointed devotee, he becomes like an ocean of jewels.

Mahāprabhu inspired the heart of Śrī Rāmānanda Rāya. Śrīman Mahāprabhu then personally listened in order to establish the topmost example, and thus encourage in others, also, an eagerness to hear. Those jewels have now appeared in the form of this book, which presents the crest jewel of all spiritual perfections.

Śrīman Mahāprabhu already knew every aspect of *bhakti-siddhānta* in full. If this were not so, how could He have empowered the heart of Śrī Rāmānanda Rāya with all devotional conclusions? Then, the question naturally arises: how was it that the Lord gained knowledge of *siddhānta* by hearing from the lotus mouth of Śrī Rāmānanda Rāya? What is the meaning of this?

The answer is that previously Śrī Caitanya Mahāprabhu's knowledge had simply been *jñāna*, theory; but after hearing from Śrī Rāmānanda Rāya, that knowledge became *vijñāna*, realized knowledge. *Jñāna* and *vijñāna* are not the same thing. Here, *jñāna* refers to ordinary knowledge, whereas *vijñāna* entails special knowledge, which is full of realization. Bhagavān Śrī Kṛṣṇa said to Lord Brahmā:

jñānaṁ parama-guhyaṁ me
yad vijñāna-samanvitam
sarahasyaṁ tad-aṅgañ ca
gṛhāṇa gaditaṁ mayā

Śrīmad-Bhāgavatam (2.9.30)

"O Brahmā, knowledge concerning Me is absolute, non-dual (*advaya*), and supremely confidential. Even though it is without differentiation, it is eternally divided into four categories: *jñāna* (theoretical knowledge), *vijñāna* (realized knowledge), *rahasya* (confidential knowledge), and *tad-aṅga* (concomitant parts of that knowledge, or the limbs of devotion). By your intelligence, as a *jīva*, you cannot understand this; by My mercy, now realize it. *Jñāna* is My *svarūpa* (original form or essential identity). *Vijñāna* is the knowledge pertaining to *bhakti* to Me. My *rahasya* (secret knowledge) is the minute *jīva*. *Pradhāna* (the unmanifested modes of material nature in its original and undifferentiated state) is My *jñānāṅga* (limb of *jñāna*, or knowledge). The eternal non-duality and confidential differences of these four *tattvas* are all transformations of My potency, which is simultaneously one with and different from Me (*acintya-bheda-abheda-śakti*)."

Here, *jñāna* indicates *kṛṣṇa-tattva*; *vijñāna* denotes *rādhā-tattva*; *rahasya* signifies the *tattva* of *prema*; and *tad-aṅga* means *tattva* of Śrīmatī Rādhā and Śrī Kṛṣṇa's loving pastimes (*vilāsa*).

One can obtain Bhagavān Śrī Kṛṣṇa, who is *acintya-bheda-abheda-tattva* (simultaneously one with and different from His own multifarious energies), only by the process of *sādhana-bhakti*. Knowledge that we grasp by hearing from another is called *jñāna*, which when realized in the heart, is then called *vijñāna*. It was *vijñāna* that Śrīman Mahāprabhu obtained from Śrī Rāmānanda Rāya.

Bhagavān Śrī Kṛṣṇa is the *viṣaya*, the enjoyer or object of *bhakti*. He is not the *āśraya*, the abode of *bhakti*. He is completely unaware of the feelings aroused in the heart of the *sādhaka* by his devotional service to Him. The devotee serves Him in one of four relationships: *dāsya* (servitorship), *sakhya* (fraternity), *vātsalya* (parental affection), or *madhura-bhāva* (amorous love).

Thus, Śrī Kṛṣṇa is the *viṣaya*, or object of devotion of all the various *āśraya-jātīya* devotees, those who are the shelters, or receptacles, of divine love. Śrī Kṛṣṇa does not have the loving sentiments of the devotees who the receptacles of divine love (*āśraya-jātīya*). He cannot taste the supreme, indescribable happiness that Śrīmatī Rādhikā feels when She sees His enchanting form. How is it possible for Śrī Kṛṣṇa to experience the state of happiness that Śrīmatī Rādhikā reaches in the stage of *rāga* and *anurāga*[3], and especially in the stage of *mādanākhya-mahābhāva*[4]?

Kṛṣṇa wanted to know: "What are the glories of Śrī Rādhā's *praṇaya*[5] (intense love)? What type of happiness does She experience in loving service to Me? How does She taste the nectar of My sweetness?"

To fulfill these desires, Śrī Kṛṣṇa accepted Her mood and complexion, and coming as the *āśraya* (the shelter or receptacle of the divine love), He appeared in this world as Śrī Gaurasundara. He infused the heart of Śrī Rāmānanda Rāya with the conclusions of His own *bhakti-rasa* (the ambrosia of devotion).

śrī-rādhāyāḥ praṇaya-mahimā kīdṛśo vānayaivā-
svādyo yenādbhuta-madhurimā kīdṛśo vā madīyaḥ
saukhyañ cāsyā mad-anubhavataḥ kīdṛśaṁ veti lobhāt
tad-bhāvāḍhyaḥ samajani śacī-garbha-sindhau harīnduḥ

Śrī Caitanya-caritāmṛta, Ādi-līlā (4.230)

It is only by the influence of His mercy potency (*kṛpā-śakti*) that the Lord's desire could be fulfilled. In *Śrī Bṛhad-bhāgavatāmṛta* it is told how Śrī Gopa-kumāra bestowed realization of ecstatic love upon his disciple in the same manner. He simply placed his lotus hand on the head of his disciple, who then realized everything. This example illuminates a secret: should the *jīva* wish to receive the ecstasy of the fundamental truths regarding Bhagavān, he should hear only from the devotee who possesses such realization. The pastimes of Śrī Hari are naturally stored only in the heart of such a devotee. Such narrations, full of transcendental knowledge and bliss, cause the listeners to also relish them.

3 When *sneha* (deep affection) is imbued with intense longing it is known as *rāga*. With the appearance of *rāga*, even a moment of separation is intolerable, and at that time even distress seems to be happiness. When *rāga* always experiences its object (the most beloved Kṛṣṇa) in ever-fresh ways then it is called *anurāga*.

4 The supreme state of exaltation in which all the various stages of *prema*, from *rati* to *mahābhāva*, are manifest simultaneously in their most radiant form is called *mādanākhya-bhāva*.

5 In *Ujjvala-nīlamaṇi*, Śrīla Rūpa Gosvāmī defines *praṇaya* as the state in which the hearts of both the hero (*nāyaka*) and heroine (*nāyikā*) become one.

Śrī Caitanya Mahāprabhu Meets Rāmānanda Rāya

8.2

jaya jaya śrī-caitanya jaya nityānanda
jayādvaita-candra jaya gaura-bhakta-vṛnda

All glories to Śrī Caitanya-deva! All glories to Śrī Nityānanda! All glories to Śrī Advaita! All glories to the devotees of Śrī Gaurāṅga!

8.3

pūrva-rīte prabhu āge gamana karilā
'jiyaḍa-nṛsiṁha'-kṣetre katadine gelā

Śrīman Mahāprabhu continued His tour, and everywhere, as previously, He converted the people into Vaiṣṇavas, and submerged them in the ocean of *prema-bhakti-rasa*. After a few days, He came to the holy place named Jiyaḍa-Nṛsiṁha.

Jiyaḍa-Nṛsiṁha kṣetra. Five miles from Viśākhāpaṭṭanam is a place named Siṁhācala, where there is now a railway station. There, upon a mountain, is a temple of Lord Śrī Nṛsiṁha-deva. This temple in Viśākhāpaṭṭanam is the most famous and affluent above all others. The excellence of its architecture captivates the minds of all. There is one engraved stone plaque commemorating that the devotionally minded wife of King Tṛtīya Goṁkāra decorated the deity with gold leaf.

The servants of Śrī Nṛsiṁha-deva reside there, along with the local people. On top of the mountain, adjoining the temple are many houses for the visiting pilgrims. The outer section of the main temple houses the *śrī vijaya-vigraha*, the smaller deity who is taken out on street processions during festivals, while the inner sanctum of the temple accommodates the original deity of Bhagavān Śrī Nṛsiṁha-deva. Devotees of the Śrī Rāmānuja Vaiṣṇava *sampradāya* perform the worship of Śrī Nṛsiṁha-deva, under the patronage of the king of Vijaya-nagara.

Some people also say that the deity of Bhagavān Śrī Nṛsiṁha-deva once gave His special mercy to a devotee named Jīyaḍa; and for this reason, the deity took the name Jiyaḍa-Nṛsiṁha. Thus the place came to be known as Jiyaḍa-Nṛsiṁha-kṣetra.

8.4

nṛsiṁha dekhiyā kaila daṇḍavat-praṇati
premāveśe kaila bahu nṛtya-gīta-stuti

Taking *darśana* of Bhagavān Śrī Nṛsiṁha-deva, Śrīman Mahāprabhu fully prostrated Himself before the deity. Then, absorbed in *prema* He sang and danced, and afterwards offered many types of prayers and glorifications of the Lord.

Here, some people may consider that because Śrī Gaurasundara is Vrajendra-nandana Śrī Kṛṣṇa, endowed with the mood and complexion of Śrīmatī Rādhikā (*rādhā-bhāva-dyuti-suvalita śrī-kṛṣṇa-svarūpa*), surely He will hold only the ecstatic mood of Śrīmatī Rādhikā, tasting exclusive *prema* for Śrī Kṛṣṇa of Vraja. Why, then, does He become absorbed in *prema* by having the *darśana* of Śrī Nṛsiṁha-deva, who is in the mood of awe and majesty?

Our Gosvāmīs provide the answer. They state that Śrī Kṛṣṇa is the quintessence of all the incarnations of Bhagavān, the Supreme Person. He is the personification of all transcendental mellows (*akhila-rasāmṛta-murti*), the shelter of unlimited varieties of *rasa*, and the personification of wonderful, extraordinary transcendental sentiments. Only by tasting each of the unique varieties of *rasa* does the taste of Śrī Kṛṣṇa's sweetness reach its fullness. Śrī Nṛsiṁha-deva is also a form of Bhagavān. Thus, there is a particular variety of *rasa*, or flavor, in Him. Therefore, on the day when Śrīman Mahāprabhu had *darśana* of Śrī Nṛsiṁha-deva, His heart developed a desire to taste that special flavor. Upon that desire being completely satisfied, He became absorbed in *prema* and began to dance and perform *kīrtana*.

8.5

"śrī-nṛsiṁha, jaya nṛsiṁha, jaya jaya nṛsiṁha
prahlādeśa jaya padmā-mukha-padma-bhṛṅga"

"All glories to Bhagavān Śrī Nṛsiṁha-deva! All glories to the Lord of Śrī Prahlāda! All glories to You who are like a bumblebee always hovering about the lotus-like face of Śrī Lakṣmī-devī. All glories to You.

Śrīdhara Svāmī has composed the following two verses in his commentary on *Śrīmad-Bhāgavatam* (1.1.1 and 10.87.1), as a means of offering his obeisances to Lord Nṛsiṁha-deva:

prahlāda-hṛdayāhlādaṁ bhaktā-vidyā-vidāraṇam
śarad-indu-ruciṁ vande pārīndra-vadanaṁ harim

vāg-īśā yasya vadane lakṣmīr yasya ca vakṣasi
yasyāste hṛdaye saṁvit taṁ nṛsiṁha ahaṁ bhaje

"I offer my prayers to Lord Nṛsiṁha-deva, who always gives happiness to the heart of His devotee Śrī Prahlāda, who always dispels the ignorance of the devotees, and who is endowed with a complexion as effulgent as the autumnal full moon. I offer my prayers to that Bhagavān Śrī Nṛsiṁha, upon whose tongue Sarasvatī, the goddess of speech, eternally stays, upon whose chest Lakṣmī always resides, and in whose heart dwells the transcendental potency of spiritual consciousness."

While describing the speciality of the mercy of Śrī Bhagavān, Śrīman Mahāprabhu glorifies Śrī Nṛsiṁha-deva through the following verse, personally composed by Śrī Śrīdhara Svāmī (in his commentary on *Śrīmad-Bhāgavatam* 7.9.1).

8.6

ugro 'py anugra evāyaṁ sva-bhaktānāṁ nṛ-keśarī
keśarīva sva-potānām anyeṣām ugra-vikramaḥ

"Just as a lion is exceedingly cruel, powerful, and a cause of great fear for others, yet is very affectionate and merciful to his own cubs, Bhagavān Śrī Nṛsiṁha-deva is exceedingly ferocious towards demons such as Hiraṇyakaśipu, yet He is always full of affection for Prahlāda and His other devotees."

8.7

ei-mata nānā śloka paḍi' stuti kaila
nṛsiṁha-sevaka mālā-prasāda āni' dila

In this way, Śrī Caitanya Mahāprabhu recited many different verses in glorification of Bhagavān Śrī Nṛsiṁha. Seeing Śrīman Mahāprabhu's devotional sentiments, Lord Śrī Nṛsiṁha-deva's servant then brought garlands and the remnants of the Lord's food and offered them to Him.

8.8

pūrvavat kona vipre kaila nimantraṇa
sei rātri tāṅhā rahi' karilā gamana

As happened before, a *brāhmaṇa* came with an invitation for Śrī Caitanya Mahāprabhu. The Lord passed the night there, and early the next morning, He again commenced His tour.

8.9

prabhāte uṭhiyā prabhu calilā premāveśe
dig-vidik nāhi jñāna rātri-divase

The next morning, Śrīman Mahāprabhu rose and being absorbed in *prema* started out again on His tour. Owing to His great ecstasy,

He had no knowledge of the proper direction, or whether it was day or night.

8.10

pūrvavat 'vaiṣṇava' kari' sarva loka-gaṇe
godāvarī-tīre prabhu āilā katadine

As before, Śrīman Caitanya-deva converted all the *jīvas* there to Vaiṣṇavism, and after some days the Lord reached the banks of the river Godāvarī.

8.11

godāvarī dekhi' ha-ila 'yamunā'-smaraṇa
tīre vana dekhi' smṛti haila vṛndāvana

As soon as Śrīman Mahāprabhu caught sight of the river Godāvarī, He remembered the river Śrī Yamunā, a vision of which manifested in His heart. Thus absorbed, when He saw the forest on the banks of the Godāvarī, Śrī Vṛndāvana appeared upon the screen of His heart. He understood the Godāvarī to be the Yamunā, and the forest there to be Vṛndāvana.

The symptom of the *mahā-bhāgavata* (the devotee on the highest platform of devotional service) is that wherever he goes and whatever he sees become *uddīpana* (stimulants or causes of remembrance) of his worshipable Lord and all that is related to Him. Seeing the purifying holy water of the Godāvarī caused within Śrīman Mahāprabhu's mind an awakening of the water-associated pastimes of Vraja. He remembered especially the emperor of all Vraja pastimes, the *rāsa-līlā*, because it occurred in Śrīdhāma Vṛndāvana on the banks of the river Yamunā. Therefore, He became immersed in the fathomless ocean of Vraja's sweetness.

8.12

sei vane kaṭakṣaṇa kari' nṛtya-gāna
godāvarī pāra hañā tāṅhā kaila snāna

Mahāprabhu remained for some time in that sanctified forest, singing and dancing. Afterwards, the Lord crossed the river and took His bath on the other bank.

8.13

ghāṭa chāḍi' kata-dūre jala-sannidhāne
vasi' prabhu kare kṛṣṇa-nāma-saṅkīrtane

After bathing in the river, Śrī Caitanya-deva left the bathing place and walked a little distance from there. Sitting near the water, He engaged in chanting the holy name of Kṛṣṇa.

Here some may enquire as to why Mahāprabhu did not remain seated at that holy bathing place to perform *nāma-saṅkīrtana*. Why did He move a little distance away on the same shore? Our Gosvāmīs have explained that the continuous traffic of persons bathing at the *ghāṭa*, or bathing place, could have presented an obstacle to His tasting the nectar of chanting the holy name. Therefore, Mahāprabhu chose a place that was more suitable for *kīrtana*.

8.14

hena-kāle dolāya caḍi' rāmānanda rāya
snāna karibāre āilā, bājanā bājāya

At that time, Śrī Rāmānanda Rāya, sitting in a special palanquin fit for a king, arrived there to take his bath. Accompanying him were musicians playing on their instruments.

Why were they playing music? Śrīla Viśvanātha Cakravartī Ṭhākura explains that it was customary at the time to have musicians preceding any famous royal officer on his journeys. Thus, Śrī Rāmānanda Rāya, seated in a palanquin and accompanied by instrumental music, was offered the appropriate royal respect as he traveled towards the bathing place where Mahāprabhu sat.

8.15

tāṅra saṅge bahu āilā vaidika brāhmaṇa
vidhi-mate kaila teṅho snānādi-tarpaṇa

Many Vedic *brāhmaṇas* were accompanying Śrī Rāmānanda Rāya, who took his bath according to the Vedic rituals and offered oblations.

In this Bengali verse, the word *vidhi-mata*, meaning "according to the Vedic system" does not indicate the *smārta* method of ritualistic worship, which is based simply on an external understanding of the system of *varṇāśrama-dharma*. Rather, it is understood that Śrī Rāmānanda Rāya performed his bathing and offering of oblations to his ancestors according to the Vaiṣṇava methods prescribed in literatures such as *Śrī Hari-bhakti-vilāsa*.

Some so-called intelligent and learned persons say that Śrī Rāmānanda Rāya was personally well-versed in the Vedas, and that although he was a pure devotee, he still followed *varṇāśrama-dharma* with complete faith; indeed, he himself was the foundation of the *varṇāśrama* system. Therefore, he performed the activities of taking bath and offering oblations to his forefathers according to the injunctions of the scriptures.

Yet the great and learned spiritual master Śrīla Viśvanātha Cakravartī Ṭhākura has refuted this by stating that Śrī Rāmānanda Rāya was a *śuddha-bhakta*, and that there is no need at all for such a pure devotee to follow the rules of *varṇāśrama-dharma*. The term *śuddha-bhakta* actually means that such a person has abandoned *varṇāśrama-dharma* and follows only devotional service to Śrī Kṛṣṇa (*śrī-kṛṣṇa-bhakti*). It is for this reason that Śrī Rāmānanda Rāya is said to be the topmost of all devotees. From this it is clearly evident that Śrī Rāmānanda Rāya was not at all a follower of *varṇāśrama-dharma*.

8.16

prabhu tāṅre dekhi' jānila—ei rāma-rāya
tāṅhāre milite prabhura mana uṭhi' dhāya

When Śrī Caitanya Mahāprabhu saw Śrī Rāmānanda Rāya, He knew immediately who he was, and a great eagerness to meet him awoke within the Lord's mind.

8.17

tathāpi dhairya dhari' prabhu rahilā vasiyā
rāmānanda āilā apūrva sannyāsī dekhiyā

Although Śrī Caitanya Mahāprabhu was very eager to meet him, He remained sitting patiently. Śrī Rāmānanda Rāya, a little distance away from the bathing place, saw the astonishing and wonderfully beautiful *sannyāsī* and came near.

8.18

sūrya-śata-sama kānti, aruṇa vasana
suvalita prakāṇḍa deha, kamala-locana

The bodily effulgence of that *sannyāsī* was as brilliant as unlimited suns. A saffron garment was covering the Lord, who was large in body and very strongly built, and whose eyes were like lotuses.

It should be known that even though His bodily effulgence was more brilliant than millions of suns, it did not give any pain to the eyes; rather it bestowed a great ecstasy.

8.19

dekhiyā tāṅhāra mane haila camatkāra
āsiyā karila daṇḍavat namaskāra

The sight of the astonishing *sannyāsī* struck the heart of Śrī Rāmānanda Rāya with wonder. He approached Him and respectfully prostrated himself, falling flat like a stick before Him.

Śrī Rāya Rāmānanda was astonished to see the extraordinary beauty of the Lord and His great otherworldly effulgence. Because he was a pure devotee, he fell flat like a stick at the divine feet of the Lord.

8.20

uṭhi' prabhu kahe,—uṭha, kaha 'kṛṣṇa' 'kṛṣṇa'
tāre āliṅgite prabhura hṛdaya satṛṣṇa

Śrīman Mahāprabhu, seeing him offering obeisances, stood up and said, "Please get up, please get up! Chant Kṛṣṇa, Kṛṣṇa!" Indeed, Śrī Caitanya Mahāprabhu was very eager to embrace him.

8.21

tathāpi puchila,—"tumi rāya rāmānanda?"
teṅho kahe,—"haṅa muñi dāsa śūdra manda"

Although Śrī Caitanya Mahāprabhu understood who he was, still He inquired, "Are you Rāya Rāmānanda?" To this, he replied with great humility, "Yes, this unfortunate *śūdra* is Your servant."

8.22

tabe tāre kaila prabhu dṛḍha āliṅgana
premāveśe prabhu-bhṛtya, doṅhe acetana

Hearing this, Śrīman Mahāprabhu then embraced Śrī Rāmānanda Rāya very firmly. Indeed, both the master and the servant, absorbed in ecstatic love, lost consciousness.

8.23

svābhāvika prema doṅhāra udaya karilā
duṅhāke āliṅgiyā duṅhe bhūmite paḍilā

Natural love for each other awakened in both their hearts, and in their embrace, they both fell down to the ground unconscious.

In Śrī Saccidānanda Bhaktivinoda Ṭhākura's *Amṛta-pravāha-bhāṣya* it is stated that the *prema* between them was natural. Actually, Śrī Rāmānanda Rāya is Viśākhā Sakhī in Śrī Kṛṣṇa's pastimes. Therefore, as Śrīman Mahāprabhu is the combined form of Śrī Rādhā and Śrī Kṛṣṇa, the natural love of the Divine Couple for Viśākhā Sakhī, and the love of Viśākhā Sakhī for Them manifested immediately upon their seeing each other.

Perfect, naturally occurring *prema* is not achievable by spiritual practice (*sādhana*). The relationship between the devotee and Bhagavān is something like this: when the devotee sees his worshipful Lord, unlimited towering waves of *prema* arise within his heart. And when Bhagavān sees His devotee, then His *bhakta-vātsalya*, or fathomless ocean of affection for the devotee, churns within His heart. Thus both of them become bewildered.

8.24

stambha, sveda, aśru, kampa, pulaka, vaivarṇya
duṅhāra mukhete śuni' gadgada 'kṛṣṇa' varṇa

When they embraced each other, the eight ecstatic transformations such as becoming stunned, perspiration, tears, shivering, paleness, and horripilation, appeared on their bodies. Their voices became choked, and both began to chant "Kṛṣṇa, Kṛṣṇa."

They both tried to conceal their natural eternally perfect love for each other, but they could not. Both became helpless due to the towering waves of *prema*, and their throats became choked.

8.25

dekhiyā brāhmaṇa-gaṇera haila camatkāra
vaidika brāhmaṇa saba karena vicāra

When the ritualistic Vedic *brāhmaṇas* who accompanied Śrī Rāmānanda Rāya saw this astonishing meeting, they were wonderstruck. They reflected within their minds:

8.26

'ei ta' sannyāsīra teja dekhi' brahma-sama
śūdre āliṅgiyā kene karena krandana

8.27

ei mahārāja—mahā-paṇḍita, gambhīra
sannyāsīra sparśe matta ha-ilā asthira'

"The effulgence of this *sannyāsī* is like Brahman itself, but despite this, He is crying upon embracing this *śūdra*, Śrī Rāmānanda Rāya. Why is this?"

The Vedic *brāhmaṇas* considered Śrī Rāmānanda Rāya to be a supremely learned personality, naturally very grave; so why did he become so excited, like a mad person, upon touching this *sannyāsī*?

The Vedic *brāhmaṇas* were considering Śrī Rāmānanda Rāya to be a *śūdra*, a member of the lowest social class. The scriptures forbid *sannyāsīs* to touch members of the *śūdra* community. "This *sannyāsī*, who is certainly very effulgent," the *brāhmaṇas* reflected, "is not only touching Śrī Rāmānanda Rāya, but He is binding him up in His tight embrace. How can this be?"

Śrī Rāmānanda had indeed described himself as a *śūdra* when he offered obeisances. In the district of Vidyānagara, he was the royal representative of King Pratāparudra and had experienced all the enjoyment befitting a ruler. Due to performing service to a king, his nature and activities should have been inclined towards irreligion. His dress and ornaments were that of a servant of the king. Therefore, it was not proper for a *sannyāsī* to touch him at all.

In fact, Śrī Rāmānanda Rāya's familial connection was with the *kṣatriya*, or administrative class of persons. Furthermore, he was a great *śuddha bhakta*, or pure devotee. By declaring himself a *śūdra*, he manifested the mood of *tṛṇād-api sunīca*, regarding himself lower in status than the straw on the street. Śrī Rāmānanda Rāya was a *parama-bhāgavata*, or a devotee of the topmost caliber, and a complete knower of *bhakti-tattva*. Because the Vedic *brāhmaṇas* did not know the factual identity of Mahāprabhu, they took Him for a mere *sannyāsī*. They also considered Śrī Rāmānanda Rāya to be a supremely learned personality, naturally very grave. Why, then, did he become so restless, like a mad person, upon touching this *sannyāsī*? This was the cause of the Vedic *brāhmaṇas*' astonishment.

8.28

ei-mata vipra-gaṇa bhāve mane mana
vijātīya loka dekhi' prabhu kaila saṁvaraṇa

Śrīman Mahāprabhu is *antaryāmī*, or the indwelling Supersoul and supreme witness in the heart of all. Knowing that the *brāhmaṇas*' sentiments were opposed to pure devotion, He concealed His emotions.

Śrīla Bhaktisiddhānta Sarasvatī Prabhupāda says that these *brāhmaṇas* were opposed to Śrīman Mahāprabhu, whereas Śrī Rāmānanda Rāya was indeed most favorably disposed to Him, and was in fact a most surrendered and intimate devotee. Despite being in close proximity to a pure devotee, those *brāhmaṇas* maintained their faith in the materialistic process of performing action with a desire for the fruits (*karma-kāṇḍa*). For precisely this reason, those *brāhmaṇas* are said to be non-devotees and opposing elements. It is proper for devotees to conceal loving exchanges in front of those who are not inclined to serving Bhagavān and who are fixed in following the materialistic path of *karma*.

8.29

sustha hañā duṅhe sei sthānete vasilā
tabe hāsi' mahāprabhu kahite lāgilā

Concealing their emotions and regaining their external consciousness, they again became sober and sat down together. Śrī Caitanya Mahāprabhu then smiled – it is never possible to obstruct the joyful bliss of the devotees – and began to speak.

8.30

"sārvabhauma bhaṭṭācārya kahila tomāra guṇe
tomāre milite more karila yatane

"O Rāya, before I came here, Sārvabhauma Bhaṭṭācārya greatly extolled your good qualities, and insisted on My meeting you.

8.31

tomā milibāre mora ethā āgamana
bhāla haila, anāyāse pāiluṅ daraśana"

"Indeed, I have come here only to meet you. It is very good that with great ease I have gotten your audience."

8.32

rāya kahe,—"sārvabhauma kare bhṛtya-jñāna
parokṣeha mora hite haya sāvadhāna

Śrī Rāya Rāmānanda replied, "Sārvabhauma Bhaṭṭācārya directly accepts me as his servant, and indirectly always acts for my welfare.

8.33

tāṅra kṛpāya pāinu tomāra daraśana
āji saphala haila mora manuṣya-janama

"Only by his mercy, I have received *darśana* of Your lotus feet today. By virtue of this, I now consider that my human birth has become successful."

Human birth is extremely rare. Only by the special mercy of Bhagavān can one attain the human form of life. It is impossible to perform *bhajana* (devotional service) of Bhagavān in any other species; it is not even possible as a demigod. The human body is itself the very root of *bhajana*. Only by this human body is it possible to hear topics of Lord Hari in the association of saintly persons (*sādhu-saṅga*), take shelter at the feet of a bona fide spiritual master, perform the limbs of devotional service, become free from unwanted habits, and develop through the stages of *niṣṭhā* (constant engagement), *ruci* (taste), *āsakti* (attachment), etc. *Śrīmad-Bhāgavatam* (11.20.17) states:

nṛ-deham ādyaṁ sulabhaṁ sudurlabhaṁ
plavaṁ sukalpaṁ guru-karṇadhāram
mayānukūlena nabhasvateritaṁ
pumān bhavābdhiṁ na taret sa ātma-hā

"It is said that the human form of life is the basis of all auspiciousness. It is a good boat by which one can cross the ocean of birth and death. In the human form of life, one may obtain the guidance of a good navigator, the spiritual master. One also gets the assistance of a favorable wind – the instructions and the mercy of Kṛṣṇa as given in the scriptures. If, however, one does not take advantage of this opportunity and wastes the human form of life, then he is a killer of his own self."

It is according to this reasoning that Śrī Rāmānanda Rāya now considered his human form of life successful, having obtained the *darśana* of the lotus feet of Śrīman Mahāprabhu.

8.34

sārvabhaume tomāra kṛpā,—tāra ei cihna
aspṛśya sparśile hañā tāṅra premādhīna

Śrī Rāmānanda Rāya continued, "I can see that You have bestowed great mercy upon Śrī Sārvabhauma. The proof of this is that, being controlled by his love, You have touched me, although I am an untouchable.

8.35

kāṅhā tumi—sākṣāt īśvara nārāyaṇa
kāṅhā muñi—rāja-sevaka viṣayī śūdrādhama

"Who are You? You are the Supreme Controller Nārāyaṇa Himself. And who am I? I am a materialist enjoying royal opulences, a most fallen *śūdra* engaged in enjoying the objects of the senses.

8.36

mora sparśe nā karile ghṛṇā, veda-bhaya
mora darśana tomā vede niṣedhaya

"The Vedic injunctions have forbidden You to even look at me, however You have not considered these prohibitions and You did not feel contemptuous of my touch. Indeed, it is forbidden for *sannyāsīs* like You to even see persons such as myself.

Śrīla Prabhupāda Sarasvatī Ṭhākura says that in this verse, Śrīla Rāmānanda Rāya sees himself as a most fallen materialistic *śūdra*. It is true that he did not take birth in a family of *brāhmaṇas*; rather, he was a transcendental *brāhmaṇa* initiated according to the *ekāyana*[6] branch of the Vedic tree.

6 *Ekāyana* means "one path" or "exclusive devotion." On December 30, 1928 the great scholar Pramathanātha Tarkabhūṣaṇa came to the Gauḍīya Maṭha and heard an extensive explanation of the *daiva-varṇāśrama* system from Śrīla Sarasvatī Ṭhākura. In January of 1929, Śrīla Sarasvatī Ṭhākura established the Ekāyana Gauḍīya Maṭha in Kṛṣṇanagara. At the opening ceremony, he gave a lecture with an original explanation on the single path of exclusive devotion (*ekāyana*), showing that it is the trunk of the Vedic tree and the various other paths (*bahvāyana*) are its branches. [Taken from Associates of Śrī Caitanya, Volume 2, by Śrīpada Bhakti-vallabha Tīrtha Mahārāja]

Thus, he was a pure *mahā-bhāgavata*, a liberated devotee of the highest order, devoid of any material desires. The high-born Vedic *brāhmaṇas* had been initiated into the performance of all varieties of *yajñas* after studying thousands of branches of the Vedas. Considering Śrī Rāmānanda Rāya to be a *śūdra*, they thus guaranteed themselves entry to the hellish regions, as is confirmed in the *Padma Purāṇa*: "*vīkṣate jāti-sāmānyāt sa yāti narakaṁ-dhruvam* – a person rushes to hell when he considers a devotee of the Lord to belong to a particular caste in terms of birth."

Whosoever is desirous of factual spiritual attainment and genuine auspiciousness should become the servant of the servant of Śrī Rāmānanda Rāya.

8.37

tomāra kṛpāya tomāya karāya nindya-karma
sākṣāt īśvara tumi, ke jāne tomāra marma

"Your mercy alone makes You perform this condemnable act. You are directly the Supreme Controller Himself, however You are controlled by *bhakti*. Who can understand Your true purpose?

Śrīla Prabhupāda says that it is improper for *sannyāsīs* to see materialistic persons or to associate with *śūdras*, but being controlled by His own mercy, Mahāprabhu did not consider Śrī Rāmānanda's position as a *śūdra*. Thus He performed the 'despicable' act of touching him. Being controlled by *prema*, Bhagavān has indeed performed dishonorable acts in repeatedly, such as becoming the chariot driver of Arjuna, eating the remnant fruits of the lowborn woman Śabarī, and associating with the hunchback woman Kubjā.

8.38

āmā nistārite tomāra iṅhā āgamana
parama-dayālu tumi patita-pāvana

"You have come here only to deliver me. You are the ultimate storehouse of mercy and You purify the fallen souls.

8.39

mahānta-svabhāva ei tārite pāmara
nija kārya nāhi tabu yāna tāra ghara

"By Your own magnanimous nature, You always deliver the fallen and sinful souls. You have no personal business of Your own, nor do You seek self-profit. Still for the benefit of the living entities, You travel from house to house. The purpose of Your life is only to deliver the fallen souls.

8.40

mahad-vicalanaṁ nṛṇāṁ
gṛhiṇāṁ dīna-cetasām
niḥśreyasāya bhagavan
nānyathā kalpate kvacit

Śrīmad-Bhāgavatam (10.8.4)

"'My dear Lord, sometimes great souls go to the homes of householders, who are generally fallen and deprived of the association of saintly persons. They do this simply for the eternal good fortune of such family persons, because often those family persons are so immersed in material affairs that they are unable even to visit the *āśramas*, or retreats of the *sādhus*. Therefore, can there be any reason that You have visited me other than for my auspiciousness?'"

Śrī Nanda Mahārāja spoke this verse on the occasion of Śrī Gargācārya's visit to his house in Nandagāoṅ, at the behest of Śrī Vasudeva. In this verse, the two words *gṛhiṇām* (attached householders) and *dīna-cetasām* (who are very lowly, being engaged in family maintenance and nothing more) indicate Śrī Nanda Mahārāja's humility. By the influence of *bhakti*, Śrī Nanda Mahārāja considered himself to be less significant than a straw in the street. "Such saints do not even bestow their mercy upon the demigods, but upon householders like us they rain a profusion of mercy. Offering us protection, they are our factual maintainers."

Commenting on the word *mahat* in this verse, Śrī Sanātana Gosvāmī says "*mahatāṁ śrī bhagavat-sevaikaniṣṭhānāṁ* – this term is used to refer only to one who is absorbed in the service of Bhagavān." Does this indicate that Śrīman Mahāprabhu is also a great devotee engaged in the service of Bhagavān? No, He is directly the source of all incarnations (*avatārī*). He is directly Nārāyaṇa Himself.

8.41

āmāra saṅge brāhmaṇādi sahasreka jana
tomāra darśane sabāra dravī-bhūta mana

Śrī Rāmānanda Rāya continued, "There are uncountable *brāhmaṇas* and other persons here with me. Behold how all of their hearts have melted simply by seeing You.

8.42

'kṛṣṇa' 'hari' nāma śuni sabāra vadane
sabāra aṅga—pulakita, aśru—nayane

"Just see! I am hearing the holy name 'Kṛṣṇa, Kṛṣṇa' coming very sweetly from everybody's mouth. Everyone's bodily hairs are standing erect with ecstasy, and tears are flowing from their eyes.

8.43

ākṛtye-prakṛtye tomāra īśvara-lakṣaṇa
jīve nā sambhave ei aprākṛta guṇa"

"One can see the symptoms of the Supreme Lord in Your bodily appearance and nature. How is it possible for the ordinary living beings (*jīvas*) to possess such transcendental qualities that are found in Śrī Kṛṣṇa alone?"

8.44

prabhu kahe,—"tumi mahā-bhāgavatottama
tomāra darśane sabāra drava haila mana

Hearing this Śrīman Mahāprabhu replied, "O Rāmānanda, you are the best even amongst the topmost devotees; therefore only by your audience, not by Mine, has everyone's heart melted.

Quoting from the *Padma Purāṇa* Śrīla Prabhupāda Sarasvatī Ṭhākura reveals for us the qualities of a *mahā-bhāgavata* devotee:

tāpādi pañca-saṁskārī
navejyā-karma-kārakaḥ
artha-pañcaka-vid vipraḥ
mahā-bhāgavataḥ smṛtaḥ

"According to the path of ritualistic worship the *uttama* or *mahā-bhāgavata* is characterized as being a *brāhmaṇa* who has undergone the five kinds of *saṁskāras*, or purificatory processes, such as austerities; who has executed the Vaiṣṇava rituals of worship such as deity worship through recital of *mantra*, and through *yoga*, *yajña* sacrifice, offering prayers, chanting the Lord's holy names, and marking the body with auspicious signs; who has worshiped the Vaiṣṇavas; and who has understood the *artha-pañcaka* (five subjects of knowledge[7])."

In *Śrīmad-Bhāgavatam* (11.2.45) Svayam Bhagavān Himself describes the symptoms of the *mahā-bhāgavata*:

sarva-bhūteṣu yaḥ paśyed
bhagavad-bhāvam ātmanaḥ
bhūtāni bhagavaty ātmany
eṣa bhāgavatottamaḥ

7 Śrī Jīva Gosvāmī explains the five subjects as the worshipable Supreme Lord; His supreme abode of Vaikuṇṭha; His assets, or *tadīya* (the pure devotees); His *mantras*; and the living entities.

"My devotees see Me as the soul of all souls within all living entities, and they see all living entities within Me. Since they see Me in all life forms, they give mercy to all beings."

8.45

anyera ki kathā, āmi—'māyāvādī sannyāsī'
āmiha tomāra sparśe kṛṣṇa-preme bhāsi

"What to speak of others, although I am a Māyāvādī *sannyāsī*, I also am drowning in the ocean of *kṛṣṇa-prema* simply by touching you.

Śrīman Mahāprabhu is calling Himself a Māyāvādī *sannyāsī* in order to reveal Himself as insignificant and worthy of rejection. It is well known that He received initiation into the ten-syllable *gopāla-mantra* from Śrī Īśvara Purīpāda. Before taking *sannyāsa*, Śrīman Mahāprabhu very cleverly chanted a Vaiṣṇava *mantra* into the ear of Śrīla Keśava Bhāratī, thus giving him initiation. In this way, He transformed him into a great devotee. Upon, receiving those *mantras* back again from Śrīla Keśava Bhāratī, Śrīman Mahāprabhu maintained the proper etiquette in regard to accepting a spiritual master, during His manifest pastimes. A Māyāvādī *sannyāsī* is a follower of *advaita-vāda* (monism), the school of thought that is opposed to *bhakti*. Śrī Caitanya Mahāprabhu however, was never a Māyāvādī *sannyāsī* in His manifest pastimes.

8.46

ei jāni' kaṭhina mora hṛdaya śodhite
sārvabhauma kahilena tomāre milite"

"Indeed, in order to purify My very hard heart (which is dry and devoid of *rasa*), Sārvabhauma Bhaṭṭācārya had asked Me to come and meet you."

8.47

ei-mata duṅhe stuti kare duṅhāra guṇe
duṅhe duṅhāra daraśane ānandita mane

In this way Bhagavān and the devotee praised each other's qualities and both fell into tremendous bliss to see each other.

8.48

hena-kāle vaidika eka vaiṣṇava brāhmaṇa
daṇḍavat kari' kaila prabhure nimantraṇa

At this time, a *brāhmaṇa* Vaiṣṇava following the Vedic principles came there. He offered *daṇḍavat praṇāma*[8] before Śrī Caitanya Mahāprabhu and invited Him for *prasāda*.

8.49

nimantraṇa mānila tāṅre vaiṣṇava jāniyā
rāmānande kahe prabhu īṣat hāsiyā

Śrī Caitanya Mahāprabhu knew that *brāhmaṇa* to be a Vaiṣṇava and accepted his invitation. Smiling, He spoke to Śrī Rāmānanda.

8.50

"tomāra mukhe kṛṣṇa-kathā śunite haya mana
punarapi pāi yena tomāra daraśana"

"Śrī Rāmānanda Rāya, I am exceedingly eager to hear from your mouth topics about Śrī Kṛṣṇa. Therefore I wish to have your *darśana* again."

---

8 *Sāṣṭānga-daṇḍavat-pranāma*. A respectful obeisance executed by prostrating eight limbs of the body, namely the thighs, feet, hands, chest, mind, head, voice, and closed eyes, by falling flat like a stick on the ground.

8.51

rāya kahe,—"āilā yadi pāmara śodhite
darśana-mātre śuddha nahe mora duṣṭa citte

Upon hearing these words from Śrīman Mahāprabhu, Śrī Rāmānanda Rāya replied, "Although You have come to cleanse the heart of this fallen soul, simply seeing You is not enough to purify my distorted and polluted heart.

8.52

dina pāṅca-sāta rahi' karaha mārjana
tabe śuddha haya mora ei duṣṭa mana"

"O Lord, please stay for at least five-seven days and kindly cleanse my contaminated heart. Only if You stay here will the consciousness of this fool become pure."

8.53

yadyapi viccheda doṁhāra sahana nā yāya
tathāpi daṇḍavat kari' calilā rāma-rāya

Although separation from one another was unbearable for both, Śrī Rāmānanda Rāya offered his obeisances to Śrī Caitanya Mahāprabhu and, on His order, departed for his royal palace.

8.54

prabhu yāi' sei vipra-ghare bhikṣā kaila
dui janāra utkaṇṭhāya āsi' sandhyā haila

Śrīman Mahāprabhu then went to the house of the *brāhmaṇa* and accepted alms, meaning took *prasāda* there. Both the devotee and Bhagavān were eager within their hearts to meet each other again. Then evening came.

8.55

prabhu snāna-kṛtya kari' āchena vasiyā
eka-bhṛtya-saṅge rāya mililā āsiyā

After finishing His bath and performing His *sandhyā* (evening *gāyatrī mantra* meditation), Śrī Caitanya Mahāprabhu sat and chanted *hari-nāma*, waiting for Śrī Rāmānanda Rāya. Then Rāmānanda Rāya, dressed as a common person and accompanied by one servant, came to meet Him.

Śrīla Bhaktivinoda Ṭhākura says that a *sannyāsī* bathes and chants the appropriate *mantras* three times per day – morning, midday and evening. Hence at dusk, according to the injunctions of Śruti, Śrī Śacīnandana sat down and chanted *hari-nāma* after taking bath and chanting the *sandhyā mantras*, otherwise known as *āhnika*.

8.56

namaskāra kaila rāya, prabhu kaila āliṅgane
dui jane kṛṣṇa-kathā kaya sei-sthāne

Śrī Rāmānanda Rāya approached and respectfully prostrated before Mahāprabhu. The Lord arose and embraced him with great *prema*. They then began to discuss topics of Kṛṣṇa in a secluded place.

Varṇāśrama-dharma

8.57

prabhu kahe,—"paḍa śloka sādhyera nirṇaya"
rāya kahe,—"sva-dharmācaraṇe viṣṇu-bhakti haya"

Śrīman Mahāprabhu began by saying, "O Rāya, what is the *sādhya* (ultimate goal) and *sādhana* (spiritual practice, or method to attain that goal) for the living entities? Please recite verses from the revealed scriptures as evidence." Receiving the order of the Lord, Rāmānanda replied that the verdict regarding the ultimate goal of life is to perform *viṣṇu-bhakti*, devotional service to Lord Viṣṇu, by executing one's prescribed duties according to his social position.

8.58

varṇāśramācāra-vatā
puruṣeṇa paraḥ pumān
visṇur ārādhyate panthā
nānyat tat-toṣa-kāraṇam

Viṣṇu Purāṇa (3.8.8)

"Lord Viṣṇu, the Supreme Controller, is worshiped by those who properly execute the system of prescribed duties according to one's *varṇa* and *āśrama* (spiritual and social classification). Apart from this there is no other way to satisfy Him."

Viṣṇu-bhakti – devotion to Lord Viṣṇu. Śrīla Sarasvatī Prabhupāda says that *bhakti* is indeed most pleasing and valuable for the human race. Apart from this, all else is undesirable and unsatisfying. Only the soul endowed with *bhakti* can accept Śrī Bhagavān. By the continuous performance of *jñāna-miśra-bhakti* and *karma-miśra-bhakti,* then gradually, a special kind of realized knowledge which pertains to the topmost form of *bhakti* (*svarūpa-siddha-bhakti*) awakens. In *Śrī Bhagavad-gītā* (18.46), Śrī Kṛṣṇa says:

sva-karmaṇā tam abhyarcya siddhiṁ vindati mānavaḥ

"Mankind can, by the constant performance of his own duty, attain all perfection."

All forms of life arise from Bhagavān, and this world itself expands from Him alone. Even knowledge of this makes a man favorably inclined towards Bhagavān. The supremely pure disciplic succession, or *paramparā*, of the path of devotional service is sanctioned by Bhagavān Bodhāyana, Ṭaṅka, Dramiḍa, Guhyadeva, Kapardi, and down to Bhāruci, in the disciplic order.

It is stated in the *Śrīmad-Bhāgavatam* (6.3.22):

bhakti-yogo bhagavati tan-nāma-grahaṇādibhiḥ

"Devotional service, beginning with the chanting of the holy name of the Lord, is the ultimate religious principle for human beings."

In this verse, the term *bhakti-yoga* alone is capable of conveying the desired meaning, but the word *bhagavati* has also been used. The special meaning is that an endeavor may be called *bhakti-yoga* only when the limbs of devotion such as chanting and remembering the holy name are performed to please Bhagavān. That type of *bhakti-yoga* is capable of bestowing *prema-bhakti.*

One is unable to apply the name *bhakti-yoga* even to such activities as *śravaṇa* and *kīrtana* when they are performed with intentions other than the desire to please Bhagavān. It is never possible to achieve the fruit of *prema-bhakti* by this. Only after the attainment of *prema* may it become possible to reach the stages of *sneha*, *māna*, *praṇaya*, etc. In devotional literatures such as the *Śrīmad-Bhāgavatam* and the *Nārada-pañcarātra*, use of the word *bhakti* exclusively indicates pure *bhagavat-bhakti*, or devotional service to Bhagavān. Therefore, it is extremely clear that the word *bhakti* only applies to *viṣṇu-tattva*[9] not to anyone or anything else.

It is only possible to know what to do and what not to do by consulting the scriptures. This is why Śrīman Mahāprabhu asked Śrī Rāmānanda Rāya to quote evidence from the scriptures. The definition of *sādhya* (goal) is "desired object" (*abhīṣṭa-vastu*). *Sādhana* (duties pertaining to the soul) is defined as service that is pleasing to Śrī Kṛṣṇa, who is *sevya* (He who is to be served). Only divine love for Kṛṣṇa, which is utterly devoid of any desire for one's own happiness, is the true goal of the soul, as per the soul's constitutional nature.

Sva-dharma-ācaraṇa – following one's prescribed duties. *Brāhmaṇas* (the priestly class), *kṣatriyas* (the warrior or managerial class), *vaiśyas* (the mercantile class), and *śūdras* (the servitor class), comprise the four *varṇas*, or divisions of society according to one's occupation; and *brahmacarya* (celibate student life), *gṛhastha* (household life), *vānaprastha* (retired, or partial renunciation from household life), and *sannyāsa* (complete renunciation) constitute the four spiritual orders, or *āśramas*.

When we adhere to the responsibilities ordained by the scriptures for these social and spiritual divisions, we are engaged in the performance of one's prescribed duties. By executing the prescribed directives that are suitable for one's social and spiritual status, it is possible to attain qualification to perform devotional service to Lord Viṣṇu. *Sva-dharma-ācaraṇa* cannot be called the *sādhana* to achieve perfect devotion to Viṣṇu, which is the goal of human life. Therefore, the words of scripture determine that devotion to Viṣṇu alone is the true goal.

Bhagavān Viṣṇu is pleased with the worship that is performed by executing the duties prescribed for one's social and spiritual status, which are determined by one's conditioned nature. *Śrīmad-Bhāgavatam* lists the respective constituent qualities of each of the four social divisions:

---

9 Lord Kṛṣṇa and His incarnations.

śamo damas tapaḥ śaucaṁ
santoṣaḥ kṣāntir ārjavam
jñānaṁ dayācyutātmatvaṁ
satyaṁ ca brahma-lakṣaṇam

śauryaṁ vīryaṁ dhṛtis tejas
tyāgaś cātmajayaḥ kṣamā
brahmaṇyatā prasādaś ca
rakṣā ca kṣatra-lakṣaṇam

deva-gurv-acyute bhaktis
tri-varga-paripoṣaṇam
āstikyam udyamo nityaṁ
naipuṇyaṁ vaiśya-lakṣaṇam

śūdrasya sannatiḥ śaucaṁ
sevā svāminy amāyayā
amantra-yajño hy asteyaṁ
satyaṁ go-vipra-rakṣaṇam

Śrīmad-Bhāgavatam (7.11.21–24)

"The symptoms of a *brāhmaṇa* are control of the mind, control of the senses, performance of austerities, cleanliness, satisfaction, forgiveness, simplicity, knowledge, compassion, truthfulness, and devotion to Bhagavān.

"To be powerful in battle, heroic, patient, influential, and charitable, in control of the senses, renounced, forgiving, devoted to the *brāhmaṇas*, merciful, and always protective of the citizens – these are the symptoms of the *kṣatriya*.

"To be ever devoted to the demigods, the spiritual master and Bhagavān; to always protect the three religious principles – religiosity (*dharma*), economic development (*artha*), and sense gratification (*kāma*); to be theistic; to always endeavor for wealth, and to be expert in trade – these are the symptoms of the *vaiśya*.

"To remain submissive to the higher sections of society [the *brāhmaṇas*, *kṣatriyas*, and *vaiśyas*], to always be very clean, to serve one's master without duplicity, to perform sacrifices without uttering

Vedic *mantras*, to not steal, to always speak the truth, and to protect the cows and *brāhmaṇas* – these are the symptoms of the *śūdra*."

In much the same way, there are four spiritual positions, or *āśramas*, namely *brahmacarya*, *gṛhastha*, *vānaprastha*, and *sannyāsa*. Every human being should please Bhagavān by executing one's prescribed duties (*dharma*) according to one's spiritual position. In the *Jāvāla Upaniṣada* (8.5) it states:

> *sa hovāca yājñavalkyaḥ, brahmacaryaṁ samāpya gṛhī bhavet, gṛhī bhūtvā vanī bhavet, vanī bhūtvā pravrajet, yadi vetarathā brahmacaryādeva pravrajed gṛhād vā vanādvā, atha punaravratī vā vratī vā snātako vā 'snātako vā utsannāgniko vā yadahareva virajet tadahareva pravrajet*
>
> "The saintly Janaka Mahārāja asked the great sage Maharṣi Yājñavalkaya: 'My lord, please be merciful and explain the qualification for the position of *sannyāsa* and the rules and regulations to be followed by one in that order.' Maharṣi Yājñavalkya replied, 'After completing one's time in the *brahmacarya-āśrama*, as a celibate student, one should accept the *gṛhastha-āśrama*, or household life. Following that, one should accept the *vānaprastha-āśrama*, in which one retires from household affairs. And after some time, one should accept the *sannyāsa-āśrama*, the renounced order of life. If feelings of renunciation arise in someone before entering the *gṛhastha-āśrama*, then one may directly enter the *sannyāsa-āśrama*.'"

One should endeavor to please Bhagavān in the prescribed manner. If one deviates from this and instead turns to illicit behavior, then the result will be greatly detrimental, and one will attain a hellish destination. To follow the path of transcendental enlightenment is the foremost responsibility of the living beings. One's acquired nature, close association, and received teachings each have a discernable effect upon one's life.

In the present verse beginning with *varṇāśramācāra-vatā*, Śrī Rāmānanda Rāya states that the *sādhya* (goal) for every living entity is the attainment of loving sentiments for Viṣṇu, and that the *sādhana* to achieve that is following the *varṇāśrama* system.

Offering the Results of One's Activities to Kṛṣṇa

8.59

prabhu kahe,—"eho bāhya, āge kaha āra"
rāya kahe,—"kṛṣṇe karmārpaṇa—sarva-sādhya-sāra"

Śrīman Mahāprabhu said, "What you have just said is external. Please tell Me something more than this." Śrī Rāya Rāmānanda replied, "To completely offer the results of one's activities to Śrī Kṛṣṇa is the essence of all perfection.

By declaring this as external, Śrīman Mahāprabhu intended to convey that yes, by following the system of *varṇāśrama-dharma*, Śrī Viṣṇu is pleased, but only partially so. *Varṇāśrama* is not directly related to the constitutional nature of the *jīva* as a servant of Śrī Kṛṣṇa, nor is it devotional practice composed entirely of the nine limbs of *bhakti* performed for the pleasure of the Lord (*svarūpa-siddhā-bhakti*).

Uttamā-bhakti, or topmost devotional service, is that *bhakti* which sets the pleasure of Śrī Kṛṣṇa as the goal, and in which the nine processes of devotional service, especially hearing and chanting, are executed. By the mercy of Bhagavān, that *uttamā-bhakti* thus attains oneness, or qualitative equality (*tādātmya*), with the special function of Bhagavān's internal potency. Even when the *sādhaka* finally attains perfection and achieves service to Bhagavān in His eternal pastimes in the spiritual realm, the activities of hearing and chanting do not subside; rather they become even more supremely relishable and keenly desirable. This taste and desire are in both the devotee and Bhagavān; indeed, they both realize ecstasy. To the liberated souls, this ecstasy is highly desirable, as it is their most treasured object and their ultimate goal.

Here the term *karma* refers to the activities mentioned in Smṛti and other scriptures that are performed on the basis of the natural inclination of the present body. The pursuance of *varṇāśrama-dharma* is *sakāma-karma* (performing acts in accordance with scriptural injunctions to fulfill one's own material desires). Offering the fruits of one's activities to Bhagavān is therefore superior to this. It is stated in the *Śrīmad Bhagavad-gītā* (3.9):

yajñārthāt karmaṇo 'nyatra
loko 'yaṁ karma-bandhanaḥ
tad-arthaṁ karma kaunteya
mukta-saṅgaḥ samācara

"O son of Kuntī, apart from offering the fruits of one's selfless activities (*niṣkāma-karma*) to Śrī Viṣṇu, other forms of *karma* are simply a cause of bondage. Therefore, remaining free from the desire to enjoy the fruits of your labor, you should perform all activities with Śrī Viṣṇu as the goal."

Whatever *karma* is performed for the pleasure of Śrī Hari is called *yajña* (sacrifice). Any other activity is the cause of bondage in this world. *Śrīmad Bhagavad-gītā* (2.51) further states:

karma-jaṁ buddhi-yuktā hi
phalaṁ tyaktvā manīṣiṇaḥ
janma-bandha-vinirmuktāḥ
padaṁ gacchanty anāmayam

"Sages who perform *buddhi-yoga* (devotional service endowed with knowledge of Śrī Kṛṣṇa) renounce the fruits of action in the material world. They become liberated from the cycle of birth and death and attain that state beyond all miseries."

Performing *karma* while free from attachment, completely eradicates the fear of all bondage. *Śrīmad Bhagavad-gītā* discusses this topic in the section on *karma-yoga*. Śrī Kṛṣṇa Himself says:

śubhāśubha-phalair evaṁ
mokṣyase karma-bandhanaiḥ

sannyāsa-yoga-yuktātmā
vimukto mām upaiṣyasi

Śrīmad Bhagavad-gītā (9.28)

"O Arjuna! In this way you will be freed from all bondage caused by the fruit of good and evil deeds, and, by the *yoga* of renouncing the fruits of action, you will be a unique soul even amongst liberated persons, and you will come to Me."

Our Gauḍīya Gosvāmīs have stated unequivocally that we should never offer any sinful activity or low-class activity to Bhagavān Śrī Kṛṣṇa. One should perform *bhakti* by offering one's very self, and abandon the mentality of being the enjoyer and the doer. As the next verse says:

śravaṇaṁ kīrtanaṁ dhyānaṁ
pāda-sevanam arcanam
vandanaṁ svārpaṇaṁ sakhyaṁ
sarvaṁ dāsye pratiṣṭhitam

Śrī Hari-bhakti-kalpa-latikā (10.3)

"The devotional processes of hearing about the Lord, glorifying Him, remembering Him, serving His lotus feet, worshiping Him, offering obeisances to Him, surrendering everything to Him, and befriending Him, all rest on service to Him."

This verse describes *dāsya-bhāva*, in which the devotee feels, "I am a servant of the Lord." When one becomes a servant, nothing remains his own – not his body, his intelligence, his senses, his speech, his heart, his religion, his desires, his wealth, or his actions. One cannot even say, "I am performing austerities," or "I am performing *bhakti*," because the consciousness that "I am the doer" also disappears. The first stage of *bhakti* is *ātma-samarpaṇa*, or self-surrender.

When we feel that all of our desires have been fulfilled by worshiping Śrī Viṣṇu, we may conclude that Bhagavān Viṣṇu is pleased with us, but really, this is not the case at all. Therefore, Mahāprabhu considered offering the fruits of one's action to be an external conception, because this method of worship is not inherently pleasing to Bhagavān. He is only superficially pleased with the devotee, for the sake of that devotee's happiness.

Such a worshiper considers the earth, the heavenly planets and other such places to be related to him. This conception has no connection whatsoever with *svarūpa-siddhā-bhakti*, or the nine limbs of devotional service performed to achieve one's perfect spiritual body. Some who follow *varṇāśrama-dharma* consider their austerities to be their own, some consider their mother to be their own, some their father, and some consider everything they have to be their personal property.

For example, once there was a *brāhmaṇa* who sat beneath a tree performing austerities. A pigeon perching on the upper branches passed stool upon him, which broke the *brāhmaṇa's* meditation. He became so angry that by his glance he burnt the pigeon to ashes. By this, he believed that his austerity had achieved perfection. So impressed was he that he became quite haughty and was not slightly concerned about pleasing Bhagavān.

Bhagavān fulfills the desires of such a devotee yet remains unattached to him. A *sādhaka* who, by the special grace of Śrī Kṛṣṇa, performs *uttamā-bhakti*, or activities exclusively for the pleasure of Śrī Kṛṣṇa, desires nothing, nor is there anything more that Śrī Kṛṣṇa possesses that is worthy to be given to him. Thus, He sells Himself to such a *sādhaka*. The *sādhana* of following *varṇāśrama-dharma* pleases Śrī Viṣṇu only fractionally. For this reason it is called external.

Śrīla Sarasvatī Prabhupāda says that the bodily achievements of those who follow *varṇāśrama-dharma* are based on the false egoism arising from the bodily conceptions of "I" and "mine" and are thus confined to this universe. *Bhakti*, on the other hand, is beyond the material universe. Bhagavān Śrī Gaurahari regards the external realization of those persons residing outside Vaikuṇṭha or Goloka-dhāma as fit to be rejected, and He does not accord any special independent recognition to the worship of Viṣṇu by the *varṇāśrama* method. *Jñānīs* direct their worship toward the formless aspect of Bhagavān (*nirviśeṣa*), and *karmīs* (reward-seeking workers) revere His variegated forms (*saviśeṣa*). Both worship Śrī Viṣṇu with some material intent.

According to Śrīla Bhaktivinoda Ṭhākura, to offer the results of one's action to Bhagavān Śrī Kṛṣṇa is the very essence of perfection when compared to the ordinary *varṇāśrama* system. *Nirviśeṣa tattva-vadīs* actually remain absorbed in *karma*, which is full of variety, or *saviśeṣa*. Even though it appears that they are engaging in *bhakti*, factually it is not so at all. Everything they offer is related to the body. Such offerings bear no relation to the soul, and so Mahāprabhu calls the offering itself, external. Undertakings such as constructing hospitals and *dharmaśālās* (guest-houses for pilgrims) and digging wells may be offered to Śrī Kṛṣṇa, but they are external and are thus an obstruction to the soul's relationship with Bhagavān. Consequently, one's devotional service is blemished with undesirable habits.

Śrīla Raghunātha dāsa Gosvāmī has said:

na dharmaṁ nādharmaṁ śruti-gaṇa-niruktaṁ kila kuru
vraja rādhā-krsna pracura-paricaryām iha tanu

Śrī Manaḥ-śikṣā (2)

"O my dear mind! Please do not perform either the *dharma* or *adharma* (religion or irreligion) prescribed in the Śrutis. Rather, you should perform profuse loving service to the Divine Couple Śrī Rādhā-Kṛṣṇa. The Śrutis have ascertained Them to be the highest principle of worship and the Supreme Absolute Truth."

8.60

yat karoṣi yad aśnāsi
yaj juhoṣi dadāsi yat
yat tapasyasi kaunteya
tat kuruṣva mad-arpaṇam

Śrīmad Bhagavad-gītā (9.27)

"Śrī Kṛṣṇa says to Arjuna: 'O son of Kuntī, whatever activities you perform, whatever you eat, whatever you sacrifice and give in charity, and whatever austerities you perform, should be done as an offering to Me. All endeavors should be to please Me alone.'"

The term *mad-arpaṇam* speaks here of the independent *saviśeṣa-tattva* (the Absolute Truth possessed of all transcendental attributes, without a touch of the material). Its use refutes the notion that the Supreme is *nirviśeṣa* (devoid of form and other characteristics). This *niṣkāma-karma* process, in which one performs one's prescribed duties and offers the results to Bhagavān, with no desire to enjoy the fruits, is also known as *jñāna-miśrā-bhakti* (devotion mixed with the desire for liberation).

Śrīla Viśvanātha Cakravartī Ṭhākura comments that in this verse Bhagavān suggests the practice of offering everything to the Lord (*bhagavad-arpita-bhakti*) for those who denounce devotion performed with personal interest (*sakāma-bhakti*) yet who are unable to abandon *karma* and *jñāna* completely, and who do not have the qualification to perform one-pointed devotion (*ananyā-bhakti*). This practice can hardly be called *śuddha-niṣkāma-karma-yoga*, as this name is awarded only to action that is performed according to the injunctions of the scriptures, as an offering to Bhagavān. A person's ordinary eating and drinking habits may not be included in this.

Those unable to understand the process of exclusive *ananya-bhajana* are instructed to offer all of their activities (like eating and drinking) to Bhagavān. In much the same way, the worship of the universal form of Bhagavān is recommended for those unable to properly conceive of the established truths regarding the actual object of worship, namely Śrī Kṛṣṇa. Thus, the performer of the activity is still the recipient of the fruit of action, which is indicated by the *ātmanepada* form of the verb *kuruṣva*, meaning "to perform." Furthermore, the verse makes no mention that this practice relates directly to Bhagavān.

The practice of the nine-fold process of devotional service known as *navadhā-bhakti* begins when the *sādhaka* completely surrenders himself to Bhagavān Śrī Viṣṇu. But here, by contrast, the activity is performed first and then offered to Bhagavān. For this reason, the type of devotion being discussed is not to be equated with *bhakti-yoga*. Indeed, it is not even considered one of the limbs of *bhakti-yoga*.

Renouncing Occupational Duties

8.61

prabhu kahe,—"eho bāhya, āge kaha āra"
rāya kahe,—"svadharma-tyāga, ei sādhya-sāra"

Mahāprabhu said, "This is also external. Speak further on this matter." Śrī Rāya Rāmānanda replied, "To give up one's *sva-dharma*, or occupational duties in the *varṇāśrama* system, is the essence of perfection.

Sva-dharma tyāga – abandoning *varṇāśrama-dharma*. There are two types of *sva-dharma*: to practice *varṇāśrama-dharma* with the desire to enjoy the fruits of one's activities and to offer one's work and its results to Śrī Kṛṣṇa without desiring to taste the fruits. Śrīman Mahāprabhu declared both of these to be external, whereupon Śrī Rāmānanda Rāya explained the topic of *sva-dharma tyāga*, or the complete abandonment of one's occupational duty.

The sequence so far has been as follows: it was first suggested that *varṇāśrama-dharma* was the perfect goal, yet Śrīman Mahāprabhu designated it as external because by this process, one cannot attain *prema-bhakti*, what to speak of mounting the staircase of *prema*. Next, offering the fruits of one's activities, or *karma-arpaṇa*, was presented as the ultimate goal, but Śrīman Mahāprabhu also determined that as external, based on the prior statement, "*bhaktyā sañjātayā bhaktyā* – *bhakti* only comes from *bhakti*" (*Śrīmad-Bhāgavatam* 11.3.31). The commentator on *Śrīmad-Bhāgavatam* Śrī Śrīdhara Svāmī writes of this verse, "*bhaktyā sādhana-bhaktyā saṁjātayā prema-lakṣaṇayā* – *prema-bhakti* only arises from *sādhana-bhakti*."

Śrīla Viśvanātha Cakravartī Ṭhākura says that for those who are incapable of entering into *bhajana*, verses such as *yat karoṣi* have been spoken. By properly performing one's role in the *varṇāśrama* system, the mind is gradually purified. By not following one's prescribed duties, one incurs a fault, therefore it is best to execute one's prescribed duties. However, he who abandons this process in order to perform *bhakti* is the topmost *sādhu*. Bhagavān Śrī Kṛṣṇa says:

tāvat karmāṇi kurvīta
na nirvidyeta yāvatā
mat-kathā-śravaṇādau vā
śraddhā yāvan na jāyate

Śrīmad-Bhāgavatam (11.20.9)

"As long as a feeling of detachment from this world of work and its concomitant fruits, culminating in the happiness of the heavenly planets, has not arisen, or in other words, as long as faith in hearing and chanting narrations of My pastimes has not awoken, the many rules and regulations in regard to the performance of *karma* must be followed."

If one who is indifferent to hearing narrations about Śrī Kṛṣṇa abandons his *sva-dharma* before a taste in hearing has arisen, he will fall into a degraded condition. Such a person surrenders to Bhagavān because he fears the results of his good and bad *karma*, not because he has *prema* for the Lord. Śrīman Mahāprabhu thus labeled abandoning the *varṇāśrama-dharma* external. Bhagavān Śrī Kṛṣṇa has clearly said:

yadṛcchayā mat-kathādau
jāta-śraddhas tu yaḥ pumān
na nirviṇṇo nāti-sakto
bhakti-yogo 'sya siddhi-daḥ

Śrīmad-Bhāgavatam (11.20.8)

"By virtue of spiritual merit attained in their previous births, those who are neither repelled nor overly attached materially, and in whom faith in discussions of My pastimes has awakened, are eligible to take to *bhakti*. Bhakti-devī then confers perfection upon them."

The execution of *sva-dharma* has been termed external because by following *varṇāśrama-dharma* one will act according to his material nature. Śrīla Rūpa Gosvāmī has said in his *Bhakti-rasāmṛta-sindhu* (1.2.60):

śāstrataḥ śrūyate bhaktau nṛ-mātrasyādhikāritā

"It is every person's birthright to accept devotional service. This is substantiated in many scriptures."

Even that person who does not follow *varṇāśrama-dharma* has the qualification to worship Viṣṇu. The partial quote from this verse is an unequivocal statement to that effect.

8.62

ājñāyaivaṁ guṇān doṣān
mayādiṣṭān api svakān
dharmān saṁtyajya yaḥ sarvān
māṁ bhajet sa ca sattamaḥ

Śrīmad-Bhāgavatam (11.11.32)

"'O Uddhava, My instructions concerning occupational duties are described in the scriptures. One who deliberates on their merits and limitations, and then gives up *varṇāśrama* to perform *bhajana* of Me is the best of perfected persons.'

The word *śāstra* in this connection refers to the Vedas and other scriptures which propound mundane moral virtues and give instruction how to progress in life. The word *ājñāya* (knowing completely or properly) is split into two parts: *ā* means "completely, or properly," and *jñāya* means "knowing, or understanding." After fully comprehending the inherent limitations and assets of one's prescribed religious duties, one should reject them.

There are three obstacles encountered in the performance of *śuddha-bhakti*:

(1) *dehātma-buddhi* – to consider the material body to be the self.

(2) *jīva-brahma-aikya-jñāna* – to cultivate knowledge that promotes the idea of oneness between the *jīva* and Brahman.

(3) *bhagavat-tattva-jñāna*, or *aiśvarya-jñāna* – to cultivate knowledge concerning the opulence of Bhagavān.

In addition, there are three kinds of people who abandon the path of *karma*:

(1) *ajña* – the ignorant who depart from the prescriptions of *nitya* (daily obligatory) and *naimittika* (occasional) duties mentioned in the Vedas.

(2) *nāstika* – the atheists who know about *karma* as presented in the Vedas but have no faith in it.

(3) *sarva-parityāgī* – those whose renunciation is complete, or who are aware that *karma* is not a limb of *śuddha-bhakti*. They have unflinching faith that through the performance of *bhakti* to Śrī Kṛṣṇa, all *karma* (prescribed duties) automatically becomes complete, meaning they have no other duties to perform.

Persons in this third category are therefore considered to be superior, and Bhagavān refers to them in this verse. In *Śrīmad-Bhāgavatam*, when Bhagavān speaks of the glories of the association of *sādhus*, He is referring to *sādhus* such as these only. For example:

satāṁ prasaṅgān mama vīrya-saṁvido
bhavanti hṛt-karṇa-rasāyanāḥ kathāḥ
taj-joṣaṇād āśv apavarga-vartmani
śraddhā ratir bhaktir anukramiṣyati

Śrīmad-Bhāgavatam (3.25.25)

"In the assembly of pure devotees, powerful discussions illuminating My heroic deeds become a rejuvenating tonic for both the ears and the heart. By hearing these narrations, one quickly advances on the path of emancipation from ignorance. First he develops *śraddhā* in Me, then *rati*, and finally he experiences the awakening of *prema-bhakti*."

He automatically attains eligibility to receive all good qualities, such as mercifulness, as stated in *Śrī Caitanya-caritāmṛta* (*Madhya-līlā* 22.75), "*kṛṣṇa-bhakte kṛṣṇera guṇa sakali sañcārī* – All the good qualities of Kṛṣṇa gradually develop in Kṛṣṇa's devotee."

8.63

sarva-dharmān parityajya
mām ekaṁ śaraṇaṁ vraja
ahaṁ tvāṁ sarva-pāpebhyo
mokṣayiṣyāmi mā śucaḥ

Śrīmad Bhagavad-gītā (18.66)

"'O Arjuna, abandon all varieties of *dharma* such as *varṇāśrama* and just surrender completely unto Me. I shall deliver you from all sinful reaction. Do not lament.'"

In *Śrī Manaḥ-śikṣā* (2) Śrī Raghunātha dāsa Gosvāmī states:

na dharmaṁ nādharmaṁ śruti-gaṇa-niruktaṁ kila kuru
vraja rādhā-kṛṣṇa pracura-paricaryām iha tanu

"Do not perform either the *dharma* (pious deeds) or *adharma* (irreligious, or impious deeds) mentioned in the Vedas. Rather you should perform profuse loving service to the Divine Couple Śrī Rādhā-Kṛṣṇa."

In his commentary to this verse, Śrīla Sarasvatī Ṭhākura presents, as an example, the following verse from the *Śrīmad-Bhāgavatam* (4.29.46):

yadā yam anugṛhṇāti
bhagavān ātma-bhāvitaḥ
sa jahāti matiṁ loke
vede ca pariniṣṭhitām

"Bhagavān bestows His mercy upon a *jīva* who meditates on Him constantly. The *jīva* then becomes free from the root cause of bondage, i.e., the attachment to all social customs and religious rituals prescribed by the Vedas."

The word *dharma* here is taken to mean all bodily and mental occupations (*dharmas*) such as adherence to the spiritual orders and social positions. The use of the prefix *pari* in the word *pariniṣṭhitām* (attached) carries a special meaning, indicating that these devotees constitutionally reject all forms of fruitive activities. The soul itself has no attraction to all of these *dharmas*. The *sādhaka* quits his *brahma-niṣṭhā* (firm faith in impersonal Brahman) and *īśvara-niṣṭhā* (firm faith in the Supreme Controller of the material world, Lord Viṣṇu) and attains *bhagavan-niṣṭhā*, or firm faith in Bhagavān.

Bhakti Mixed with Empiric Knowledge

8.64

prabhu kahe,—"eho bāhya, āge kaha āra"
rāya kahe,—"jñāna-miśrā bhakti—sādhya-sāra"

Upon Śrīman Mahāprabhu saying that renouncing one's *sva-dharma*, or occupational duties, is external, Rāmānanda Rāya proposed that *jñāna-miśrā-bhakti*, or devotion mixed with empiric speculation, is the essence of perfection.

Jñāna-miśrā-bhakti – *bhakti* mixed with empiric knowledge. *Jñāna* (knowledge) has three divisions: *tat-padārtha-jñāna* – knowledge of the Absolute Reality (*para-tattva*), or the Lord (*bhagavat-tattva*); *tvaṁ-padārtha-jñāna* – knowledge of the constitutional position of the *jīva*, which includes knowledge of the relationship between the *jīva* and Brahman; and *jīva-brahma-aikya-jñāna* – knowledge of the oneness between the *jīva* and Brahman.

This last limb, namely, *jīva-brahma-aikya*, is completely opposed to devotion because therein, knowledge of the constitutional relationship between Brahman as master and the *jīva* as servant cannot manifest, or rather, awaken. The first two limbs of *jñāna*, namely knowledge of *jīva-tattva* and knowledge of *brahma-tattva*, or *bhagavat-tattva*, are not in opposition to *bhakti*, because they do not hinder nourishment of a master-servant relationship.

The meaning of the word *jñāna* in the current verse might be stretched, and thus interpreted in such a way as to suggest that *bhakti* mixed with these three limbs of *jñāna* is called *jñāna-miśrā-bhakti* (devotional service to Śrī Kṛṣṇa with a desire to enjoy the fruits of transcendental knowledge), but that would not be correct.

It is worth considering here that without the help of *bhakti*, *nirviśeṣa-jñāna* (knowledge of the impersonal Brahman effulgence) on its own is completely incapable of bestowing *sāyujya-mukti*, or impersonal liberation. Thus, in the verse under consideration the *jñāna-miśrā-bhakti* referred to specifically indicates the third type of *jñāna*, or *jīva-brahma-aikya-jñāna*, which promulgates knowledge of the non-difference between the individual soul and the Supreme Soul.

In addition, there are even some *sādhakas* on the path of *bhakti-yoga* whose predominant goal is to attain knowledge that does not obstruct *bhakti*, such as *bhagavat-tattva-jñāna* (knowledge of the reality about the Supreme Personality of Godhead), *jīva-tattva-jñāna* (knowledge about the reality of the minute spiritual living entity), and *sambandha-jñāna* (the accompanying knowledge of the relationship between both), as well as *māyā-tattva-jñāna* (knowledge about the reality of the illusory energy). For this reason, their practice of the limbs of *bhakti* also remains mixed with *jñāna*. Therefore, one might include their practice in the definition of *jñāna-miśrā-bhakti*.

Regardless, the *jñāna-miśra-bhakti* referred to in this verse by Śrī Rāmānanda only equates with that *bhakti* which is mixed with *jīva-brahma-aikya-jñāna*. We shall see that this is indicated directly in the next verse, *brahma-bhūtaḥ prasannātmā*. In their commentaries on this verse, Śrī Śaṅkarācārya, Śrīpāda Śrīdhara Svāmī, and Śrī Viśvanātha Cakravartī Ṭhākura have all accepted that the *jñāna* mentioned here is *jīva-brahma-aikya-jñāna*.

Although on the path of *śuddha-bhakti* there is a statute allowing one to abandon his *sva-dharma*, a certain level of qualification to do this is required. An edict to that effect appears in the *Śrīmad-Bhāgavatam*:

tāvat karmāṇi kurvīta
na nirvidyeta yāvatā
mat-kathā-śravaṇādau vā
śraddhā yāvan na jāyate

Śrīmad-Bhāgavatam (11.20.9)

"As long as disinterest in *karma* has not arisen, or until, by the mercy of some *mahā-puruṣa*, one experiences the awakening of faith in the process of hearing and chanting *bhagavat-kathā*, one should continue to perform *karma*."

It is only upon the awakening of extremely thick *śraddhā* by the grace of a pure devotee that one receives the qualification to enter *kevalā-bhakti*, or exclusive devotion, and it is then that one becomes qualified to abandon prescribed duties (*sva-dharma*).

When an unqualified person renounces prescribed duties, there is fear of an inauspiciousness occurrence. For this reason, Śrīman Mahāprabhu is saying that it is external. If hearing and chanting are not coming from love within the heart, but rather from some mentally conceived sense of duty, then this practice, too, is external or superficial. Śrīman Mahāprabhu is looking for an explanation of something superior; therefore, Śrī Rāmānanda Rāya describes *jñāna-miśrā-bhakti* as the *sādhya*, or state of perfection.

Śrīla Bhaktisiddhānta Sarasvatī Prabhupāda explains that while in this universe, one who is advancing in his activities along the path of self-realization will still be subject to some *asmitā*[10], or material identification, but when that false conception of the self is dispelled, he crosses over the Virajā River, which is beyond the influence of the three modes of material nature, and reaches the neutral (*sāmya*) or unmanifest (*avyakta*) state of the three modes.

The material universe manifests from the external energy, whereas Vaikuṇṭha *dhāma*, the abode of the Lord, is manifest from the internal potency. In between the two are Brahma-loka and the Virajā River. This river is the place of shelter for those *jīvas* who are detached from dull matter and who deny the material varieties within the material creation. Those who have acquired this unmanifest state may not enter Vaikuṇṭha but must remain outside; therefore it is termed as *bāhya*, or external. Just as the realization of the *sādhakas* who have abandoned their prescribed duties within this world does not equate to realization

10 *Asmitā*: the false egoism arising from the conceptions of "I" and "mine" in relation to the material body.

of Vaikuṇṭha or Goloka-dhāma, similarly those who make their goal detachment from material enjoyment only receive realization of a non-conscious impersonal reality. For this reason, it is also external. In fact, only *prema-bhakti* qualifies as *parā-bhakti* (transcendental devotional service to the Supreme Lord). Unless one reaches the state of *sāmya* or *avyakta* (the neutral state of the three modes), it is actually impossible to attain *prema-bhakti.*

In *jñāna-miśrā-bhakti*, *jñāna* remains prominent, and thus it is not *bhakti* at all. Rather, it is merely an offense at the lotus feet of Bhagavān. It becomes possible to obtain *bhakti* from the *sāmya* or *avyakta* platform if one somehow gets the association of a pure *guru* and Vaiṣṇavas. If a piece of gold, the size and shape of a mustard seed, is mixed into a huge heap of golden mustard seeds, it is extremely difficult to distinguish it, but once the pile of seeds is set on fire and reduced to ashes it is easy to find that piece of gold.

In the same manner, in the saintly association of the pure spiritual master and Vaiṣṇava devotees, that mountain-like heap of *jñāna* is burned to ashes by the fire of hearing and chanting, whereupon pure *bhakti* (that piece of gold) may easily be obtained. Accordingly, where *jñāna-miśrā-bhakti* ends, *śuddha-bhakti*, or pure devotion, begins. *Jñānīs* desire to obtain *sāyujya*, which is the liberation of merging with the effulgence of the Lord, yet they cannot attain their goal by the process of *jñāna* alone. They may obtain it only by virtue of mixing this *jñāna* with *bhakti.*

The practice of this *jñāna-miśrā bhakti* is never capable of awakening *prema*; therefore, this type of *jñāna* presents an obstruction to *śuddha-bhakti. Śrīmad-Bhāgavatam* (11.20.31) states:

tasmān mad-bhakti-yuktasya
yogino vai mad-ātmanaḥ
na jñānaṁ na ca vairāgyaṁ
prāyaḥ śreyo bhaved iha

"Thus the *yogī* who is connected with My *bhakti* and absorbed in thinking of Me, need not cultivate *jñāna* or renunciation. His auspiciousness is achieved only through devotion to Me."

8.65

brahma-bhūtaḥ prasannātmā
na śocati na kāṅkṣati
samaḥ sarveṣu bhūteṣu
mad-bhaktiṁ labhate parām

Śrīmad Bhagavad-gītā (18.54)

"'A person happily absorbed in Brahman neither laments for nor desires anything. Being equipoised in his vision of all living beings, he obtains *parā-bhakti* (transcendental devotional service to Me) which is endowed with the symptoms of *prema*.'"

There is a multitude of *mantras* in the Vedas establishing the difference between the *jīva* and Brahman. Some examples are given here:

(1) "*Pradhāna-kṣetra-jña-patir guṇeśaḥ* – that Paramātmā is the controller of the *guṇas* and master of the living entities" (*Śvetāśvatara Upaniṣad* 3.6.16).

(2) "*Tam āhur agryaṁ puruṣaṁ mahāntam* – sages declare Him to be the foremost and greatest of persons" (*Śvetāśvatara Upaniṣad* 3.3.19).

(3) "*Yāthātathyato 'rthān vyadadhāt* – it is He who awards the many *jīvas'* necessities" (*Īśopaniṣad* 3.8).

(4) "*Tenedaṁ pūrṇaṁ puruṣeṇa sarvam* – by that Person's arrangement, this universe is complete in every respect" (*Śvetāśvatara Upaniṣad* 3.3.9).

(5) "*Nityo nityānāṁ* – He is supreme among all eternal beings" (*Kaṭha Upaniṣad* 2.2.13, *Śvetāśvatara Upaniṣad* 3.6.13).

This compilation of *sutras* directly demonstrates that the *jīva* can never dissolve and become one with Brahman in any situation. Persons who attain the *brahma-bhūta* platform are in one of two categories. One type, despite reaching this platform, disrespects the names, forms, qualities, and pastimes of Bhagavān, as well as His devotees. Such persons continue to endeavor exclusively for *sāyujya-mukti*. The *brahma-bhūta* (self-realized) persons of this category are offenders. Instead of achieving liberation, this kind of person continues to rotate in the cycle of birth and death, taking birth in demonic species. The other kind of *brahma-bhūta* souls, being non-offenders, easily achieve the shelter of the devotees and attain *parā-bhakti*.

Bhakti Devoid of Empiric Knowledge

8.66

prabhu kahe,—"eho bāhya, āge kaha āra"
rāya kahe,—"jñāna-śūnyā bhakti—sādhya-sāra"

After hearing this, Śrīman Mahāprabhu said, "This is also external. If there is anything more than this, please speak further." Rāmānanda Rāya replied, "Pure devotional service without any touch of speculative knowledge (*jñāna-śūnyā-bhakti*) is the topmost perfection.

Jñāna-śūnyā-bhakti – devotion free from *jñāna*. As mentioned earlier, there are three limbs of *jñāna*: knowledge of *bhagavat-tattva*, knowledge of *jīva-tattva*, and knowledge of the oneness between the *jīva* and Brahman. Now in this verse, there is mention of a variety of *bhakti* untouched by these three types of *jñāna*. *Jñāna-śūnyā-bhakti* is superior *to jñāna-miśrā-bhakti*, primarily in that there is no trace of knowledge of the oneness between the *jīva* and Brahman (*jīva-brahmaika-jñāna*), which is directly opposed to the cultivation of a master-servant relationship. Moreover, this *jñāna-śūnyā-bhakti* is not mixed with the excessive insistence to collect knowledge about the nature of Bhagavān (*bhagavat-tattva-jñāna*) or knowledge about the nature of the living entity (*jīva-tattva-jñāna*), which generate obstacles in the path of *śuddha-bhakti*.

In *jñāna-śūnyā-bhakti*, there is a complete manifestation of *sambandha-jñāna*, or knowledge of one's relationship with Bhagavān. However in the path of *jñāna-miśrā-bhakti*, the *jīva* simply becomes a dry speculator (*śuṣka-jñānī*). Upon the awakening of good fortune, by the influence of the association of pure devotees, one very quickly achieves *prema-bhakti*. In such a position all obstacles are gradually destroyed. The *sādhaka* goes far beyond having material desires, and gradually obtains a proper level of realization of *prema-bhakti*.

In relation to *jñāna-śūnyā-bhakti*, Śrī Rāmānanda Rāya quotes evidence from the *Śrīmad-Bhāgavatam*:

8.67

jñāne prayāsam udapāsya namanta eva
jīvanti san-mukharitāṁ bhavadīya-vārtām
sthāne sthitāḥ śruti-gatāṁ tanu-vāṅ-manobhir
ye prāyaśo 'jita jito 'py asi tais tri-lokyām

Śrīmad-Bhāgavatam (10.14.3)

"Śrī Brahmā is saying to Śrī Kṛṣṇa: 'The *sādhana* to obtain an object that is beyond the senses, with the help of knowledge obtained by the senses, is called *āroha-vāda* (the futile and laborious ascending process) or *aśrauta-panthā* (the path devoid of aural reception of the Vedic principles). However, those who do not make any endeavor for *jñāna*, and who instead maintain their lives by exclusively rendering service to the descriptions of Your pastimes flowing from the mouths of the *sādhus*, by body, mind, and words, are able to conquer You. Despite their not making any other endeavor, and despite Your being unconquerable, such persons control You by their *prema*.'"

"**Bhakti-vaśaḥ puruṣaḥ** – the Supreme Person is controlled by devotion" (*Māṭhara-śruti*). One may attain *ānanda*, or bliss, through *jñāna-śūnya-bhakti*, even though relationship with Śrī Kṛṣṇa, or a sense of ownership and intimacy with Him, is lacking, just as one feels ecstasy witnessing the moon even though one has no relation with it.

There are two types of *jñāna*: *tat-padārtha-jñāna* (that which is related to the Lord) and *tvaṁ-padārtha-jñāna* (that which is related to the *jīva*). Śrī Bhagavān is worshipful by all, and the *jīva* is His eternal servitor. Yet *nirviśeṣa-jñāna* completely opposes this conception. Thus it stands contrary to *bhakti* and should be rejected entirely. This alone is the reason that *jñāna-śūnyā-bhakti* is accepted as superior to *jñāna-miśrā-bhakti*. By presenting this verse from *Śrīmad-Bhāgavatam*, Śrī Rāmānanda Rāya has made it totally clear that the *sādhaka* is able to achieve everything by only hearing *hari-kathā* from the mouths of the unalloyed devotees. To obtain *sambandha*, *abhidheya*, and *prayojana* (knowledge of the relationship, process, and ultimate goal) rests on the basis of this *hari-kathā*, which is both the *sādhya* (goal) and the *sādhana* (process).

When Śrī Kṛṣṇa went to Mathurā, He sent His friend Uddhava to Vraja with the tattered garment of *jñāna*. The *gopīs* took that garment and after tearing it to shreds threw it straight into the Yamunā River. The Yamunā then carried it to Prayāga and from there it continued until it reached the ocean. Submerged in the salty water of the ocean, those shreds of *jñāna* dissolved and lost their very existence. Even opulence (*aiśvarya*) cannot find any right to render service in Vraja, what to speak of *nirviśeṣa-jñāna*, which the *gopīs* did not permit to exist inside Vraja even by name. If opulence desires to perform any service there, it is subsumed within Vraja's bottomless, fathomless, and limitless oceanic sweetness.

Take the example of a piece of straw placed in a large pot of boiling milk. That straw remains visible on the surface only for a second before totally disappearing into the milk. One will not be able find it. *Aiśvarya*, likened to the straw in that milk, is concealed by the fathomless ocean of *mādhurya* in Vraja. One has no way of knowing that it is there. To support this Śrī Śukadeva Gosvāmī has said:

tasmin mahan-mukharitā madhubhic-caritra-
pīyūṣa-śeṣa-saritaḥ paritaḥ sravanti
tā ye pibanty avitṛṣo nṛpa gāḍha-karṇais
tān na spṛśanty aśana-tṛḍ-bhaya-śoka-mohāḥ

Śrīmad-Bhāgavatam (4.29.40)

"In the society of *sādhus*, many rivers of pure nectar in the form of discussions of Śrī Kṛṣṇa flow in all directions, from the mouths of the pure devotees present there. Persons who, with their well-like ears, drink this nectar without getting full, are not disturbed by hunger, thirst, fear, lamentation, illusion, etc."

The Śruti confirms:

tam eva, viditvāti mṛtyum eti nānyaḥ panthā vidyate 'yanāya

"By knowing that Supreme Person, who is the embodiment of knowledge, bliss, and eternity (*sat-cit-ānanda-svarūpa*), the *jīva* can cross this ocean of birth and death. Apart from knowing Him, there is no other method of liberating oneself from the blazing fire of material existence."

Just by thirstily endeavoring to hear the topics of Śrī Kṛṣṇa (*hari-kathā*), a person is not merely liberated, but he subjugates Śrī Bhagavān. If someone tries to obtain *jñāna* alone, then, just like a person threshing empty husks of rice, he achieves nothing.

śreyaḥ-sṛtiṁ bhaktim udāsya te vibho
kliśyanti ye kevala-bodha-labdhaye
teṣām asau kleśala eva śiṣyate
nānyad yathā sthūla-tuṣāvaghātinām

Śrīmad-Bhāgavatam (10.14.4)

"O Lord, devotional service unto You is the main source of all kinds of auspiciousness. Those who give up this path only to cultivate *jñāna* will simply undergo hard labor, pain, and difficulty, just as the only gain of a person who beats empty husks is hard work, not rice."

Narrations about Bhagavān become supremely attractive and full of *rasa* when infused with the nectar of Bhagavān's form, pastimes, and qualities. Śrī Bhagavān Himself has said to Śrī Durvāsā Ṛṣi: "*ahaṁ bhakta-parādhīno hy asvatantra iva dvija* – O *brāhmaṇa*, the *sādhus*, My topmost devotees, hold complete possession of My heart. Their love for Me is so great that I accept their control. And because their heart is so infused with *prema-rasa*, I have no desire to leave it" (*Śrīmad-Bhāgavatam* 9.4.63).

After *jñāna-śūnyā-bhakti*, the propensity to bring Bhagavān under one's loving control begins to develop. This ability is also a measure of one's *bhakti*. We can therefore say that this *jñāna-śūnyā-bhakti* is the first milestone on the path to attain *prema-bhakti*; one controls the Lord in proportion to its progressive development.

The primary cause of this wonderful phenomenon of being able to control Bhagavān is the variegatedness of the *sādhakas'* tastes, natures, and tendencies. Each person's *bhakti* and their practices of the limbs of *bhakti* are unique. From here begins the description of the performance of devotion that pertains to one's eternal constitutional relationship with Bhagavān. The *bhakti* that was described before this verse is performed in connection with the body.

Prema-bhakti

8.68

prabhu kahe,—"eho haya, āge kaha āra"
rāya kahe,—"prema-bhakti—sarva-sādhya-sāra"

Śrīman Mahāprabhu said, "O Rāmānanda, this may be called the *sādhya*, but please speak something more." Śrī Rāmānanda Rāya said, "*Prema-bhakti* is the essence of all perfection.

Up until now, Śrīman Mahāprabhu had only responded to all proposals with "*eho bāhya* – this is external," but now He says, "*Eho haya* – this may be." When *jñāna-śūnyā-bhakti* was proposed, He said, "This is good," because whatever Śrī Rāmānanda Rāya had explained before had not been conducive for the progressive understanding of the master-servant relationship. However, this *jñāna-śūnyā-bhakti* is favorable for its development.

Mahāprabhu's request for him to speak further on this point reveals that Śrī Rāmānanda Rāya has now reached the correct path but should proceed further. From the verse from *Śrīmad-Bhāgavatam* (10.14.3) which Śrī Rāmānanda Rāya spoke to illuminate *jñāna-śūnyā-bhakti*, one may comprehend that practicing *jñāna-śūnyā-bhakti* and hearing *hari-kathā* is so powerful that Bhagavān becomes controlled by the *sādhaka* who does so. The Śruti also confirms that Bhagavān is controlled by *bhakti* (*bhakti-vaśaḥ purusaḥ*), yet the degree to which He is controlled is also gradated. He is not controlled equally by all the *bhaktas*.

Sādhakas engage in devotional services according to their individual tastes and desires, and thus they control Bhagavān to the degree of their devotion. They may even be performing the same limb of *bhakti* as each other, but due to the *sādhakas'* individual natures, there will be differences in their practice, so they will not control Bhagavān to the same degree. Essentially, this means that to the degree of intensity with which a devotee desires to perform service, Bhagavān is then accordingly inclined to manifest His quality of being controlled by him. It is for this reason that the devotees of *śānta*, *dāsya*, *sakhya*, *vātsalya*, and *kānta-bhāva*[11] do not each control Bhagavān to the same extent.

There is another point to consider: Is Bhagavān controlled simply by hearing the *hari-kathā* that comes from the mouth of His devotees? Or is Bhagavān controlled by a listener who attains some special state on hearing *hari-kathā*? It is with the intention of clarifying this that Mahāprabhu asked Śrī Rāmānanda Rāya to speak a little further on the subject. The listener controls Bhagavān just by listening to the narrations of Bhagavān's pastimes – this is fine, but this takes place only when the hearer of *hari-kathā* is situated in the stage of *prema*.

Prema-bhakti – devotion endowed with the characteristics of divine love. That proclivity to render such service that it gives excessive happiness to Śrī Kṛṣṇa is called *prema*. Through the performance of hearing and chanting performed in the stage of *jñāna-śūnyā-bhakti*, by the mercy of Bhagavān, the contamination of the heart is gradually dispelled. Thereafter, knowledge of the servant's relationship with the Lord as well as the tendency to serve Śrī Kṛṣṇa, manifest in the heart. Then, by the mercy of the *svarūpa-śakti*, the essence of the *hlādinī* and *saṁvit-śaktis* (Kṛṣṇa's transcendental bliss and knowledge potencies) enters the heart of the *sādhaka*. The fully ripened, or mature, stage of *śuddha-sattva* is called *prema*. This devotional service to Śrī Kṛṣṇa, which is filled with pure love, is known as *prema-bhakti*.

Bhagavat-kathā is both our *sādhya* and our *sādhana*; similarly, so is *prema-bhakti*. If there is *prema* within the heart of the *sādhaka* then he will perform all the limbs of *bhakti* with deep love, and Śrī Kṛṣṇa is pleased with him. Without *prema*, the *sādhaka* may perform *bhakti* but that *bhakti* will never satisfy Śrī Kṛṣṇa. For a person who is hungry, even dry bread seems most appealing, but if someone is neither hungry nor

11 *Kānta-bhāva* – another name for *mādhurya-bhāva*.

thirsty then he can easily ignore a delicious feast replete with the six types of tastes (salty, sweet, pungent, bitter, sour, and astringent).

Controlled by the *prema* of Vidura, Śrī Kṛṣṇa ate even banana skins, yet because Duryodhana had no *prema*, Śrī Kṛṣṇa abstained from a huge feast, composed of all six tastes, served by him. Śrī Kṛṣṇa ate the rice and yoghurt offered with *prema* by the wives of the *brāhmaṇas*, Śrī Rāmacandra ate the remnant fruits of Śabarī (a low-caste lady dwelling in the forest), and Śrīman Mahāprabhu consumed vegetables snatched from the devotee Śrīdhara. Bhagavān, hungry to eat whatever a *premī-bhakta* offers Him, very lovingly and enthusiastically accepts foodstuffs presented with *prema*.

Although Śrī Lakṣmī resides eternally on the chest of Śrīman Nārāyaṇa, she identifies as being the wife of a *brāhmaṇa*. Proud of this designation, her serving attitude was slackened and she was thus precluded from entering the pastimes of Vraja. When one has knowledge of the relationship between the master (*sevya*) and servant (*sevaka*), the tendency or desire to render service transforms into *prema* and the *premī-bhakta* chants the holy name, maintaining a vow to chant a fixed number of names daily. The devotee engages in *sādhana-bhajana*, absorbed in the moods expressed in these songs:

rādhā-kuṇḍa-taṭa-kuñja-kuṭīra, govardhana-parvata, yāmuna-tīra

"A bower on the bank of Rādhā-kuṇḍa, as well as Govardhana Hill, and the banks of the Yamunā River – all these places are my life and soul."

he rādhe vraja-devīke ca lalite he nanda-sūno kutaḥ
śrī-govardhana-kalpa-pādapa-tale kālindī-vane kutaḥ

"O Rādhā, mistress of Vṛndāvana! O Lalitā! O son of Nanda Mahārāja! Where are all of you now? Are you seated beneath the *kalpa-vṛkṣa* (desire trees) of Śrī Govardhana Hill? Or are you roaming in the forests along the soft sandy banks of the Yamunā?"

A devotee who performs *sādhana-bhajana* in this way very much pleases Bhagavān, who becomes restless to taste even his ordinary offerings. In order to taste *prema*, He will dance for just a cup of buttermilk.

8.69

nānopacāra-kṛta-pūjanam ārta-bandhoḥ
premṇaiva bhakta-hṛdayaṁ sukha-vidrutaṁ syāt
yāvat kṣud asti jaṭhare jaraṭhā pipāsā
tāvat sukhāya bhavato nanu bhakṣya-peye

Padyāvalī (13)

"'As long as one feels acute hunger and thirst, one enjoys eating and drinking. In the same way, even if one worships *ārtta-bandhu* Bhagavān (the Lord who is the friend of the distressed) with many different types of paraphernalia, only when that *pūjā* is performed with *prema* will that devotee's heart melt with happiness.'

The essential meaning is that if very strong hunger and thirst are not present, then even if one is offered very tasty, fragrant, and appetizing dishes, one will still not have a desire to eat. Likewise, if there is no *prema*, then even if one worships Śrī Kṛṣṇa with many, many different articles, still He is not pleased. And, on the other hand, if one has a raging hunger and thirst, then one will appreciate and be greatly satisfied by taking common rice and water. Similarly, if *prema* is present in a devotee's heart, Śrī Kṛṣṇa receives great happiness by accepting even ordinary items the devotee gives Him.

Some people may doubt that the example and the idea being clarified actually correspond because, in the example it says that only if a person is hungry and thirsty can taking simple rice and water give him happiness. Yet in the idea being clarified, it says that Bhagavān indeed feels hungry upon being given anything with *prema*. Thus the doubt may come in the mind that, if the devotee is hungry to serve, then how does this makes Bhagavān hungry? Yet such a doubt is unfounded.[12]

12 Here in this verse Rāya Rāmānanda is explaining, that when the devotee has *prema* and yearns for Kṛṣṇa to accept his offering, then the love in the devotee causes a hunger and thirst in Kṛṣṇa. The devotee's affection creates in Kṛṣṇa a hunger and thirst to accept the offering. The offering itself may consist of

We can thus see that since Bhagavān lovingly accepts a devotee's service, according to the degree of strong love that he has for Bhagavān, that such a doubt has no basis. If *prema* is not present in the heart of the devotee, then the desire to accept service cannot possibly awaken in the heart of Bhagavān. Once *prema* awakens in the heart of the devotee and reaches the stage of extreme eagerness and longing to serve, then the desire to accept service awakens in the heart of *bhakta-vatsala* Bhagavān (the Lord who is always affectionate to the devotee). That is why here, Bhagavān is called *ārtta-bandhu* (friend of the distressed). With regard to the object of *sādhana*, Śrī Rūpa Gosvāmī has said:

kṛti-sādhyā bhavet sādhya-
bhāvā sā sādhanābhidhā
nitya-siddhasya bhāvasya
prākaṭyaṁ hṛdi sādhyatā

Bhakti-rasāmṛta-sindhu (1.2.2)

"*Sādhana-bhakti* is the engagement of the mind and senses in the limbs of *bhakti* for the purpose of attaining *bhāva-bhakti*. This *bhāva* is a potentiality which eternally exists in the heart of the *jīva* and is manifested in the heart purified by *sādhana* (through the mercy of a *nitya-siddha*, a living *sad-guru*)."

Pure devotion is the ever-present, eternal constitutional position of the *jīva*. The living being is a tiny particle of blissful consciousness, likened to a spark of sunshine (*cit-kaṇa*) of the all-blissful spiritual sun (*cit-sūrya*) Śrī Kṛṣṇa. This naturally occuring happiness is known as *nitya-siddha-bhāva* (eternally present love for Kṛṣṇa) and it is awakened in the heart of the *jīva* by the practice of *sādhana-bhakti*. In this stage, the eternally perfect object, namely, the potency of pure love for Godhead, reaches its perfection. When the bound *jīvas*, endeavoring by their senses, strive to attain *bhāva*, their practice is called *sādhana-bhakti*. The goal of *sādhana-bhakti* is to awaken *bhāva-bhakti*.

---

ordinary items, but still Kṛṣṇa comes, and with great relish He tastes what the devotee has offered. Why? It is because the *prema* in the heart of the devotee has created a great hunger in Him.

At the time of initiation, or *dīkṣā*, the holy master instructs the *sādhaka* on his relationship with Śrī Bhagavān. Fixed in this relationship, the devotee performs *sādhana* with firm determination, and thus he achieves *bhāva-bhakti*. When this *bhāva-bhakti* reaches a completely ripened condition it is known as *prema-bhakti*. The *sādhaka-bhakta* becomes extremely blessed when *śrī guru* bestows realization of his position as a maidservant of Śrī Rādhā. Only by the devotion of His devotees does Śrī Kṛṣṇa's love swell. The term *sādhana-bhakti* includes all of the progressive stages of *bhakti* – *śraddhā* (faith), *sādhu-saṅga* (association with pure devotees), *bhajana-anuṣṭhāna* (performance of devotional service to Kṛṣṇa), *anartha-nivṛtti* (the diminishing of all unwanted habits), *niṣṭhā* (firm faith), *ruci* (taste), and *āsakti* (attachment).

8.70

kṛṣṇa-bhakti-rasa-bhāvitā matiḥ
krīyatāṁ yadi kuto 'pi labhyate
tatra laulyam api mūlyam ekalaṁ
janma-koṭi-sukṛtair na labhyate

Padyāvalī (14)

"'O men of virtue, if consciousness that is saturated and perfumed with the nectar of *kṛṣṇa-bhakti* is available anywhere, then purchase it at once without delay. The only price to get it is greed to obtain *vraja-rasa* (the moods of Vraja). Without this divine greed, then even heaps of spiritual credits (*sukṛti*) accumulated over millions of lives will not be enough to procure that *bhakti* for Śrī Kṛṣṇa.'"

Śrīla Bhaktivinoda Ṭhākura says that this type of devotion, where the heart is soaked in *kṛṣṇa-bhakti-rasa* (the nectar of loving service to Kṛṣṇa), has only one price and that price is greed. *Bhakti* is of two types: the first is *śāstra-avadhāraṇā-mayī vaidhī-bhakti*, the path of *bhakti* inspired by the governing principles of the scriptures, and the second is *lobha-mūlaka rāgānuga-bhakti*, devotion impelled by greed to follow the loving sentiments of the eternally perfected residents of Vraja. Here Śrī Rāmānanda Rāya is alluding solely to this second type of devotion, namely *lobha-mūlaka rāgānuga-bhakti.* Śrīla Cakravartī Ṭhākura tells us that the only method to give happiness to Śrī Kṛṣṇa is *kṛṣṇa-bhakti-bhavitā mati*, to have a consciousness infused with the flavors of loving service to Him. A fortunate person may enter this *rāgānuga-bhakti*, spontaneous devotion.

In this case "Śrī Kṛṣṇa" means "Vrajendra-nandana Śrī Kṛṣṇa, the son of the king of Vraja," and *bhakti* signifies *bhāva-bhakti*, the initial stage of perfection in devotion, which matures into *prema-bhakti.* The phrase *prema-bhakti-rasa-bhāvitā mati* refers to that person whose every pore is utterly saturated with *śrī-kṛṣṇa-bhakti-rasa*, and whose intelligence has become one with that *bhakti-rasa*[13]. This mood may only be attained by the mercy of Bhagavān. In *Śrīmad-Bhāgavatam* it has been said:

satāṁ prasaṅgān mama vīrya-saṁvido
bhavanti hṛt-karṇa-rasāyanāḥ kathāḥ
taj-joṣaṇād āśv apavarga-vartmani
śraddhā ratir bhaktir anukramiṣyati

Śrīmad-Bhāgavatam (3.25.25)

"In the assembly of pure devotees, powerful discussions illuminating My heroic deeds become a rejuvenating tonic for both the ears and the heart. By hearing these narrations, one quickly advances on the path of emancipation from ignorance. First he develops *śraddhā*, then *rati*, and finally *prema-bhakti.*"

This *bhakti-bhāva* is received by two methods – by the mercy of the devotee (*bhakta-prasādaja*) and by the mercy of Bhagavān (*bhagavat-prasādaja*). The mercy of Bhagavān strictly follows the mercy of the devotee. This is the very reason why Svayam Bhagavān Śrī Kṛṣṇa descended in the form of the topmost devotee, Śrī Caitanya Mahāprabhu, and poured His mercy everywhere.

---

13 *Bhakti-rasa* – attachment to Śrī Kṛṣṇa in the mood and manner of those eternally perfected devotees, particularly the Vrajavāsīs.

Śrīla Narottama Ṭhākura has prayed to Śrī Lokanātha Gosvāmī:

kabe lokanātha more saṅge laiyā jābe
śrī rūpera pāda-padme more samarpibe

"O Gurudeva! When will you bestow upon me your mercy and offer me to the feet of Śrīla Rūpa Gosvāmī?"

In the same manner we see Śrī Kṛṣṇadāsa Kavirāja praying at the end of almost every chapter of *Śrī Caitanya-caritāmṛta*:

śrī-rūpa-raghunātha-pade yāra āśa
caitanya-caritāmṛta kahe kṛṣṇa dāsa

"Always praying at the lotus feet of Śrī Rūpa and Śrī Raghunātha for their mercy, I, Kṛṣṇadāsa Kavirāja, recite this *Śrī Caitanya-caritāmṛta*."

Bhagavān can give *bhakti* but not a mood of service to Him. Along with *bhakti*, the devotee can also give his own *bhāva* and his own personal realizations. By accepting these *bhāvas*, or moods, it no longer remains difficult for one to attain *bhakti*. In the same way that sugar syrup permeates every atom of a *rasagullā*, similarly every pore of the body of a *vraja-rasa-rasika guru* or Vaiṣṇava is completely saturated with *prema-bhakti-rasa*. At every moment, the *rasika* Vaiṣṇava continuously distributes the most purifying sweet discussions of Śrī Rādhā-Kṛṣṇa's pastimes. His mind, intelligence, affection, and character are all completely filled with Śrī Kṛṣṇa's *rasamayī-bhakti* (ambrosial devotion).

By associating with these *rasika* devotees, greed is awakened to serve Śrī Kṛṣṇa with *prema*. If due to that greed, one has to give up his very life, Bhagavān will indeed become dearer to him than his own existence. We all possess this *prema-rasa* in our hearts, but now it is dormant. It is by hearing discussions saturated with *bhakti-rasa* that this *prema* will be awakened. The devotee hears *bhakti-śāstras* (devotional scriptures) and cultivates his Kṛṣṇa consciousness by following the instructions given in them; thus he becomes immersed in this *bhakti-bhāva*.

Dāsya-prema – the love of a servant for Kṛṣṇa

8.71

prabhu kahe,—"eho haya, āge kaha āra"
rāya kahe,—"dāsya-prema—sarva-sādhya-sāra"

Śrīman Mahāprabhu said, "This is fine, but please speak something more." Śrī Rāmānanda Rāya replied, "Loving service in servitude (*dāsya-prema*) – as exchanged by master and servant – is the essence of all perfection.

The *bhakti* of all devotees is not equal. There is a gradation. "*Jīvera svarūpa haya nitya kṛṣṇa-dāsa* – It is the living entity's constitutional position to be an eternal servant of Kṛṣṇa." This *dāsya-bhāva* also has gradations within it. If rain falls at the time of the *svāti-nakṣatra* and falls upon an oyster, then that rain produces a pearl. If it falls on a banana plant it produces camphor, and if it falls on the head of an elephant it gives rise to *gaja-muktā*, a pearl found in the projections of an elephant's forehead, and thus known as an elephant pearl. If that same rain falls upon the feet of a cow it makes a yellow pigment called *gorocanā*, and if it falls on bamboo, then *vaṁśa-locana*, which is a milky colored substance is formed in the hollow of the bamboo.

Different transformations take place, depending on the objects the rain falls upon. Similarly, if a variety of seeds, such as mango, neem, and tamarind, are planted in the same garden and watered with the same Ganges water, three different kinds of fruit-bearing trees will appear. In the same way, despite the fact that everyone is a servant of Śrī Kṛṣṇa, each person's eternal constitutional service mood is different, and because these service moods are variegated, the happiness derived from the service, is also variegated. By performing service, worship, and *sādhana* under the guidance of *śrī gurudeva* and Vaiṣṇavas, the eternal constitutional position of the *sādhaka*, the *nitya-svarūpa*, manifests itself. Beforehand, *śuddha-sattva* must necessarily manifest in the heart.

The essential meaning of *dāsya-bhāva* is as follows: "Śrī Bhagavān is the object of service. He is my master (*prabhu*) and I am His servant (*dāsa*)." The service propensity (*sevā-vāsanā*) that accompanies this mood of servitorship is called *dāsya-prema*. Service rendered to Bhagavān that is devoid of this *dāsya-bhāva* and its accompanying feelings of possessiveness (*mamatā*), is called ordinary *prema-bhakti*, or *śānta-prema*; it cannot establish a relationship with Bhagavān.

When one's feeling of possessiveness of the Lord gradually increases, this ordinary *prema* (*śānta-prema*) transforms into the mood of a servant (*dāsya-bhāva*). More complete feelings of servitorship are found within all the Lord's associates who participate in His pastimes. This mood of servitude is present completely in the devotees in *dāsya-rasa*, more completely in the devotees in the mellow of friendship (*sakhya-rasa*), most completely in the devotees in the parental mood (*vātsalya-rasa*), and is totally complete in the devotees in the amorous mellow (*madhura-rasa*).

In the *dāsya-bhakti* of the devotees of Vraja, *mamatā* (excessive feelings of intimacy, or possessiveness) are mixed with feelings of fraternity and parental affection for Śrī Kṛṣṇa. The various types of wonderment of *prema*, all of which consist of the desire to please Śrī Kṛṣṇa, present themselves through devotional service rendered in the mood of servitude (*dāsya-sevā*). For the glorification of *dāsya-prema*, Śrī Rāmānanda Rāya quotes the following verse from *Śrīmad-Bhāgavatam*:

8.72

yan-nāma-śruti-mātreṇa pumān bhavati nirmalaḥ
tasya tīrtha-padaḥ kiṁ vā dāsānām avaśiṣyate

Śrīmad-Bhāgavatam (9.5.16)

"Śrī Durvāsā, the best of *ṛṣis*, said to Ambarīṣa Mahārāja, 'Simply by hearing the all auspicious names of Bhagavān, the *jīva* becomes pure, so for those who are the servants of the lotus feet of *tīrtha-pada* Bhagavān, what desirable object remains to be still attained?'

8.73

bhavantam evānucaran nirantaraḥ
praśānta-niḥśeṣa-mano-rathāntaraḥ
kadāham aikāntika-nitya-kiṅkaraḥ
praharṣayiṣyāmi sa-nātha-jīvitam

Stotra-ratna (43)
by Śrī Yāmuna Muni (Śrī Yāmunācārya)

"'O Lord, when will I become Your eternal, one-pointed servant, renouncing all desires apart from serving You, and always feeling joyful because of having such a glorious master?'"

Śrī Cakravartī Ṭhākura explains that it is clear from both of these verses that there is nothing the servant of Bhagavān cannot attain. In both cases, the devotee's only prayer is for the feeling of eternal exclusive servitorship. Service to Śrī Kṛṣṇa is the only success of life.

In *dāsya-prema*, the specialty of *prema-bhakti* is concealed. This *dāsya-rasa* flows continuously in Vaikuṇṭha, Ayodhyā, Dvārakā, Mathurā, and Vraja; yet throughout these holy abodes, *dāsya-rasa* exists in special types of gradation. The feelings of awe and reverence (*aiśvarya*) diminish as one progresses from Vaikuṇṭha to Ayodhyā, to Dvārakā, and finally to Vraja. As one advances towards Vraja, the feelings of reverence that are present in the devotees in the mood of servitorship of Vaikuṇṭha are gradually concealed. Also, as one approaches Vraja, the sweetness of *prema* as well as feelings of possessiveness for the Lord increase.

In his *Śrī Bṛhad-bhāgavatāmṛta* Śrī Sanātana Gosvāmī says that the minds of the *dāsya-bhaktas* of Vṛndāvana are attracted only to the service of Vrajendra-nandana Śrī Kṛṣṇa, and nothing else. On the other hand, when the *dāsya-bhaktas* of Vaikuṇṭha, Ayodhyā, Dvārakā, and Mathurā see the service of the *dāsya-bhaktas* of Vraja, their greed awakens for that. It is not that there is no opulence in Vraja; indeed it exists in great profusion. Kṛṣṇa's lifting Śrī Govardhana for seven days with one hand, killing demons such as Pūtanā and Aghāsura, showing Mother Yaśodā unlimited universes within His mouth – all these pastimes are full of opulence, but the Vrajavāsīs considered such displays of majesty to be the power of Nārāyaṇa, the influence of the illusory energy, or the spell of some witch.

For this reason, when Kanhaiyā (a pet name of Śrī Kṛṣṇa) displayed unlimited universes within His mouth, Mother Yaśodā thought, "Some witch has attacked my son." In order to protect Him, the controller of all, she bathed Him in cow dung and cow urine, engaged the *brāhmaṇas* in chanting protective *mantras* and incantations for Him, and gave away charity on His behalf.

In fact, in *dāsya-bhāva*, one constantly ponders, "What service can I do?" Hence in this present verse, the word *kiṅkara*[14] has been used for the devotees of *dāsya-bhāva*. It has already been mentioned that there is no *śuddha-dāsya* (feelings of pure, unmixed servitorship) in the *dāsya* devotees of Vraja; rather their mood of *dāsya* is mixed with feelings of friendship (*sakhya*) and parental affection (*vātsalya-bhāva*).

Another speciality of the *dāsya-bhaktas* of Vraja is that again, unlike the *dāsya* devotees of other places, there are no feelings of pure respect and reverence. Śrīla Viśvanātha Cakravartī Ṭhākura reveals that devotees of *dāsya-bhāva* in the mood of awe and reverence have a concept that offenses can be committed in their service; therefore for them, there is no deluge of *prema*. In *dāsya-prema*, service is not fully developed.

The service of the *dāsya-bhaktas* Jaya and Vijaya in Vaikuṇṭha, composed of feelings of pure awe and reverence, is extraordinarily beautiful, but in those *bhaktas*, we cannot see the mood of *viśrambha-sevā*, pure service performed with intimacy and devoid of feelings of awe and reverence. In order to fulfill the desire of their Lord, during the pastimes accomplished by Śrī Kṛṣṇa's creative internal potency (*yogamāyā*), they accepted three births in demonic species. By doing

14 The word *kiṅkara* comes from *kiṁ karomi*, meaning, "What may I do? What service can I do?"

so they gave their Lord an opportunity to taste *vīra-rasa*, or happiness obtained in fighting, in its completeness. In one form they were providing Him with a taste of this chivalrous mellow (*vīra-rasa*), and simultaneously, in another form, or *svarūpa*, they were engaged in their service in Vaikuṇṭha.

Almost all the devotees in Ayodhyā are in *dāsya-bhāva*. Amongst all of the servants there, Śrī Hanumān is the topmost. Hanumān serves his Lord, Śrī Rāma, with his full life force. Because of his great thirst for service, he warmly welcomes any type of service to Śrī Rāma.

Rāma is present in every pore of his entire being, and his every breath contains Rāma. Rāma is his life and soul. When by trickery, Ahi-Rāvaṇa, the adopted younger brother of Rāvaṇa, took Śrī Rāma and Lakṣmaṇa to Pātāla-loka as a human sacrifice, then and there Hanumān killed him, and seating Rāma and Lakṣmaṇa upon his shoulders, he took them away from there. But he cannot serve the Lord like the *dāsya-bhaktas* of Vraja; he cannot take his Lord on his lap, nor can he kiss Him.

It can be accepted that the *dāsya-bhaktas* of Dvārakā are superior to the *dāsya-bhaktas* of Ayodhyā, but even within them, there is not so much as a scent of *sakhya* (friendship).

Śrīman Mahāprabhu, thinking that now Śrī Rāmānanda Rāya was approaching the desired *sādhya*, said:

Sakhya-prema – the love of a friend for Kṛṣṇa

8.74

"prabhu kahe,—"eho haya, kichu āge āra"
rāya kahe,—"sakhya-prema—sarva-sādhya-sāra"

Śrīman Mahāprabhu said, "This *dāsya-prema* is perfection. What you have said is correct, but please speak something beyond this." Śrī Rāmānanda Rāya replied, "*Sakhya-prema*, or *prema-bhakti* infused with the feelings of fraternity, is the essence of all perfection.

The devotee who in the profusion of *prema* considers himself to be as good as Śrī Kṛṣṇa, does not accept that Kṛṣṇa is superior to him in any way. There is a saying, *khelata meṁ ko kāko gusaiyāṅ*, which means, "In play, who is the master of anyone?" Such devotees are called the *sakhās* of Śrī Kṛṣṇa. The name of their favorable service mood to Śrī Kṛṣṇa is *sakhya-prema*. The fixed devotion (*niṣṭhā*) of *śānta-bhāva*, the service mood imbued with possessiveness (*mamatā*) of *dāsya-bhāva*, and the mood of service with intimacy (*viśrambha-sevā*) of *sakhya-bhāva* are all present in this *sakhya-prema*.

When one compares these *bhāvas*, it can be seen that even though there is so much sense of possessiveness in *dāsya-prema*, it still retains *sambhrama-bhāva*, or feelings of respect. "Śrī Kṛṣṇa is my master and I am His servant." All the friends in Vaikuṇṭha, Ayodhyā, Dvārakā, and Mathurā accept Śrī Kṛṣṇa and Śrī Rāma as Bhagavān. However, in the *sakhya-prema* of Vraja, the devotee maintains the feelings of great intimacy (*viśrambha-bhāva*), so he feels, "Śrī Kṛṣṇa is a cowherd boy, just like me; He is not superior to me in any way. We are equal as cowherd boys and friends." In addition, whatever is done by the devotee in *sakhya-prema* will certainly please Śrī Kṛṣṇa.

While eating, should the *sakhās* think that any foodstuff is especially tasty, they place their remnants into Śrī Kṛṣṇa's mouth, saying, "Kanhaiyā, just eat this *pakorā* and see how tasty it is!" They do not feel shy in feeding their remnants to Him. The fear, hesitation, and respect of *dāsya-bhāva* are not present in *sakhya-prema*. Only the feeling of equality (*sama-bhāva*) remains.

Sakhya-prema is characterized by *viśrambha*, one-pointed affection full of loving trust, and includes feelings of possessiveness between Śrī Kṛṣṇa and His devotees. Even though Arjuna and the other sons of Pāṇḍu are eternal associates of the Lord, their affection for Śrī Kṛṣṇa in *sakhya-bhāva* is full of awe and reverence for Him. But in Vraja, such friends as Subala and Madhumaṅgala possess *sakhya-rati*, which is composed of sweetness (*mādhurya*).

Śrīman Rāya Rāmānanda here presents evidence from *Śrīmad-Bhāgavatam*:

8.75

itthaṁ satāṁ brahma-sukhānubhūtyā
dāsyaṁ gatānāṁ para-daivatena
māyāśritānāṁ nara-dārakeṇa
sākaṁ vijahruḥ kṛta-puṇya-puñjāḥ

Śrīmad-Bhāgavatam (10.12.11)

"Śrī Śukadeva Gosvāmī said to Mahārāja Parīkṣit, 'He who manifests Himself to the *jñānīs* as the happiness of the Brahman effugence, who manifests Himself to the devotees of *dāsya-rasa* as the supremely worshipful Lord, and who appears to those under the spell of illusory *māyā* as an ordinary boy – that same Bhagavān Śrī Kṛṣṇa plays in *sakhya-rasa* with the most fortunate cowherd boys of Vraja, who are receiving the fruit of their profuse pious activities.'"

There are three different types of *sādhakas*: *jñānīs*, *karmīs*, and *bhaktas*. According to their own particular devotional practices, they each realize Śrī Kṛṣṇa in different ways. The verse currently under consideration, which depicts the realization of these different *sādhakas*, glorifies above all the good fortune of the cowherd boys of Vraja, in whom *sakhya-bhāva* has arisen.

Satām. The *jñānīs*, taking the help of *bhakti*, worship Bhagavān by the process of *jñāna*, or speculative knowledge. Without *bhakti* it is impossible for the *jñānī-sādhakas* to gain knowledge. Thus, in order to achieve perfection in *jñāna*, they take the shelter of *bhakti*. We should understand the word *satām* here to indicate the followers of the path of *jñāna* mixed with *bhakti*.

Brahma-sukhānubhūtyā. *Jñānīs* worship *nirviśeṣa-brahma*, the impersonal Brahman effulgence, as the Absolute Truth, desiring *sāyujya-mukti*, or to merge into the impersonal Brahman effulgence of the Lord. Once they have achieved the perfection of this practice, they derive happiness from the perception, or realization, of this *nirviśeṣa-brahma*, which is, in fact, the effulgence emanating from the bodily limbs of Śrī Kṛṣṇa. How is it possible for the *jñānīs* to sport with this *nirviśeṣa-brahma*?

Dāsyaṁ gatānāṁ refers to devotees who worship Śrī Kṛṣṇa in *dāsya-bhāva*, nurturing feelings of respect and seeing Him as their most worshipful Lord. They worship Śrī Kṛṣṇa in the form of *paradevatā*, *iṣṭadevatā*, or *paramārādhya devatā*. Due to feelings of reverence for Śrī Kṛṣṇa, it is not possible for them to joke or play with Him.

Māyāśritānāṁ – *jīvas* who are attached to fruitive activities and bound by *māyā*, only recognize Bhagavān Śrī Kṛṣṇa as an ordinary human child. Such souls under the shelter of the illusory potency neither undertake the *bhajana* of Śrī Kṛṣṇa, nor do they love Him. What to speak of playing with Him, such people are unable to have realization of Him in any form.

Kṛta-puṇya-puñjā – those who have collected huge amounts of pious activities – the cowherd boys of Vraja who have achieved *sakhya-rasa*, the mood of friendship. In his commentary on this verse, Śrīla Sarasvatī Prabhupāda says that it describes the vast fortune of the *sakhās* of Vraja, who go to the forest to picnic with Śrī Kṛṣṇa, binding Him with the rope of *prema* that is full of intimacy and devoid of reverence. These cowherd boys of Vraja are said to have accumulated unlimited pious activities, or *kṛta-puṇya-puñjā*. The fruitive workers (*karmīs*), the impersonalist philosophers (*jñānīs*), and the mystics (*yogīs*) can never eat and drink or play with Śrī Kṛṣṇa under any circumstances. Here the verse tells us that these *sakhās* are so fortunate that they sit on Śrī Kṛṣṇa's shoulders and also have Him sit on their shoulders.

Śrī Sanātana Gosvāmīpāda says: *kṛtānāṁ caritānāṁ bhagavataḥ parama-prasāda-hetutvena, puṇyāścāravaḥ puñjā yeṣāṁ te ityrthaḥ*. *Kṛta* means the "behavior or character of the cowherd boys." *Puṇya* means "mind-enchanting." The behavior of the *sakhās* is indeed the cause of Śrī Kṛṣṇa's topmost mercy upon them; thus they are called *puṇya-puñja*, which means "very beautiful" or "enchanting." *Puñjā* here means "group." The *sakhās* of Vraja possess matured *mamatā* (sense of possessiveness) for Śrī Kṛṣṇa, which is generated from *prema*.

Itthaṁ – sinking or immersed in *prema*. There are examples of this in *Śrīmad-Bhāgavatam* (10.12.4–10) describing how Śrī Kṛṣṇa and the *sakhās* decorate each other with leaves and flowers, and how they steal each others' flutes and sticks. When for some reason Śrī Kṛṣṇa goes some distance away, the *sakhās* then run to catch Him. They imitate the calls of bees and peacocks with their forest bugles and flutes, dance with the peacocks, and sit like cranes on the bank of the Yamunā. They contort their faces to resemble the cranes' mouths, jump like frogs, challenge their own shadows, and perform other mind-enchanting activities. The *sakhās*, completely devoid of reverence and full of intimacy (*viśrambha-bhāva*), exclaim as they climb on Śrī Kṛṣṇa's shoulders, "*tumi kon baḍa loka,—tumi āmi sama* – What kind of big man are You? You and I are equal!" (*Śrī Caitanya-caritāmṛta, Ādi-līlā* 4.25).

They shout, "Oh, come on, Kanhaiyā! What? Do You consider Yourself a great person? You don't know anything! Your father only has nine hundred thousand cows, while my father has one million one hundred thousand cows."

If Kṛṣṇa is sleeping and the cowherd boys arrive, they ask, "O Mother, where is Kanhaiyā? What is He doing?" Mother Yaśodā replies, "Now He is sleeping. Do not wake Him up." But before her reply is heard, all the boys jump onto His bed and wake Him, saying "Kanhaiyā! Are You still sleeping? The time for taking the cows out to graze is passing."

Here is a sign of *sama-bhāva* (the mood of equality) in the intimate friendship between Śrī Kṛṣṇa and His friends. There are *sakhās* in Dvārakā like Arjuna and also others, but they can never act like this. As soon as Śrī Kṛṣṇa shows His *virāṭa-svarūpa* (universal form) to Arjuna, he begins shaking in fear and joins his hands together in prayerful supplication. Likewise in Ayodhyā, *sakhās* such as Sugrīva, Vibhīṣaṇa, Lakṣmaṇa, Bharata, and Śatrughna are the friends and brothers of Śrī Rāma. Even though they are His brothers and *sakhās*, they can never act so intimately with Him. Bharata, Lakṣmaṇa, and Śatrughna cannot sit on the same seat as Śrī Rāma because of their feelings of reverence and respect for Him. These emotions make it impossible for them to have the same feelings of complete equality and intimacy (*viśrambha-bhāva*) as the *sakhās* of Vraja. In Vraja there is friendship, love, possessiveness, and sweetness.

kāndhe caḍe, kāndhe caḍāya, kare krīḍā-raṇa
kṛṣṇe seve, kṛṣṇe karāya āpana-sevana!

viśrambha-pradhāna sakhya—gaurava-sambhrama-hīna
ataeva sakhya-rasera 'tina' guṇa—cihna

'mamatā' adhika, kṛṣṇe ātma-sama jñāna
ataeva sakhya-rasera vaśa bhagavān

Śrī Caitanya-caritāmṛta, Madhya-līlā (19.223–225)

"The devotee in *sakhya-rasa* sometimes offers Kṛṣṇa service and sometimes he makes Kṛṣṇa serve him. As they playfully fight, the *gopas* sometimes climb on Kṛṣṇa's shoulders, and sometimes they have Him climb on their shoulders. This *sakhya-rasa* possesses three qualities: *viśrambha-pradhāna* (a prominence of intimacy), *sakhya* (friendship), and *gaurava-sambhrama-hīna* (a lack of feelings of deference and reverential respect)."

Kṛṣṇa's *sakhās*, the cowherd boys of Vraja, have not attained their position by the fruit of any *puṇya*, or pious material activities, or by observing any *sādhana*. They are all eternally perfect associates of the Lord (*nitya-siddha-parikara*), and they have been engaged eternally in the loving service of Śrī Kṛṣṇa. For tasting *sakhya-rasa*, Svayam Bhagavān Śrī Kṛṣṇa, the Supreme Personality of Godhead, has manifested Himself as all the cowherd boys from time eternal. All the cowherd boys are personified forms of the *sandhinī* portion of the *svarūpa-śakti*. To the ultimate degree that the tendency to serve is developed, then to that degree Śrī Kṛṣṇa, who is to be served as the object of service (*sevya-vastu*) will also reveal Himself. The service tendency of the eternal associates is fully developed in their *svātantrya-mayī-sevā* (independent service). And by following *ānugatya-mayi-sevā* (service performed under their guidance) then our own service tendency unfolds correspondingly.

Vātsalya-prema – the love of a parent for Kṛṣṇa

8.76

prabhu kahe,—"eho uttama, āge kaha āra"
rāya kahe,—"vātsalya-prema—sarva-sādhya-sāra"

Śrīman Mahāprabhu said, "O Rāmānanda, that is the topmost, but please speak something beyond this." Śrī Rāmānanda Rāya then said that *vātsalya-prema* (parental love for Śrī Kṛṣṇa) is indeed the essence of all perfection.

In his commentary on this statement, Śrī Bhaktivinoda Ṭhākura says that *sakhya-rasa* is superior to *dāsya-rasa*, but one can find a goal that is superior even to this. Śrī Rāya replied, "*Vātsalya-prema* is the essence of all perfection." Śrīla Sarasvatī Prabhupāda expressed this inner intention thus: "Śrīman Mahāprabhu heard Śrī Rāmānanda Rāya's conclusion that the ultimate goal is *sakhya-rasa*. Thereupon, Śrīman Mahāprabhu said that *sakhya-prema* is superior to *dāsya-prema*. When Śrīman Mahāprabhu requested that he expand further upon the subject, he described *vātsalya-prema*, love in the mood of parental affection.

Up until this point, Śrīman Mahāprabhu has said, "*Eho haya* – this is good," but now to this He replies, "*Eho uttama* – this is the topmost." Prior to *sakhya-rasa* being mentioned, whatever scriptural evidence that had been presented had mainly referred to the practitioner who comes in the category of an ordinary living entity; but here the discussion embarks upon the subject of the *nitya-siddha-parikaras*, or the eternally perfected associates of the Lord. The devotees of *śānta* and *dāsya-rasa* are controlled by Bhagavān, but from the stage of *sakhya-rasa* onward, Bhagavān is controlled by His devotee.

Some of those eternally perfect associates, in the form of Śrī Kṛṣṇa's mother and father, consider themselves to be superior to Him. They regard themselves as His maintainers, and they see Him as the object of their mercy. Their mood to maintain Kṛṣṇa is called *vātsalya-prema*, or parental love, which demonstrates even more *mamatā* than *sakhya-rasa*. Within *vātsalya*, we find the firm faith and determination (*niṣṭhā*) of *śānta-rasa*, the service mood of *dāsya-rasa*, and especially the fraternal love devoid of shyness or reserve that is peculiar to *sakhya-rasa*. In addition, we find in *vātsalya* a mood that Kṛṣṇa must be sustained. Such devotees are His complete protectors, and will even punish, scold, and bind Him.

vātsalye śāntera guṇa, dāsyera sevana
sei sei sevanera iṅhā nāma—'pālana'

sakhyera guṇa—'asaṅkoca', 'agaurava' sāra
mamatādhikye tāḍana-bhartsana-vyavahāra

āpanāre 'pālaka' jñāna, kṛṣṇe 'pālya'-jñāna
'cāri' guṇe vātsalya rasa—amṛta-samāna

se amṛtānande bhakta saha ḍubena āpane
'kṛṣṇa—bhakta-vaśa' guṇa kahe aiśvarya-jñāni-gaṇe

Śrī *Caitanya-caritāmṛta*, *Madhya-līlā* (19.226–229)

"In parental love, all of the qualities found in *śānta-rasa*, *dāsya-rasa*, and *sakhya-rasa* become transformed into a particular service called maintainanence.

"The essence of *sakhya-rasa* is intimacy devoid of the formality and reverence of *dāsya-rasa*. It is because of this increased sense of intimacy that one chastises and admonishes Kṛṣṇa.

"One with *vātsalya-prema* considers oneself to be Kṛṣṇa's nourisher and maintainer, and cares for Him as one does a son. The four qualities found in the other four *rasas* are all within this *vātsalya-rasa*, which is just like nectar.

"The reciprocation of nectarean bliss between Kṛṣṇa and the devotee is such that Kṛṣṇa is completely subjugated by the devotee. This happiness is compared with an ocean of nectar into which the devotee and Kṛṣṇa plunge. This is the conclusion of the *aiśvarya-jñānīs*, those with knowledge of Kṛṣṇa's opulence."

8.77

nandaḥ kim akarod brahman
śreya evaṁ mahodayam
yaśodā vā mahā-bhāgā
papau yasyāḥ stanaṁ hariḥ

Śrīmad-Bhāgavatam (10.8.46)

"Śrī Parīkṣit Mahārāja enquired from Śrī Śukadeva Gosvāmī, 'What auspicious pious activities did Śrī Nanda Bābā perform so that Śrī Kṛṣṇa agreed to become his son? And what did Śrī Yaśodā do that led to the Absolute Truth Śrī Kṛṣṇa sucking that most fortunate woman's breast milk?'

Śrī Rāya Rāmānanda then presented one more verse from *Śrīmad-Bhāgavatam*:

8.78

nemaṁ viriñco na bhavo
na śrīr apy aṅga-saṁśrayā
prasādaṁ lebhire gopī
yat tat prāpa vimukti-dāt

Śrīmad-Bhāgavatam (10.9.10)

"Śrī Śukadeva Gosvāmī said to Śrī Parīkṣit Mahārāja, 'O saintly King, the mercy that the *gopī* Yaśodā received from Śrī Kṛṣṇa, the giver of liberation, was not given to Brahmā, or Śiva, or even to Lakṣmī, who always resides on the chest of Śrī Viṣṇu.'"

Here, we see Śrī Kṛṣṇa being controlled by *vātsalya-bhāva*, parental affection. Despite being the supreme Lord Himself and full of unlimited opulence, He was completely controlled by Mother Yaśodā's *prema*, and thus He allowed her to bind Him. Who can bind Him, who is unlimited, having no inside, outside, top, or bottom?

However, due to excessive feelings of possessiveness she thinks Śrī Kṛṣṇa to be the object of protection and maintenance and herself to be His guardian and maintainer, and for His welfare, she bound Him. But no, this is not so. He was bound by *vātsalya-prema*; this was His mercy upon Mother Yaśodā. Such mercy was never achieved by anyone else. Even Brahmā, who is the son of the Lord, or Śrī Śiva, who has emanated from the Lord's own body, or even Lakṣmī herself, who resides eternally on the Lord's chest, cannot obtain such mercy as Śrī Yaśodā received.

Bhagavān has said that He is always subservient to the devotee – *ahaṁ bhakta-parādhīnaḥ* (*Śrīmad-Bhāgavatam* 9.4.63). In the pastime of His mother binding Him to the grinding mortar, known as *dāma-bandhana-līlā*, His affection for His devotee is displayed to its highest degree.

With reference to the *sukṛti* (devotional merits) of Nandarāya and Yaśodā, our *ācāryas* (recognized preceptors) have said that both are eternally perfect associates. It was Śrī Droṇa and Dharā, who are actually partial expansions (*aṁśas*) of Śrī Nanda and Yaśodā respectively, who had performed austerities. They had begged from Lord Brahmā the benediction of receiving a relationship with Bhagavān in *vātsalya-prema*. Lord Brahmā knew them to be partial expansions of Śrī Nanda and Yaśodā. Thus Brahmā, desiring to be the object of Śrī Kṛṣṇa's affection, said to both of them, "*Tathāstu* – So be it." If one does not have *vraja-prema* himself, how can he grant it to someone else?

The query may arise here that since Nanda Bābā and Yaśodā-māiyā are Śrī Kṛṣṇa's eternal parents, what is the need for them to perform austerities? All of this is arranged by Yogamāyā to carry out the Lord's human-like pastimes. Lord Brahmā knew that this incident marked the start of the manifestation of Bhagavān's human-like pastimes in the material world. It is also worth noting that when Droṇa and Dharā requested this benediction, some great sages were assembled there who had faith in *bhakti* that is mixed with knowledge of the Lord's opulence.

Therefore, Droṇa and Dharā directly requested the benediction of *para-bhakti*, which automatically transformed into their innate *vātsalya-prema*. Actually, no one can become the mother and father of Śrī Kṛṣṇa by the blessings of Lord Brahmā.

The fact is that when the *aṁśīs* (full, original forms of Śrī Nanda and Yaśodā) appear in this world, their respective *aṁśas* (partial expansions) again enter into their bodies. This principle is indicated by Lord Brahmā using the word *tathāstu*. Lord Brahmā is very far from the position of Śrī Nanda-Yaśodā, so how can he give this type of benediction to another? He himself hankers to take birth in any lower species in Vraja – a deer, animal, bird, tree, or creeper – and considers his life successful if he will be able to obtain the footdust of any resident of Vraja:

tad bhūri-bhāgyam iha janma kim apy aṭavyāṁ
yad gokule 'pi katamāṅghri-rajo-'bhiṣekam
yaj-jīvitaṁ tu nikhilaṁ bhagavān mukundas
tv adyāpi yat-pada-rajaḥ śruti-mṛgyam eva

Śrīmad-Bhāgavatam (10.14.34)

Just as Śrī Nanda and Yaśodā are eternally perfected personal associates of Śrī Kṛṣṇa, so too is their *vātsalya-prema* eternally existent. Thus, the question may arise that if *vātsalya-prema* cannot be achieved by the performance of austerities, then are the spiritual practices and the worship performed by those *sādhakas* who desire *vātsalya-bhāva* also worthless? No, it is not like this. One will definitely achieve *vātsalya-bhāva* in service to Śrī Kṛṣṇa if one worships under the guidance of Śrī Nanda and Yaśodā, but no one can become either Śrī Nanda or Yaśodā.

While discussing this subject it is also worth mentioning that Śrī Nanda had five brothers, Upānanda being the eldest. His father Parjanya wanted to make Upānanda king, but Upānanda told his father, "I am neither qualified nor able to become king. You will only find such qualification in my younger brother Nanda." Hearing this Parjanya became very happy and announced that Nanda would be the king of Vraja. All the people welcomed Parjanya's declaration.

On the other hand, Nanda was completely renounced, and furthermore, he had no son, but as soon as Śrī Kṛṣṇa took birth in his home, all of his detachment was transformed into attachment. His house, kingdom, and every object contained in them were all for the enjoyment of Śrī Kṛṣṇa. Both husband and wife performed their endeavors so that there would be no shortcomings in the rearing of Śrī Kṛṣṇa. Both became absorbed in feeding their son fresh butter, placing Him on their laps and caressing Him. They chastised Him lovingly and Yaśodā bound Him to a grinding mortar.

Nanda and Yaśodā learned that the daughter of Vṛṣabhānu Mahārāja, Rādhā, had obtained from Durvāsā Muni a benediction, that whoever would eat the *prasāda* cooked by Her lotus hands would always enjoy good health and long life. Upon hearing this, with great respect they invited Rādhā to their palace so that Kṛṣṇa would eat the *prasāda* prepared by Her hand. Even when Rādhā was married, Mother Yaśodā would patiently tolerate the curses and complaints of Śrī Rādhā's mother-in-law, Jaṭilā, to whom she would continue to humbly send gifts and requests to send Rādhā to cook for Śrī Kṛṣṇa. Nanda and Yaśodā loved Rādhā as much as they loved Kṛṣṇa. Herein lies the great specialty of Nanda Bābā and Mother Yaśodā's parental affection. We find testimony to this in *Padyāvalī* (126):

śrutim apare smṛtim itare
bhāratam anye bhajantu bhava-bhītāḥ
aham iha nandaṁ vande
yasyālinde param brahma

"In a world frightened by birth and death, some people take shelter of the Śrutis, some of the Smṛtis, and some of the *Mahābhārata*. But I pay my homage to Śrī Nandarāya, in whose courtyard Parabrahma is playing as a child."

By this and other prayers, all *ṛṣis*, *munis*, and Śrī Nārada himself have glorified Śrī Nanda and Yaśodā. Śrī Kṛṣṇa performed so many pastimes, but nowhere else was He ever bound. When He became an envoy of peace and went to Hastināpura, Duryodhana attempted to bind Him with ropes, but Śrī Kṛṣṇa showed His universal form and everyone in the whole assembly, including Duryodhana, became fearful. We cannot find it described anywhere that Bhagavān was bound by Mother Devakī or Kauśalyā; but He was bound by the hand of Mother Yaśodā. Nanda-Yaśodā's human-like dealings (*laukika sad-bandhuvat*) with Śrī Kṛṣṇa are not found anywhere else.

The source of all expansions, the unlimitedly opulent Supreme Lord Śrī Kṛṣṇa, being controlled by the fully ripened *vātsalya-prema* of Śrī Yaśoda, allowed Himself to be bound, and by accepting this He experienced supreme happiness. Indeed, He was extremely anxious to taste this *vātsalya-rasa*. In this way, Yaśodā, who is so proud of feeling that she is Kṛṣṇa's mother, became even more fortunate in this *līlā*, which combines both *aiśvarya* and *mādhurya*.

It is not possible to describe Nanda and Yaśodā's pain of separation from Kṛṣṇa when He was going to Mathurā. At that time Yaśodā became just like a piece of dry wood. Śrī Nanda Bābā quit speaking with others and stopped coming outside of the palace. Remembering his son he simply would continuously call for Him and weep. Immersed in the bottomless ocean of *vātsalya-prema*, he remained searching for his son. Every second he would turn his face towards Mathurā, waiting expectantly: "Now He will come, now He will come."

When Uddhava came and tried to pacify Nanda Bābā, it only increased his feelings of separation one hundred times over. Uddhava said, "O Nanda Mahārāja, come and wander outside for a bit. Your mind may find some distraction." Nanda Baba replied, "Please tell me, Uddhava, where should I go? Wherever I go, I remember Kanhaiyā and become even more distressed. Every object I see reminds me of Kṛṣṇa and pierces me like a spike. My misery and suffering simply increase, but my life does not leave me."

Uddhava said, "O Nanda! Your son is directly Bhagavān, the Supreme Lord." Hearing this Nanda Baba exclaimed, "Uddhava, I was thinking that you were extremely intelligent, but this is not so. Uddhava, you do not know the symptoms of Bhagavān. Does Bhagavān ever become hungry? Come on, if Kṛṣṇa's mother is just a little bit late in bringing a ball of butter, He breaks all the pots in the house. Does Bhagavān ever go house to house stealing? Our boy wanders everywhere in Vraja, stealing.

"O my son Uddhava, if ever there were a real father, then that was Mahārāja Daśaratha. After Śrī Rāma went to the forest, he could not wait even one second – immediately his life left him. But see, Uddhava, I do not wish to die like Daśaratha Mahārāja. Before leaving, Kanhaiyā said, 'I will definitely return,' so surely He will come back to Vraja. If I were to die before His return, then, not seeing me, He will ask His mother after me, and when His mother answers, 'My son, Your father has died,' He will be so unhappy. Wherever I may go, if He is unhappy, my unhappiness will only increase. I will tolerate my own unhappiness, but Uddhava, I never want to see any unhappiness in my son."

The greatly learned sage Uddhava became dumbstruck; the parental affection of Śrī Nanda and Yaśodā was beyond his understanding. From the day that Kṛṣṇa went to Mathurā, food had not been prepared, even once. For whom would they cook? All the pots were kept upside-down and the stove was covered with cobwebs.

What sweet and charming pastimes are found in *vātsalya-rasa*! Just seeing Yaśodā's upraised stick, Śrī Kṛṣṇa's opulence and position as Bhagavān ran away. When Mother Yaśodā looked into Kṛṣṇa's mouth after He ate dirt, she saw all of the moving and non-moving entities in the universe. Thinking this to be the work of some witch, she continued to caress her son, as her affection for Him simply swelled higher. Even today the personified Vedas are searching for the foot dust of these Vrajavāsīs.

Kāntā-prema – the love of a beloved for Kṛṣṇa

8.79

prabhu kahe,—"eho uttama, āge kaha āra"
rāya kahe,—"kāntā-bhāva—prema-sādhya-sāra"

Śrīman Mahāprabhu said, "This *vātsalya-prema* is the topmost, but please speak something more." Śrī Rāmānanda Rāya replied, "*Kāntā-prema* is the essence of all perfection.

Kāntā-prema – one thinks of Śrī Kṛṣṇa as one's beloved. In other words, considering herself to be His sweetheart to be enjoyed by Him, she abandons her own happiness. Even the desire to meet and be with Śrī Kṛṣṇa is only for His happiness. Śrī Bhaktivinoda Ṭhākura says that *vātsalya-prema* can be accepted as topmost, but superior still is one more *rasa*, which is said to be the essence of all perfection. This *kāntā-bhāva* (the mood of a ladylove) is indeed the supermost level of *prema*. In ordinary *prema* (*śānta-prema*) there is an absence of a sense of possessiveness (*mamatā*), in *dāsya-rasa* there is an absence of intimacy and confidence (*viśrambha* and *viśvāsa*), in *sakhya-rasa* there is an absence of overflowing affection, and in *vātsalya-rasa* there is an absence of freedom from shyness or hesitancy. Because there is an assortment of shortcomings in all these *rasas*, the *prema* in these respective *rasas* cannot be said to have reached completeness. When *kāntā-bhāva* for Śrī Kṛṣṇa awakens in the heart, then these shortcomings disappear totally. In other words all that is lacking becomes fulfilled, and the wellspring of the entire *prema-tattva* begins to flow continuously; thus it is the essence of the topmost goal.

Śrīla Sarasvatī Prabhupāda says that *vātsalya-prema* is superior to *sakhya-prema*, yet Mahāprabhu desires to hear still more. Therefore, Rāmānanda Rāya explains Mahāprabhu's desired intention by explaining that the essence of all perfection is *kāntā-bhāva*. Actually, the real meaning of *kāntā-bhāva* is the extramarital mood (*parakīyā-bhāva*) of the *vraja-gopīs*, which extends from *bhāva* right up to *mahābhāva*, whereas *vātsalya-prema* can only develop up to the stage of *anurāga*. In *kāntā-bhāva*, the *gopīs* have the good fortune to engage all their limbs in the most complete mood of service to Śrī Kṛṣṇa. The desire to perform service is developed to its ultimate extremity:

madhura-rase—kṛṣṇa-niṣṭhā, sevā atiśaya
sakhyera asaṅkoca, lālana-mamatādhikya haya

kānta-bhāve nijāṅga diyā karena sevana
ataeva madhura-rasera haya 'pañca' guṇa

ākāśādi guṇa yena para para bhūte
eka-dui-tina-cāri krame pañca pṛthivīte

ei-mata madhure saba bhāva-samāhāra
ataeva āsvādādhikye kare camatkāra

Śrī Caitanya-caritāmṛta, Madhya-līlā (19.231–234)

"In *madhura-rasa*, the qualities available in the previously mentioned relationships, such as attachment for Kṛṣṇa, rendering service unto Him, uninhibited feelings of fraternity, and the feelings of being His maintainer, all increase. The heroine serves her beloved with her entire body. Hence, all five transcendental qualities are present, just as all material qualities manifest one after another in the material elements, starting from ether. First one quality develops, then two, three and four, culminating with all five qualities being present in the earth element. This union of the moods of the other *rasas* in amorous love produces an intensified taste that is quite astonishing."

8.80

nāyaṁ śriyo 'ṅga u nitānta-rateḥ prasādaḥ
svar-yoṣitāṁ nalina-gandha-rucāṁ kuto 'nyāḥ
rāsotsave 'sya bhuja-daṇḍa-gṛhīta-kaṇṭha-
labdhāśiṣāṁ ya udagād vraja-sundarīṇām

Śrīmad-Bhāgavatam (10.47.60)

"'In the *rāsa* festival, Bhagavān Śrī Kṛṣṇa embraced the Vraja *gopīs* with His vine-like arms, and fulfilled all of their desires. The mercy that was given to them by Bhagavān was not even received by the most loving Lakṣmī, who is eternally present on the chest of Bhagavān. That mercy cannot be achieved by the ladies of the heavenly planets, whose complexion and bodily aroma are like that of a lotus, what to speak of other women.'

There are many different ways to explain this verse.

Rāsotsave – in the *rāsa-līlā* festival. The word *utsava* (festival) has a very special intonation here. That festival is the pastime wherein the *gopīs* fully blossom after giving Śrī Kṛṣṇa complete happiness. Within *rāsa-līlā*, all other types of *līlās* are also included. From *rasa*, *rāsa* (*rāsa-līlā*) arises; *rāsa* is performed on the platform made of *rasa*, or bliss.

Bhuja-daṇḍa-gṛhīta-kaṇṭha-labdhāśiṣāṁ – arms like sticks, which are nicely rounded and gradually increasing in beauty from the shoulders to the hands. With these arms, He embraced the beautiful necks of the *gopīs* and thus fulfilled their hearts' desires.

Here our worshipable predecessor Gosvāmīs have given the understanding that *rasika-śekhara* Śrī Kṛṣṇa is placing His beautiful, playful, attractively decorated, delightful, extremely soft, gentle, and cooling arms around the *gopīs'* conch-shaped necks, which are marked with three graceful lines. He is hanging there as if swinging with intense love and begging them to fulfill His innermost desires: "O *gopīs*, do not leave Me and go elsewhere, and do not let Me go anywhere else; otherwise I shall be swept far away in this nectarean ocean of *prema*. You are My only saviors."

Prasāda – mercy. Here, this means the qualification the *gopīs* received from Śrī Kṛṣṇa by serving Him with their entire bodies. Qualification means the supreme happiness of intimate, personal association with Śrī Kṛṣṇa. Not even Lakṣmī could receive this happiness, what to speak of the Apsarās, the society girls of heaven, or the wives of the demigods.

Aṅge – this refers to the golden line on Kṛṣṇa's chest. This line is in fact none other than His most beloved Lakṣmī, who is eternally seated upon the chest of Śrī Nārāyaṇa, who is the *vaibhava-svarūpa* (opulent manifestation) of Śrī Kṛṣṇa.

Nitānta-rateḥ – She who is passionately in love with Śrī Kṛṣṇa. When Lakṣmī observed the great fortune of the *gopīs* with Śrī Kṛṣṇa, she too hankered to join in the *rāsa-līlā* festival. To attain the same good fortune, she began to perform austerities, yet still to this day, her desire remains unfulfilled.

Śriyaḥ. Even Lakṣmī could not attain the good fortune of the beautiful Vraja *gopīs*.

Nāyaṁ. The word *ayaṁ* again indicates Lakṣmī, and it can also apply to the queens of Dvārakā. Despite greatly coveting *rati* for Śrī Vrajendra-nandana's lotus feet, still they could not achieve it. They could not realize the uniqueness of *rasa* in Śrī Kṛṣṇa which is not found in Śrī Nārāyaṇa.

8.81

tāsām āvirabhūc chauriḥ
smayamāna-mukhāmbujaḥ
pītāmbara-dharaḥ sragvī
sākṣān manmatha-manmathaḥ

Śrīmad-Bhāgavatam (10.32.2)

"Śrī Śukadeva Gosvāmī said to Parīkṣit Mahārāja, 'After the *gopīs* sang their lament of separation, Bhagavān Madana-mohana, who churns and bewilders the mind of Kāmadeva (Cupid) himself, suddenly appeared in the midst of the *gopīs* wearing a golden yellow cloth, a garland of forest flowers, and a smile on His lotus face.'

The particular image of Bhagavān portrayed here only manifests in *kāntā-rasa*. This attractively sweet form constitutes the center of focus and attraction for the assembly of Śrī Kṛṣṇa's beloveds, the beautiful *vraja-gopīs*. In separation from that astonishingly attractive form, the *gopīs* experienced a mere second like millions of years. In the pain of their separation, the form that Śrī Kṛṣṇa assumed pierced the core of the *gopīs'* heart and seemed to only increase their suffering more and more. This type of sweetness can be experienced only in *kāntā-bhāva*, not in any other *rasa*.

8.82–83

kṛṣṇa-prāptira upāya bahu-vidha haya
kṛṣṇa-prāpti-tāratamya bahuta āchaya

kintu yāṅra yei rasa, sei sarvottama
taṭastha hañā vicārile, āche tara-tama

"There are various means to attain Śrī Kṛṣṇa, and they afford many levels in the degree of that attainment. Whatever relationship a particular devotee has with the Lord is the best for him. Still, when we consider all the differences from a neutral position, we can understand that there are gradations of *prema*.

There are many spiritual practices available to attain Śrī Kṛṣṇa, many varieties of tastes, and many devotional moods also. In accordance with the undertaking of a specific *sādhana*, one will achieve a particular form of Śrī Kṛṣṇa. By performing devotion mixed with speculative knowledge (*jñāna-miśrā-bhakti*), one attains the *brahmajyoti*, which is the bodily effulgence of Śrī Kṛṣṇa. By performing devotion in the mood of reverence (*aiśvarya-miśrā-bhakti*), one achieves Śrī Kṛṣṇa's opulent pastime expansion (*vilāsa-mūrti*) named Śrī Nārāyaṇa. And by the practice of pure devotion (*śuddhā-bhakti*) a person may attain Śrī Kṛṣṇa Himself.

There is a gradation in the specialty of the form of Śrī Kṛṣṇa that manifests, depending on whether He is attained by the devotional moods of *dāsya*, *sakhya*, *vātsalya*, or *mādhurya*. For those in *dāsya-bhāva* He is the Lord, in *sakhya-bhāva* He is a friend, in *vātsalya-bhāva* He is a son, and He is one's most beloved to those in *kāntā-bhāva*. Whatever mood each person has, that particular *bhāva* is indeed the topmost. Śrī Kṛṣṇa is *akhila-rasāmṛta-mūrti*, or the complete personification of the nectar of all *rasas*, in whom there are five primary *rasas* and seven secondary *rasas*. Śrī Śukadeva Gosvāmī says:

mallānām aśanir nṛṇāṁ nara-varaḥ strīṇāṁ smaro mūrtimān
gopānāṁ sva-jano 'satāṁ kṣiti-bhujāṁ śāstā sva-pitroḥ śiśuḥ
mṛtyur bhoja-pater virāḍ aviduṣāṁ tattvaṁ paraṁ yogināṁ
vṛṣṇīnāṁ para-devateti vidito raṅgaṁ gataḥ sāgrajaḥ

Śrīmad-Bhāgavatam (10.43.17)

"O Parīkṣit, when Śrī Kṛṣṇa, the embodiment of all *rasas*, entered the wrestling arena with His brother Śrī Balarāma, the various groups of people present regarded Kṛṣṇa in different ways according to the mood in which they were situated, and they also realized that particular *rasa* itself. The huge wrestlers witnessed Kṛṣṇa to be as hard as a lightning bolt; the young women, possessing a high degree of *mādhurya-rasa*, saw Him as Cupid personified, and within their heart of hearts they became absorbed in thinking of Him with amorous intentions. The ordinary men regarded Him as jewel-like among men, and the *gopas* recognized Him as their relative. The impious rulers considered Him to be a severe chastiser of the wicked; and the older men and ladies, who were like His father and mother, viewed Him as their most beautiful child. Kaṁsa, the king of the Bhojas, knew Him as time personified or death; the unintelligent materialists saw Him as the universal form; the *yogīs* as the Absolute Truth, and the Vṛṣṇis, who are devotees and lovingly disposed to the Lord, honored Him as their supreme worshipable deity."

Thus the *yogīs* developed *śānta-rasa* (neutrality); the Vṛṣṇis developed *dāsya-rasa* (servitorship); the cowherd boys, who are fond of joking, developed *sakhya-rasa* (friendship); and *hāsya-rasa* (laughter); Nanda Bābā and the other cowherd men developed *vātsalya-rasa* (parental feelings); and *karuṇa-rasa* (compassion). The ladies experienced *madhura-rasa* (amorous feelings), the wrestlers developed *vīra-rasa* (chivalry), the ordinary persons felt *adbhuta-rasa* (astonishment), the fearful kings *raudra-rasa* (anger), Kaṁsa developed *bhayānaka-rasa* (fear), and the materialists experienced *vībhatsa-rasa* (disgust).

Śrī gurudeva, by means of *mantra*, establishes this type of relationship with Bhagavān, according to the specific taste in each individual *jīva*. The *jīva* also should then remain attentive and absorbed in executing the process of worship as given by the spiritual master until he reaches his desired goal. Of all the devotional moods, *kāntā-bhāva* is undoubtedly the most excellent.

8.84

yathottaram asau svāda-
viśeṣollāsa-mayy api
ratir vāsanayā svādvī
bhāsate kāpi kasyacit

Bhakti-rasāmṛta-sindhu (2.5.38)

"'There is an increase in degree of taste, pleasure, and intensity enjoyed in each subsequent kind of *rati*. The sequence culminates with the highest taste manifesting in *madhura-rasa*, amorous love.'

In his *Amṛta-pravāha-bhāṣya* on this verse Śrīla Bhaktivinoda Ṭhākura has written: Śrī Rāya Rāmānanda said, "I had previously mentioned many different types of goals and methods to attain Śrī Kṛṣṇa, but now I will describe the gradation that exists between them. According to a person's qualification, he will follow one of these methods to achieve his ultimate goal, the *kṛṣṇa-prema* that is suitable for his particular level of eligibility. In every case, such *prema*, or *rasa*, will bring about his ultimate happiness.

The attainment of Kṛṣṇa is indeed the only worthwhile and auspicious achievement. Of the four highest types of *rasa*, namely, *dāsya*, *sakhya*, *vātsalya*, and *madhura*, the *rasa* a person is qualified will be the best for him. When someone qualifies for entering one particular *rasa*, he cannot understand the gradation when compared with another *rasa*. However, when the five types of *rasas* – *śānta*, *dāsya*, *sakhya*, *vātsalya*, and *madhura* – are viewed from a neutral position, a gradation is seen; and among them *madhura-rasa* is considered the most excellent.

8.85–88

pūrva-pūrva-rasera guṇa—pare-pare haya
eka-dui gaṇane pañca paryanta bāḍaya

guṇādhikye svādādhikya bāḍe prati-rase
śānta-dāsya-sakhya-vātsalyera guṇa madhurete vaise

ākāśādira guṇa yena para-para bhūte
dui-tina gaṇane bāḍe pañca pṛthivīte

paripūrṇa-kṛṣṇa-prāpti ei 'premā' haite
ei premāra vaśa kṛṣṇa—kahe bhāgavate

"There is a gradual increase in transcendental mellows from the first *rasa* onward. Each subsequent mellow possesses the qualities of the previous ones, thus two qualities are found in the second *rasa*, three in the third, and finally five in the fifth. As the number of qualities increases, also the taste increases in each subsequent mellow. Therefore, the qualities found in *śānta*, *dāsya*, *sakhya*, and *vātsalya-rasa* all manifest in *madhura-rasa*. There is a nice example that illustrates this. The number of qualities in each of the five material elements (sky, air, fire, water, and earth) gradually increases one by one until finally, in the fifth element, earth, all five qualities are fully present. Thus, because all the qualities of the previous four *rasas* are present in *kāntā-prema*, it is considered to be the most excellent of all. Actually, this *kāntā-prema* completely controls Śrī Kṛṣṇa, as *Śrīmad-Bhāgavatam* testifies.

The five material elements are sky, air, fire, water, and earth. From these come the five corresponding sensory qualities: sound, touch, form, taste, and fragrance. Sky (ether) possesses the single quality of sound. Two qualities – sound and touch – are present in the element air. Fire contains sound, touch, and form. Water possesses four qualities: sound, touch, form, and taste. All five qualities – sound, touch, form, taste, and fragrance – exist in the element earth. Just as sky, air, etc., are present in the element earth, simultaneous with its own natural quality of fragrance, similarly, *kāntā-bhāva* possesses the qualities of the other four *rasas* starting with *śānta-rasa*, but it has the additional quality of utilizing all the bodily limbs in the service of Śrī Kṛṣṇa. Therefore, *kṛṣṇa-prema* has arisen most completely in *madhura-rasa*, because this *prema*, which is blossoming with *rasa*, accords the use of the entire body in service. Only this *rasa* provides the possibility of bringing Kṛṣṇa completely under one's control.

Kāntā-bhāva includes all of the services performed by the associates of Kṛṣṇa who act as His servants, friends, and parents. The *kṛṣṇa-niṣṭhā* (resolute steadfastness in Kṛṣṇa) of *śānta*, the service mentality of *dāsya*, the intimate service of *sakhya*, and the pervasive desire in *vātsalya* for Kṛṣṇa's auspiciousness and for His maintenance and the well-being of He who is subordinated by *prema* – all of these qualities are included in *madhura-rasa*. Furthermore, there is one more quality: offering one's entire body in the service of Śrī Kṛṣṇa, which is exclusively available in *madhura-rasa*. The love-struck Vraja *gopīs*, who are the heroines of this *kāntā-bhāva*, have distanced themselves from material desires and even their own family members, having completely renounced body, home, and dear friends as if insignificant dry grass.

8.89

mayi bhaktir hi bhūtānām
amṛtatvāya kalpate
diṣṭyā yad āsīn mat-sneho
bhavatīnāṁ mad-āpanaḥ

Śrīmad-Bhāgavatam (10.82.44)

"'O *gopīs* of Vraja, devotional service to Me bestows immortality upon all living entities, but it is a matter of great fortune and joy that you nurture intense affection for Me, as this is the means to attain Me.'

A discussion of the *gopīs*' pain of separation is found in the account of the meeting at Kurukṣetra. Śrī Kṛṣṇa glorifies them, declaring them to be supremely fortunate, since this *kāntā-prema* is the only means by which He can be completely controlled. The *prema* of the other *rasas* is not able to do this.

8.90

kṛṣṇera pratijñā dṛḍha sarva-kāle āche
ye yaiche bhaje, kṛṣṇa tāre bhaje taiche

"Śrī Kṛṣṇa has taken a solemn oath that for all eternity He will reciprocate accordingly with the manner in which one serves Him.

In *Śrīmad Bhagavad-gītā* (4.11)[15], He has also mentioned:

ye yathā māṁ prapadyante
tāṁs tathaiva bhajāmy aham
mama vartmānuvartante
manuṣyāḥ pārtha sarvaśaḥ

"O Pārtha, in whichever way a person renders service to Me, I serve him in that very same way. Everyone follows My path in all respects."

The worshipful Śrīla Bhaktivinoda Ṭhākura has said in his commentary on this verse that whatever a person desires as the fruit of their worship of the Lord, Bhagavān in return awards the result

15 In some versions of *Śrī Caitanya-caritāmṛta*, this verse is included in the dialogue as the 91st verse, but Śrīla Sarasvatī Ṭhākura has given this verse in his commentary on the 90th verse, drawing reference from other versions of *Śrī Caitanya-caritāmṛta*.

accordingly. The *sādhaka* of *śuddha-bhakti* worships Bhagavān only to achieve eternal service to the transcendental form of the Lord; and the Lord rewards His loving devotee according to his desire by making him His eternal associate, and giving him eternal love-filled service to Bhagavān. Bhagavān fulfills the desires of the impersonalists by bestowing upon them liberation, or *nirviśeṣa-nirvāṇa*, whereupon they enter into the impersonal effulgence of the Lord. As the Supreme Controller, the Lord bestows the material fruits desired by the reward-seeking workers, and in the same manner He bestows opulences or liberation upon the *yogīs*. Of all these various attainments, service to Śrī Vrajendra-nandana Śrī Kṛṣṇa in Goloka Vṛndāvana is the best.

Thus, we should understand from the commentary to this *Bhagavad-gītā* verse that the fruit of each individual's worship is not identical. Depending on the type of *bhajana* one performs, the fruit received is indeed in accordance with one's desires.

Some learned persons have interpreted the phrase *manuṣyāḥ pārtha sarvaśaḥ* in this verse to mean that, no matter what form one's worship takes, since all are on the path of worshiping Bhagavān, the Lord will give the same result to all. This conception is completely erroneous. *Śrīmad-Bhāgavatam* and other scriptures have thoroughly refuted the foolish theory that the deluded materialists (*karmīs*), the speculators (*jñānīs*), and the pure devotees (*premi-bhaktas*) will ultimately all arrive at the same destination. Further on, *Śrīmad Bhagavad-gītā* (9.25) states:

yānti deva-vratā devān
pitṝn yānti pitṛ-vratāḥ
bhūtāni yānti bhūtejyā
yānti mad-yājino 'pi mām

"Those who worship the demigods will go to the demigods; those who worship ghosts and spirits will take birth among such beings; those who worship ancestors go to the ancestors; and those who worship Me will come to Me."

In this above-mentioned verse Bhagavān says, "With whatever mood one surrenders to Me, I reciprocate in a like manner. Factually, it is Me alone whom everyone is worshiping. Truly, I am the topmost and only valid goal of all conceptions. The pure devotees receive the ultimate bliss of eternal service to My transcendental person in the supreme abode. The impersonalists destroy their very selves through the attainment of *nirvāṇa-mukti* (liberation characterized by the cessation of material existence) in impersonal Brahman effulgence. For the *śūnya-vādīs* (voidists), I manifest myself as emptiness and nullify their very existence as well. For the gross materialists attached to matter, I cover their soul and make their consciousness like dull matter; and they attain Me in the form of matter. In the *yogis'* case, I manifest Myself as the Supreme Lord and offer them all types of opulences [in the form of various yogic perfections] and liberation. According to the various types of faith, I sometimes give them birth in a perishable body. In this way, I manifest Myself as everything and it is only I who am attained by all these different practitioners. However, one should understand that out of all of these attainments, service to Me is supreme. Certainly, the many paths followed by humanity all lead exclusively to Me."

8.91

ei 'preme'ra anurūpa nā pāre bhajite
ataeva 'ṛṇī' haya—kahe bhāgavate

"'If according to My vow I cannot fully reciprocate with someone who does *bhajana* of Me, then I become indebted to him.' This is stated by Śrī Kṛṣṇa in *Śrīmad-Bhāgavatam*.

Reciprocating with someone's *bhajana* means that when a devotee performs devotional service with a particular motive, then Śrī Kṛṣṇa fulfills that desire. This is known as Śrī Kṛṣṇa reciprocating with His devotee's *bhajana*. Another type of befitting reciprocation is where, in whatever *bhāva* one wishes to please Śrī Kṛṣṇa, He makes every effort to satisfy that devotee. However, Śrī Kṛṣṇa cannot reciprocate with both types of devotee. And considering that the perfected *gopīs* do not have even the slightest scent of desire for their own enjoyment, what is the question of Śrī Kṛṣṇa reciprocating by bestowing great happiness upon them? They only wish to give happiness and pleasure to Śrī Kṛṣṇa; if Śrī

Kṛṣṇa wishes to fulfill their desire, then He alone receives happiness by doing that. The *gopīs* of Vraja have completely abandoned everything to offer their whole selves to Śrī Kṛṣṇa. However, Śrī Kṛṣṇa can never abandon any number of *gopīs* for a single *gopī*. What to speak of many *gopīs*, He cannot even abandon one of His ordinary devotees. Thus He cannot reciprocate with the service of the *gopīs*. Śrī Kṛṣṇa Himself has accepted this fact in *Śrīmad-Bhāgavatam* (10.32.22):

8.92

na pāraye 'haṁ niravadya-saṁyujāṁ
sva-sādhu-kṛtyaṁ vibudhāyuṣāpi vaḥ
yā mābhajan durjara-geha-śṛṅkhalāḥ
saṁvṛścya tad vaḥ pratiyātu sādhunā

"'My darling *gopīs*, your meeting Me is innocent and immaculate in every respect because it is devoid of even a single iota of desire for your own happiness. It is overflowing with supremely pure love. Although the bonds of affection for the members of one's own home are impossible to overcome, you have completely demolished them. Thus, for loving service to Me, you have transgressed the moral laws of this world. Even if I lived as long as the gods I would be unable to requite even one drop of your love, sacrifice, and service. All of you may free Me from debt simply by your own gentle nature, but I am forever the debtor of your *prema*, and will always continue to be.'

The quality that makes this *kāntā-prema* the most excellent is that only in this *rasa* has Śrī Kṛṣṇa allowed Himself to fall into debt. This *prema-mādhurya* of the *gopīs* is the axle and Śrī Kṛṣṇa is the wheel upon that axle, resting and rotating upon that central object. If one removes the axle, or the *gopīs*, from the wheel, Śrī Kṛṣṇa, then He becomes *nirviśeṣa*, or featureless (impersonal), in the sense that He can do nothing. The sentiments of the *gopīs* are the cause of the increase in Śrī Kṛṣṇa's beauty.

When and why did Śrī Kṛṣṇa become indebted to the *gopīs*? The reply is that when *rāsa-līlā* was going on, the other *gopīs* developed pride in their own good fortune, and the daughter of Śrī Vṛṣabhānu Mahārāja, Śrī Rādhā, became sulky. To establish in this world the super-excellence of Śrīmatī Rādhikā's mood of separation and also in order for Śrī Kṛṣṇa to directly taste and hear the nectar of Śrī Rādhā and the other *gopīs*' talks in separation from Him, He disappeared from *rāsa-līlā*.

The *gopīs*, absorbed in their moods of separation from Kṛṣṇa, began inquiring about Him from the trees, creepers, *tulasī*, and the Yamunā, but they received no reply from them. Suddenly they saw Śrī Kṛṣṇa's footprints, and with them the footprints of a young girl. The other *gopīs* began to extol the good fortune of that particular *gopī*, who was alone with Śrī Kṛṣṇa. They began to follow the footprints until they encountered Śrī Rādhā lying upon the ground, unconscious in separation from Śrī Kṛṣṇa, looking like a golden doll. The other *gopīs* pacified Her. After this all the *gopīs* gathered together on the banks of the river Yamunā in like-minded groups, and while weeping they began *kīrtana*. This singing of the *gopīs* is known as the G*opī-gīta*. Upon hearing this song, Śrī Kṛṣṇa could not check Himself and came into their presence.

All the *gopīs* took their veils, which were covered with *kuṅkuma* from their breasts, and laying them upon the ground they prepared a seat for Him, on which He was seated. The *gopīs*, being situated in *mādhurya-rasa*, proceeded to ask Śrī Śyāmasundara a variety of questions, and He cleverly answered all of them. But those questions that were completely overflowing with *prema*, Śrī Kṛṣṇa could not answer, and He became eternally indebted to the *gopīs*.

Our most worshipful Gosvāmīs mention that not even the eulogies composed by Lord Brahmā can give Him the joy He experienced in becoming indebted to the *gopīs*. At certain opportune instances, Śrī Kṛṣṇa has released Himself from His indebtedness to the devotees of all the other *rasas*, but when He attempted to free Himself from His debt to the *gopīs* in *mādhurya-rasa*, He became even more indebted.

8.93

yadyapi saundarya kṛṣṇa-mādhuryera dhurya
vraja-devīra saṅge tāṅra bāḍaye mādhurya

"Although Śrī Kṛṣṇa represents the ultimate limit of unparalleled beauty and sweetness, still in the association of the Vraja *gopīs* His beauty and sweetness increases ad infinitum.

Although Śrī Kṛṣṇa's beauty and sweetness, upon reaching their utmost limit, have no opportunity for increasing any further, whenever the *gopīs* and Kṛṣṇa see one another, His beauty and sweetness repeatedly increase. This sweetness contains such inconceivable and astonishing power that when the *gopīs* encounter His beauty and sweetness they become filled with joy, and when Śrī Kṛṣṇa sees their joyful happiness, then He becomes exceedingly pleased. Śrī Kṛṣṇa understands that He is giving happiness to the *gopīs*, and the *gopīs* become joyful because they know that their service is giving Him happiness. In this mutual dealing of pleasing one another, there exists an eternal rivalry.

8.94

tatrātiśuśubhe tābhir bhagavān devakī-sutaḥ
madhye maṇīnāṁ haimānāṁ mahā-marakato yathā

Śrīmad-Bhāgavatam (10.33.6)

"'In the midst of the dancing *gopīs*, Bhagavān Śrī Kṛṣṇa appears most beautiful, like an exquisite sapphire in the midst of golden ornaments.'"

Haimānāṁ – looking like a jewel encrusted in a golden necklace.

Mahā-marakata – a brilliant blue sapphire. The *gopīs* resemble golden beads, and Śrī Kṛṣṇa, due to His dark bodily effulgence, appears like a blue sapphire.

Madhye maṇīnāṁ yathā. As a blue sapphire appears beautiful when set in a golden necklace, so the sapphire-like Śrī Kṛṣṇa is exquisite when surrounded by the golden ornament-like *gopīs*.

Tatrātiśuśubhe. While *mahā-rāsa* was going on, both Śrī Kṛṣṇa, surrounded by the *gopīs*, and the *gopīs*, surrounded by Śrī Kṛṣṇa, appeared extraordinarily beautiful. In fact, Śrī Kṛṣṇa's natural beauty and sweetness were unparalleled, but being in the presence of His special associates, His beauty and sweetness increased. Only amidst the beauty of the *gopīs* does He reveal the summit of His beauty and sweetness.

When Śrī Kṛṣṇa went to Dvārakā, He experienced complete absorption in the emotions of Vraja and went mad. When Lord Brahmā saw Him in this condition, he created another Vṛndāvana named Nava-vṛndāvana to revive Him from His internal state. While He was in Nava-vṛndāvana, Śrī Kṛṣṇa looked upon the statue of the daughter of Śrī Vṛṣabhānu Mahārāja surrounded by Her friends. At that time, His nature as the very charmer of Cupid himself was enhanced even more. When Padmā, Kaṁsa's mother, saw this form, she could not check herself and in *kāntā-bhāva*, she ran towards Śrī Kṛṣṇa. Finally, Mother Rohiṇī caught hold of her.

Bhagavān:

aiśvaryasya samagrasya
vīryasya yaśasaḥ śriyaḥ
jñāna-vairāgyayoś caiva
saṇṇāṁ bhaga itiṅgana

Viṣṇu Purāṇa (6.5.47)

"Śrī Bhagavān is the Supreme Truth (*parama-tattva*), who is fully endowed with six inconceivable qualities: complete wealth, strength, fame, beauty, knowledge, and renunciation."

Regarding the incarnations, some are portions of Kāraṇābdhiśāyī Mahā-Viṣṇu (Viṣṇu lying on the Causal Ocean) and others are empowered incarnations. According to *Śrīmad Bhagavad-gītā* (4.7):

yadā yadā hi dharmasya glānir bhavati bhārata
abhyutthānam adharmasya tadātmānaṁ sṛjāmy aham

"O Bhārata, whenever there is a decline in religious practice, and an increase of irreligion, I personally descend."

The incarnations of Bhagavān appear in every millenium (*yuga*) in order to protect the earth when it is oppressed by the demons. Even Mahā-Viṣṇu, who is the root of all these incarnations and the origin of the other *puruṣa-avatāras*, is but a plenary expansion of Vrajendra-nandana Śrī Kṛṣṇa. This is stated in *Śrīmad-Bhāgavatam*:

ete cāṁśa-kalāḥ puṁsaḥ kṛṣṇas tu bhagavān svayam
indrāri-vyākulaṁ lokaṁ mṛḍayanti yuge yuge

Śrīmad-Bhāgavatam (1.3.28)

At this point a question may arise: When the *rāsa-līlā* is saturated with unlimited sweetness, why has the word *bhagavān*, which denotes opulence, been used here – *tatrātiśuśubhe tābhir bhagavān devakī-sutaḥ*? The reconciliation comes by understanding that there were many different types of listeners in the assembly of Śrī Parīkṣit Mahārāja. There were *karmīs*, *jñānīs*, *yogīs*, *tapasvīs* (ascetics or performers of various types of austerities), devotees of mixed moods, and pure devotees. In order that those seated at this gathering would not think Śrī Kṛṣṇa to be an ordinary mortal, and His pastimes, associates and holy abode to be in any way mundane, the word *bhagavān* has been used. It is only Bhagavān Himself who may enact pastimes such as these.

Here our worshipful Gosvāmīs have presented the additional *siddhānta* that it is not possible for Bhagavān to perform any pastime without the foundation of *aiśvarya* (opulence). It is never possible for Śrī Kṛṣṇa to divest Himself of His opulence in any condition. However, because of excessive sweetness, or the profuse overflowing of that *mādhurya* in the pastimes of Vraja, the *aiśvarya* becomes integrated into *mādhurya*. Thus in order to temper or pacify unqualified persons, opulence is sometimes shown. But then it immediately becomes hidden once more, just as a blade of grass in a large pot of boiling milk may be seen for a moment before again being submerged in the unlimited ocean of sweetness.

Devakī-suta. It is definitely incorrect to take this word as an indication that Kṛṣṇa who is performing the *rāsa-līlā* is the son of Devakī and Vasudeva. Here, Śrī Śukadeva Gosvāmī is actually indicating the son of Yaśodā. In his commentary, Śrī Viśvanātha Cakravartī Ṭhākura has also directly explained that another name of Yaśodā was Devakī. Evidence of this is found in *Bṛhad-viṣṇu Purāṇa*:

dve nāmnī nanda-bhāryāyā
yaśodā devakīti ca
ataḥ sakhyam abhūt tasya
devakyā śauri-jāyayā

"The wife of Nanda had two names, Yaśodā and also Devakī. Because of their natural friendship, she [the wife of Nanda] and Devakī, the wife of Śauri [Vasudeva] share the same name."

Only one Kṛṣṇa danced with countless millions of *gopīs*, assuming as many forms as there were *gopīs*. It is also stated that Śrī Kṛṣṇa danced with such velocity that, just as the whirling of a burning torch in complete circle gives the appearance of an unbroken circle of fire, He appeared simultaneously at the side of each of the countless *gopīs*.

8.95

prabhu kahe,—"ei 'sādhyāvadhi' suniścaya
kṛpā kari' kaha, yadi āge kichu haya"

Śrīman Mahāprabhu replied, "This conclusion – that *kāntā-prema* is certainly the highest limit of perfection – is incontrovertible. However, Śrī Rāya, please speak more if there is something else."

8.96

rāya kahe,—"īhāra āge puche hena jane
eta-dina nāhi jāni, āchaye bhuvane

Śrī Rāya Rāmānanda replied, "Until this day I did not know anyone within the three worlds who could inquire beyond this.

Rādhā-prema – Śrī Rādhā's love for Kṛṣṇa

8.97

iṅhāra madhye rādhāra prema—'sādhya-śiromaṇi'
yāṅhāra mahimā sarva-śāstrete vākhāni

"Within the *kāntā-prema* of the *gopīs*, Śrī Rādhā's *prema* for Śrī Kṛṣṇa is the topmost essence of all perfection, and the glories of Her love are described in all the revealed scriptures.

The proper understanding of *kāntā-prema* is the *prema* of the *gopīs* of Vraja for Śrī Kṛṣṇa. Śrī Rāya Rāmānanda became amazed to hear how deeply Mahāprabhu could relate to the astonishing moods that he had just described. It is impossible for *sādhakas* to attain the *prema* of Śrī Rādhā, which is the crown jewel of all perfections. However, in the stage of perfection, the *jīva* becomes qualified for the highest mood of *kṛṣṇa-prema* (love for Śrī Kṛṣṇa), which is subservient to and follows the loving moods of Śrīmatī Rādhikā. In the stage of practice, or *sādhana*, the *jīva* must practice under the guidance of Śrī Rādhikā's female companions, or *sakhīs*. (This is called *mañjarī-bhāva*.) Uddhava witnessed these moods of Śrī Rādhā, and we can also observe them in the life and character of Śrīman Mahāprabhu. Mahāprabhu tasted the moods of Śrī Rādhā in both Her separation from Śrī Kṛṣṇa and Her meeting with Him.

8.98

yathā rādhā priyā viṣṇos tasyāḥ kuṇḍaṁ priyaṁ tathā
sarva-gopīṣu saivaikā viṣṇor atyanta-vallabhā

Padma Purāṇa, Laghu Bhāgavatāmṛta (2.1.45)

"'Just as Śrī Rādhā is most dear to Śrī Kṛṣṇa, Her lake, Rādhā-kuṇḍa, is also exceedingly dear to Him. Among all the *gopīs*, Śrī Rādhā is Śrī Kṛṣṇacandra's most dearly beloved.'

When the treasured daughter of Śrī Vṛṣabhānu Mahārāja, Śrī Rādhā, enters into *māna* (jealous anger) and when, being unable to break that anger, Śrī Kṛṣṇa is defeated, He goes to Rādhā-kuṇḍa, because He accepts Her lake to be Śrī Rādhā Herself. Hoping to gain Śrīmatī Rādhikā's merciful glance, He performs austerities to fulfill His heart's desire, and finally Rādhā-kuṇḍa indeed answers His prayer:

agha-ripur api yatnād atra devyāḥ prasāda-
prasara-kṛta-kaṭākṣa-prāpti-kāmaḥ prakāmam
anusarati yad uccaiḥ snāna-sevānubandhaiḥ
tad ati-surabhi rādhā-kuṇḍam evāśrayo me

Śrī Rādhā-kuṇḍāṣṭaka (3)
by Śrī Ragunātha dāsa Gosvāmī

"For the pleasure of Śrīmatī Rādhikā, even Śrī Kṛṣṇa Himself, yearning to attain Her merciful sidelong glance, performs difficult austerities at the very precious and fragrant Rādhā-kuṇḍa, regularly bathing and carefully observing all the appropriate rituals. May that supremely enchanting Rādhā-kuṇḍa be my shelter."

8.99

anayārādhito nūnaṁ bhagavān harir īśvaraḥ
yan no vihāya govindaḥ prīto yām anayad rahaḥ

Śrīmad-Bhāgavatam (10.30.28)

"'O *sakhīs*, the *gopī* whom Kṛṣṇa has taken away to a secluded place, leaving aside all of us, must have definitely worshiped the Supreme Controller Śrī Hari very grandly.'"

This verse has a confidential meaning. The special *gopī* mentioned here is the crown jewel of all of Śrī Kṛṣṇa's beloveds; therefore Her name is "Rādhikā."

These words were spoken by the *vipakṣā-gopīs*, Śrīmatī Rādhikā's rivals, during the *mahā-rāsa-līlā* that took place under the full autumn moon. This verse firmly proves the super-excellence of Śrīmatī Rādhikā's *prema*. At the time of the *rāsa-līlā*, Śrī Kṛṣṇa performed a vast variety of loving pastimes with the Vraja *gopīs*, which caused them to experience such pleasure that they became proud of their good fortune. Furthermore, Śrīmatī Rādhikā fell into a jealous pout when She noticed that while Śrī Kṛṣṇa was dancing and singing amorously with Her, displaying a variety of poses, He was doing the very same with the other *gopīs*. Thus, to pacify Śrīmatī Rādhikā's anger and to check the other *gopīs*' false pride in their good fortune, Śrī Kṛṣṇa disappeared from the *rāsa-līlā*, taking Rādhikā with Him.

As Śrī Rādhā and Kṛṣṇa were moving from one secluded *kuñja* to another, Śrī Rādhikā's footprints left special marks in the sand: beneath the big toe on the right foot was a barleycorn, beneath the second toe was a wheel, below this was an umbrella, and underneath that was a bangle. In between the big toe and the second toe was a long vertical line reaching down to the middle of Her foot; under the middle toe was a lotus-flower, beneath which was a flag. Below this flag was a creeper, which bore one flower. Beneath the mount of the little toe was an elephant goad, and on the heel was a half-moon. In the left footprint, there was a conch shell at the base of the big toe, and under this was a club; on the mount of the little toe was an altar, below which there was an earring, and below this a spear. Below the second, third, fourth, and little toes were mountains, underneath them was a chariot, and on the heel a fish. Similarly, Śrī Kṛṣṇa's footprints also left their characteristic marks in the sand – flag, thunderbolt, elephant goad, lotus, etc.

padāni vyaktam etāni nanda-sūnor mahātmanaḥ
lakṣyante hi dhvajāmbhoja-vajrāṅkuśa-yavādibhiḥ

Śrīmad-Bhāgavatam (10.30.25)

[Seeing the footprints, the *gopīs* spoke among themselves:] "Without a doubt these footprints belong to the most illustrious son of Nanda Mahārāja, Śrī Śyāmasundara, because the marks of a flag, lotus, thunderbolt, elephant goad, barleycorn, and so forth are clearly seen."

Śrī Rādhā Herself was unaware of Her own footprints.

Under the cover of a very dense grove of trees, Śrī Śyāmasundara appeased the angry Rādhā by decorating Her and performing other services. By so doing, He managed to pacify Her *māna*, which was extremely strong and difficult to curb. Not being able to see Śrī Kṛṣṇa once He had disappeared from *rāsa*, the other *gopīs* became extremely distressed, as if their lives had left them. They began searching for Śrī Kṛṣṇa everywhere.

After some time they saw His footprints and also noticed that next to them were the footprints of a lady. Seeing them, the rival *vipakṣā-gopīs* said to each other, "Just as a she-elephant accompanies her beloved king of elephants, similarly that greatly fortune girl walked away with Nanda-nandana Śyāmasundara, keeping Her hand on His shoulder. Who is She? She must definitely have worshiped the omnipotent Bhagavān Śrī Hari very grandly, because Her worship has pleased Him so much that our beloved Śrī Śyāmasundara has taken Her away to a solitary place, leaving all of us behind."

The *svapakṣā-gopīs* (Śrī Rādhā's own group) could recognize that these were the footprints of their *sakhī* Śrī Rādhā, and although this fact made them blossom with happiness, they did not manifest any emotions outwardly, because other groups of *gopīs* – *vipakṣā* (those who are opposed to Her), *taṭasthā* (those who are neutral), and *suhṛdā* (those who are friendly) – were also present. If these other groups had understood that the footprints belonged to Śrī Rādhā, their anger toward Her and their jealousy of Her would have only increased. Therefore, as if ignorant of whom the footprints belonged to, the *svapakṣā-gopīs* continued following them. Śrīla Bhaktivinoda Ṭhākura has written:

rādhikā-caraṇa-padma, sakala śreyera sadma,
yatane ye nāhi ārādhila

rādhā-padāṅkita-dhāma, vṛndāvana yāṅra nāma,
tāhā ye nā āśraya karila (1)

rādhikā-bhāva-gambhīra, citta jebā mahādhīra,
gaṇa-saṅga nā kaila jīvane
kemane se śyāmānanda, rasasindhu-snānānanda,
labhibe bujhaba ekamane (2)

rādhikā ujjvala-rasera ācārya
rādhā-mādhava-śuddha-prema vicārya (3)

ye dharila rādhā-pada parama yatane
se pāila kṛṣṇa-pada amūlyaratane (4)

rādhā-pada binā kabhu kṛṣṇa nāhi mile
rādhāra dāsīra kṛṣṇa, sarva-vede bale (5)

choḍata dhana-jana, kalatra-suta-mita,
choḍata karama-geyāna
rādhā-pada paṅkaja, madhurata-sevana,
bhakativinoda paramāṇa (6)

"For those who never take shelter of Śrīmatī Rādhikā's abode, Śrī Vṛndāvana, which is beautified by the marks of Her lotus feet, which are the abode of all good fortune; for those who never worship Śrī Rādhā's lotus feet; for those who never take the association of Śrī Rādhā's devotees, whose hearts are fixed in Her worship and whose moods are very deep and grave – please consider how it will ever be possible for them obtain the joy of bathing in the ocean of bliss that comes from serving Śrī Śyāmasundara?

"Śrīmatī Rādhikā is the *ācārya* of amorous love. The pure love between Śrī Rādhā-Mādhava is meant to be discussed and contemplated. Only those who carefully take full shelter of the lotus feet of Śrīmatī Rādhikā may very easily attain the priceless jewels of Śrī Kṛṣṇa's lotus feet. Without taking Her shelter, it is simply not possible. All of the Vedic scriptures declare that those who within their hearts consider themselves to be maidservants of Śrī Rādhā, can easily attain Śrī Kṛṣṇa."

8.100

prabhu kahe,—"āge kaha, śunite pāi sukhe
apūrvāmṛta-nadī vahe tomāra mukhe

Upon hearing the previous verse, Mahāprabhu's voice choked up and He said, "Speak more, Rāya! Hearing this gives Me tremendous joy. An unprecedented, unparalleled, and astonishing river of nectar is flowing from your mouth.

8.101

curi kari' rādhāke nila gopī-gaṇera ḍare
anyāpekṣā haile premera gāḍhatā nā sphure

"Rāya, by the verse *anayārādhito nūnam*, you have implied that Śrī Kṛṣṇa secretly took Śrī Rādhā to a solitary place out of fear of the other *gopīs*. Consequently, one might think that She is just like the other *gopīs*, since it may be understood that He did not steal Śrī Rādhā away directly before them as He loves them as well. If He had stolen Her away directly in front of the others, they would have become angry. Seeing that Śrī Kṛṣṇa is dependent on other *gopīs*, the intensity of Śrīmatī Rādhikā's *prema* is not established as superior to theirs.

8.102

rādhā lāgi' gopīre yadi sākṣāt kare tyāga
tabe jāni,—rādhāya kṛṣṇera gāḍha-anurāga"

"If Śrī Kṛṣṇa had rejected all the other *gopīs* by taking Śrī Rādhā away directly before them, then one could understand that Śrī Kṛṣṇa's passion for Śrī Rādhā was deeper."

Śrīla Bhaktivinoda Ṭhākura explains how Śrī Kṛṣṇa's profound, exclusive love for Śrīmatī Rādhikā could not manifest in front of the other *gopīs*. Fearing them, Śrī Kṛṣṇa secretly stole Rādhā away from the other *gopīs* during the *rāsa-līlā*. Only in this way was the complete and ultimate mellow actually reached, and *rāsa-līlā* was accomplished. Removing Rādhā from that situation pacified Her *māna*, and then it was possible to quell the other *gopīs'* pride in their own good fortune. In addition, it enabled the other *gopīs'* hearts to come together in a sweet way, mitigating all differences between them.

Śrīman Mahāprabhu concealed the depth of Rādhā's *prema*, and He raised a doubt concerning Śrī Kṛṣṇa's love for Her. Without this question, it would otherwise have been impossible to establish the full glories of Rādhā's *prema*. The conceptual streams originating from our worshipful Gosvāmīs regarding Their disappearance from *rāsa-līlā* are herewith presented.

(1) When both *ārādhikā* (the worshiper, or Śrī Rādhā) and *ārādhya* (the worshiped, or Śrī Kṛṣṇa) disappeared from the arena of *rāsa-līlā*, the *gopīs* of Śrī Rādhā's group could not at first understand that their mistress and Śrī Kṛṣṇa had disappeared together. Therefore, at the same time that the other *gopīs* began to search for Śrī Kṛṣṇa, the *gopīs* of Śrī Rādhā's group also began looking for their mistress. They were not sure whether She had departed with Śyāmasundara or had left separately.
(2) Once they had begun their search, the *svapakṣā-gopīs* (the *gopīs* in Śrī Rādhā's group) then observed a set of footprints which they immediately understood as Śrī Rādhā's, because they had received the good fortune of serving Her lotus feet. This put all of their doubts to rest and thus Śrī Rādhā was perfectly established as the most beloved of all of Śrī Kṛṣṇa's dear *gopīs*.

It was Mahāprabhu's intention here that Śrī Rāya Rāmānanda should further explain the super-excellence of the glories of Śrī Rādhā's *prema*.

8.103

rāya kahe,—"tabe śuna premera mahimā
trijagate rādhā-premera nāhika upamā

Śrī Rāmānanda Rāya said, "Now listen to the glories of Rādhā's *prema*. There is nothing superior to Her *prema* within the three worlds.

8.104

gopī-gaṇera rāsa-nṛtya-maṇḍalī chāḍiyā
rādhā cāhi' vane phire vilāpa kariyā

"Śrī Kṛṣṇa left the other *gopīs* in the dancing arena. Lamenting over Śrī Rādhā's disappearance, He began wandering through in the forest in search of Her.

With great expertise, Śrī Rāya Rāmānanda refuted Śrīman Mahāprabhu's objection, saying, "O Lord, in *śāradiya-rāsa* Śrī Kṛṣṇa secretly took Śrī Rādhā away from the other *gopīs* in order to associate with Her alone." That is true! Furthermore, it is an established and likewise proven fact that Śrī Kṛṣṇa also remains dependent on the other *gopīs*, but we do not always find this to be the case. The Vaiṣṇava poet, Śrī Jayadeva, has conclusively proved this in his description of *vāsantī-rāsa-līlā*, which took place in the springtime at Govardhana.

Rāsa-līlā started with countless millions of *gopīs* being present. Suddenly Śrī Kṛṣṇa noticed that Rāseśvarī Śrī Rādhā (the presiding Goddess of *rāsa-līlā*) was no longer present. That very instant, He abandoned the *rāsa-līlā* arena, and lamenting with a saddened heart, He ran from forest to forest, searching for Her everywhere. Millions of *gopīs* were still waiting at the dance arena, but Śrī Kṛṣṇa did not once look at them again, not even to tell them where He was going. He ran off in front of everyone, not waiting for any other *gopī*. From this account, we can identify Śrī Kṛṣṇa's unwavering and heightened attraction for Śrī Rādhā.

Even if we derive our understanding from Śrīman Mahāprabhu's description, our worshipful Gosvāmīs have explained that when Śrī Kṛṣṇa sometimes shows attachment to other *gopīs*, the desire to taste varieties of *rasa* must be the cause. If Śrī Kṛṣṇa had stolen Śrī Rādhā away, directly in front of the other *gopīs*, their pride would not have been destroyed. Rather, jealousy would have arisen in them instead, and then the great *rāsa* festival would have been over. By referring to this verse, Śrīman Mahāprabhu draws further attention to the description of *vāsantī-rāsa* in *Śrī Gītā-govinda*, composed by the great poet Śrī Jayadeva Gosvāmī.

8.105

kaṁsārir api saṁsāra-
vāsanā-bandha-śṛṅkhalām
rādhām ādhāya hṛdaye
tatyāja vraja-sundarīḥ

Gītā-govinda (3.1)

"'His heart bound by the chain of Rādhā's love, Kaṁsāri Śrī Kṛṣṇa, the enemy of Kaṁsā, firmly clasped Her to His chest and, taking Her away from the site of the *rāsa-līlā*, which is the complete essence of all His desires, He left aside all the other beautiful Vraja maidens.'

8.106

itas tatas tām anusṛtya rādhikām
anaṅga-bāṇa-vraṇa-khinna-mānasaḥ
kṛtānutāpaḥ sa kalinda-nandinī
taṭānta-kuñje viṣasāda mādhavaḥ

Gītā-govinda (3.2)

"'Struck by Cupid's arrows, Mādhava ran here and there along the banks of the Yamunā searching for Śrī Rādhā. Becoming despondent at not finding Her, He wept in a *kuñja* (forest bower).'"

During the *vāsantī-rāsa*, as soon Śrī Rādhā left the *rāsa-līlā* arena, the flow of nectar immediately stopped, despite millions of *gopīs* being there. When Śrī Kṛṣṇa saw that Rāseśvarī Śrī Rādhā was not there, He also left straight away to go looking for Her. He did not even tell the other *gopīs*, "Wait for Me for a moment. I am coming right back."

In fact, in the presence of Śrī Rādhā, He does not maintain an attachment for any other *gopī*. The arrows of Kāmadeva (Cupid) mentioned here are the arrows of Rādhā's *prema* specifically. These arrows so much wound Śrī Kṛṣṇa that He cannot even remain on His feet. Just as a diseased person has need of a healthy person's assistance, similarly the afflicted Śrī Kṛṣṇa can only again become healthy by the medicine of Śrī Rādhā's *darśana*. Do any of the other *gopīs* possess this kind of power? It is only Śrī Rādhā who completely fulfills every object of Śrī Kṛṣṇa's desires.

Afflicted by the fire of Cupid, Śrī Kṛṣṇa searched for Śrī Rādhā but in vain. He became so deeply affected by separation that, upon remembering Her *prema*, He fell into an unfathomable ocean of self-reproach. He understood that He had indeed behaved with Śrī Rādhā as He had with the other *gopīs*, even though She deserved greater honor. Repeatedly falling down and getting up, all the while reproaching Himself, He came to a *kuñja* on the bank of the river Yamunā, where He thought, "Prāṇeśvarī Śrī Rādhā, the mistress of My life, must have come to this *kuñja*." But when He did not find Her there, He fell into an ocean of despair and began lamenting.

8.107

ei dui-ślokera artha vicārile jāni
vicārite uṭhe yena amṛtera khani

Śrīman Mahāprabhu pondered the meaning of these two verses and understood that they were a reservoir of nectar. Repeatedly chewing them, He began to taste ambrosia, cup after cup.

8.108

śata-koṭi gopī-saṅge rāsa-vilāsa
tāra madhye eka-mūrtye rahe rādhā-pāśa

Śrī Rāmānanda continued: "Śrī Kṛṣṇa performed the *rāsa-līlā* with millions of *gopīs*, and in their midst He stayed by Śrī Rādhā's side with one of His forms.

8.109

sādhāraṇa-preme dekhi' sarvatra 'samatā'
rādhāra kuṭila-preme ha-ila 'vāmatā'

"Seeing that Śrī Kṛṣṇa's love for Her was the same as His love for the other *gopīs*, Śrī Rādhā exhibited a contrary, or leftist mood (*vāmya-bhāva*), because it is the nature of *prema* to be crooked.

Although both *mādhurya* (sweetness) and *aiśvarya* (opulence) are not only present but also complete in Vraja, the opulence stays in a hidden form, under the auspices of sweetness. Whenever the necessity to present itself arises, majesty manifests to serve Śrī Kṛṣṇa; opulence cannot abandon Him. When millions of *gopīs* gathered for the *rāsa* festival, *aiśvarya-mūrti* (the personification of opulence, Yogamāyā) manifested millions of forms of Śrī Kṛṣṇa. However, the power of His own *aiśvarya-śakti* prevented He Himself from realizing this fact. Every *gopī* thought that Śrī Kṛṣṇa was there with her exclusively. If Śrī Kṛṣṇa, the very form of fully condensed ecstasy, were right there next to oneself, then why would one look to see what another *gopī* was doing?

Suddenly Śrī Rādhā glanced at another *gopī* and realized that Śrī Kṛṣṇa was with her, and She also noticed Him with all the other *gopīs*. She could perceive that Śrī Kṛṣṇa would leave one *gopī* and move to the next, then leave that *gopī* and go on to the next, and dance with each of them. Suddenly She beheld Śrī Kṛṣṇa there, with Her also. Seeing this She became very angry, because She understood that all along He had been sporting with other *gopīs*. "He has come to Me last. He is a magician and a debauchee. He loves all the other *gopīs* just as much as He loves Me!" Śrīmatī Rādhikā's crooked *prema* took on a leftist mood, and becoming angry, She indignantly left the *rāsa* arena.

8.110

aher iva gatiḥ premṇaḥ svabhāva-kuṭilā bhavet
ato hetor ahetoś ca yūnor māna udañcati

Ujjvala-nīlamaṇi (15.102)

"'The movements of *prema* are naturally crooked like a snake; therefore, young lovers experience *māna*, that is, they become sulky, sometimes with cause and sometimes without.'

8.111–114

krodha kari' rāsa chāḍi' gelā māna kari'
tāṅre nā dekhiyā vyākula haila hari

samyak vāsanā kṛṣṇera, icchā rāsa-līlā
rāsa-līlā-vāsanāte rādhikā śṛṅkhalā

tāṅhā vina rāsa-līlā nāhi tāṅra citte
maṇḍalī chāḍiyā gelā rādhā anveṣite

itas-tataḥ bhrami' kāṅhā rādhā nā pāñā
viṣāda karena kāma-bāṇe khinna hañā

"Śrī Rādhā became jealous, and with good reason; thus She left the site of the *rāsa-līlā*. Śrī Hari experienced extreme distress at not seeing Her. *Rāsa-līlā* is the condensation of all Śrī Kṛṣṇa's yearnings, and thus, certainly, it is His most prominent desire. Śrī Rādhā is surely the vital link of the chain of His desire to perform *rāsa-līlā*. Without Her presence, Śrī Kṛṣṇa did not feel happy within His heart, and therefore He left the *rāsa-līlā* to search for Her. He looked everywhere but when He could not find Her, being pierced by the arrows of amorous desire, He became hopeless and wept.

Here, the purpose of Rādhā's anger is not to fulfill Her own desires, because She does not have even the slightest desire for Her own happiness. *Prema* is crooked by nature, thus contrariety automatically arises, which enhances the taste of *prema*. Because all of Śrī Kṛṣṇa's desires are present within His *rāsa-līlā*, it was His primary desire to perform this *līlā*. And in fulfilling His desires, Śrī Rādhā is the crucial link. Actually, Śrī Rādhā Herself is the reason that Kṛṣṇa desires to enact *rāsa-līlā* and thus She is the supreme abode of this pastime. This is why, despite the presence of millions of other *gopīs*, right in front of them, Śrī Kṛṣṇa also left that place.

It is obvious that Śrī Kṛṣṇa did not take away Rādhā by stealth. The statement here is very clear: owing to *māna*, She left *rāsa-līlā* on Her own. Śrī Kṛṣṇa was wounded by *kāma*, but this does not mean material lust; rather it is the mutual eagerness between lovers to give one another happiness. Śrī Rādhā's tendency to perform amorous service is of the highest standard. Furthermore, as long as Śrī Kṛṣṇa has not fulfilled Her desire He feels pain in His heart.

8.115

śata-koṭi-gopīte nahe kāma-nirvāpaṇa
tāhātei anumāni śrī-rādhikāra guṇa

"Even millions of *gopīs* were not able to extinguish the *kāma* of Śrī Kṛṣṇa. From this alone, one can infer the greatness of Śrī Rādhā's qualities. Without Her, Śrī Kṛṣṇa's desire to taste *kāntā-prema* would not be met."

8.116

prabhu kahe—"ye lāgi' āilāma tomā-sthāne
sei saba tattva-vastu haila mora jñāne

After hearing the deep explanation of *prema-tattva* from Śrī Rāya Rāmānanda, Mahāprabhu became very satisfied, and with a choked voice He explained, "Rāya, I have come to see you to receive knowledge of all these *tattvas*. My coming to you has proven successful.

8.117

ebe se jāniluṅ sādhya-sādhana-nirṇaya
āge āra āche kichu, śunite mana haya

"I have understood the *tattva* of both the *sādhya* (goal) and the *sādhana* (means to achieve it); but please speak further, for my mind desires to hear more.

Even after hearing such a deep deliberation on *sādhya-sādhana-tattva* from the lotus mouth of Śrī Rāmānanda Rāya, Śrīman Mahāprabhu's curiosity was still not pacified. It seemed that He wanted to know more about the special glories of Śrī Rādhā's nature. Therefore, He cleverly yet indirectly asked:

8.118–119

'kṛṣṇera svarūpa' kaha 'rādhāra svarūpa'
'rasa'—kon tattva, 'prema'—kon tattva-rūpa

kṛpā kari' ei tattva kaha ta' āmāre
tomā-vinā keha ihā nirūpite nāre"

"O Rāmānanda, what is the nature of Śrī Rādhā and of Śrī Kṛṣṇa? What is *rasa-tattva*? In addition, what is the intrinsic nature of *prema-tattva*? Please be merciful and explain all of these truths to Me. Except for you there is no one else who can explain these things."

8.120–122

rāya kahe,—"ihā āmi kichui nā jāni
tumi yei kahāo, sei kahi āmi vāṇī

tomāra śikṣāya paḍi yena śuka-pāṭha
sākṣāt īśvara tumi, ke bujhe tomāra nāṭa

hṛdaye preraṇa kara, jihvāya kahāo vāṇī
ki kahiye bhāla-manda, kichui nā jāni"

Hearing Śrīman Mahāprabhu's question, Śrī Rāmānanda Rāya said, "I do not know anything about this subject. I utter only those instructions You speak through me. Whatever teachings I receive from You, I recite just like a parrot. You are directly the Supreme Controller – who can understand Your drama? My tongue will vibrate those very same instructions You have inspired within my heart as the Supersoul. Whether I am speaking correctly or incorrectly, I do not know."

8.123

prabhu kahe,—"māyāvādī āmi ta' sannyāsī
bhakti-tattva nāhi jāni, māyāvāde bhāsi

Hearing Rāmānanda Rāya's humble words Mahāprabhu said, "I am a Māyāvādī *sannyāsī*. How can I understand *bhakti-tattva*? I always remain entangled in *māyāvada* philosophy.

We should understand that these words, spoken by Śrīman Mahāprabhu in full humility, were actually meant to conceal His real identity.

8.124–125

sārvabhauma-saṅge mora mana nirmala ha-ila
'kṛṣṇa-bhakti-tattva kaha', tāṅhāre puchila

teṅho kahe,—'āmi nāhi jāni kṛṣṇa-kathā
sabe rāmānanda jāne, teṅho nāhi ethā'

"Staying with Sārvabhauma Bhaṭṭācārya My mind has been purified. I inquired from him about the fundamental truth of *kṛṣṇa-bhakti*. However, he said to Me, 'I do not know topics of Kṛṣṇa. Śrī Rāya Rāmānanda knows everything, but he is not here now.'

8.126

tomāra ṭhāñi āilāṅa tomāra mahimā śuniyā
tumi more stuti kara 'sannyāsī' jāniyā

"O Rāmānanda Rāya, hearing of your glories I have come to you, but understanding Me to be a *sannyāsī* you began to praise Me.

8.127

kibā vipra, kibā nyāsī, śūdra kene naya
yei kṛṣṇa-tattva-vettā, sei 'guru' haya

"Whether or not one is a *brāhmaṇa*, a *sannyāsī* or a *śūdra*, if one knows *kṛṣṇa-tattva*, he in reality is *guru*.

By this statement, Mahāprabhu's intention is that Rāmānanda Rāya should not entertain the idea that because Mahāprabhu has accepted birth in a *brāhmaṇa* family and is also a *sannyāsī*, He cannot take religious instructions from a *śūdra*.

For anyone following *varṇāśrama-dharma* who desires to receive religious instruction and initiation, a *guru* from the *brāhmaṇa* caste is indispensable. Yet because knowledge of *kṛṣṇa-tattva* is the supreme goal of all *jīvas*, the scriptural conclusion is that anyone who knows *bhakti-tattva* is actually a spiritual master. It is said:

tad-vijñānārthaṁ sa gurum evābhigacchet
samit-pāṇiḥ śrotriyaṁ brahma-niṣṭham

Muṇḍaka Upaniṣad (1.2.12)

"In order to obtain knowledge of the Supreme Truth, one must approach a bona fide *guru* who knows the Vedas and is fixed in the Absolute Truth, taking ingredients for sacrifice in hand."

varṇottame 'tha ca gurau
sati yā viśrute 'pi ca
sva-deśato 'tha vānyatra
nedaṁ kāryaṁ śubhārthinā

Śrī Hari-bhakti-vilāsa (1.51)

"If a famous *brāhmaṇa* spiritual master is present in one's own district, a person who desires auspiciousness will not travel elsewhere to accept initiation from someone other than him."

A person from a low caste should not undertake the work of bestowing *mantras* [thus becoming an initiating spiritual master]. A qualified person of a high caste should not receive a *mantra* from one in a lower caste. These are ordinary mundane instructions, meant for those who have pride in their caste. However, for those pure persons devoted to *bhakti*, who are devoid of the false ego arising from caste, this regulation does not apply. Instead, the prescription for them is that only those who are knowledgeable in the science of Śrī Kṛṣṇa, expert in the process of devotional service, and expert in tasting devotional mellows should be accepted as spiritual masters, whether they are from a *brāhmaṇa* family or from a *śūdra* family.

The *sāttvata* scriptures (the Vaiṣṇava scriptures) explain that those who have taken initiation into a *viṣṇu-mantra* are known as *dvijādhika*, meaning they are even superior to the *dvijas*, or twice-born *brāhmaṇas*. This is because an ordinary *vipra* (*brāhmaṇa*) is only qualified for *karma-kāṇḍa*, whereas a person initiated into a *viṣṇu-mantra* possesses the qualification for the topmost religious process called *bhāgavata-dharma*. It is stated in *Śrī Caitanya-bhāgavata* that such *darśana* of the Absolute Truth (Parabrahman) as was revealed to Śrī Haridāsa Ṭhākura, who was born into a *yavana* (outcaste) family, was rarely achieved, even by Lord Brahmā, the creator of the material castes, what to speak of those who merely belong to the highest castes.

In *Bhakti-sandarbha*, Śrī Jīva Gosvāmī draws evidence from *Garuḍa Purāṇa* (as quoted below), and stipulates that a single *brāhmaṇa* who performs many sacrifices, is superior to one thousand ordinary *brāhmaṇas*, but one devotee of Viṣṇu is superior to one thousand of these *yājñika-brāhmaṇas*. And just one exclusive devotee of Śrī Kṛṣṇa is superior to one thousand devotees of Lord Viṣṇu:

brāhmaṇānāṁ sahasrebhyaḥ satra-yājī viśiṣyate
satra-yāji-sahasrebhyaḥ sarva vedānta-pāragaḥ
sarva-vedānta-vit-koṭyā viṣṇu-bhakto viśiṣyate
vaiṣṇavānāṁ sahasrebhya ekānty eko viśiṣyate

Gauḍiya *ācāryas*, like Śrī Narottama Ṭhākura, Śrī Narahari Sarakāra Ṭhākura, Śrī Mukunda Datta, Śrī Kānu Ṭhākura, Śrī Śyāmānanda

Prabhu, and Śrī Rasikānanda Prabhu, appeared in other castes such as *kāyastha*, *vaidya*, *gopa*, and *karaṇa*. Nevertheless, many *brāhmaṇas* and *kṣatriyas* accepted initiation from them. The verdict of all bona fide scriptures is that, regardless of the *varṇa* or *āśrama* from which the spiritual master comes, the real prerequisite is that he must be a Vaiṣṇava. With regard to this point, *Śrī Hari-bhakti-vilāsa* (1.40–41) quotes these verses from the *Padma Purāṇa*:

mahākula prasūto 'pi
sarva yajñeṣu īkṣitaḥ
sahasra śākhādhyāyī ca
na guruḥ syād avaiṣṇavaḥ

"Even if someone takes birth in a high-class family, is initiated into the performance of all Vedic sacrifices, and is even a *brāhmaṇa* learned in a thousand branches of the Vedas but yet is not a Vaiṣṇava, then he is not qualified to be a *guru*."

gṛhīta-viṣṇu-dīkṣāko
viṣṇu-pūjā-paro naraḥ
vaiṣṇavo 'bhihito 'bhijñair
itaro 'smād avaiṣṇavaḥ

"A Vaiṣṇava is one who is properly initiated into a *viṣṇu-mantra* and who is dedicated to the worship of Viṣṇu. Apart from these there are no other Vaiṣṇavas."

To be "properly initiated into the chanting of a *viṣṇu-mantra*" signifies that the practitioner must have a connection with and receive the *mantra* from a genuine *guru* in a bona fide and unbroken disciplic succession, or *sampradāya*. *Śrī Gautamīya-tantra* states: "*sampradāya-vihīnā ye mantrās te niṣphalā matāḥ* – That *mantra* which is not taken from the *āmnāya-paramparā*, or in other words, heard directly from the *guru-paramparā* that begins with Śrī Kṛṣṇa and descends down to Brahmā, Nārada, and other *ṛṣis*, is *niṣphala*, or fruitless."

Śrī Jīva Gosvāmīpāda conveys the meaning of the word *vipra* as one who is expert in *parā-vidyā*, or the topmost knowledge. Actually, this *parā-vidyā* is synonymous with *bhakti*. Thus a *vipra* is really one who is expert in the performance of *bhakti*. *Śrī Saṅkṣepa-vaiṣṇava-toṣaṇī* (10.16.2) may be cited in support of this *siddhānta*, wherein it states "*veda pāṭhād bhaved vipraḥ* – one who recites the Vedas is termed a *vipra*." The principle result of reading the Vedas is that one receives *divya-jñāna*, or transcendental knowledge. This knowledge goes hand-in-hand with *vaiṣṇava-dīkṣā*, because an understanding of one's relationship with Bhagavān comes through the *mantra* one obtains upon initiation. Thus by receiving *dīkṣā*, the status of *vipra* is attained as a concomitant result.

8.128

'sannyāsī' baliyā more nā kariha vañcana
kṛṣṇa-rādhā-tattva kahi' pūrṇa kara māna"

"O Rāmānanda Rāya, do not cheat Me by thinking of Me as a *sannyāsī*. Please fulfill My heart's desires by describing the *tattva* of both Śrī Kṛṣṇa and Śrī Rādhā."

8.129–130

yadyapi rāya—premī, mahā-bhāgavate
tāṅra mana kṛṣṇa-māyā nāre ācchādite

tathāpi prabhura icchā—parama prabala
jānileha rāyera mana haila ṭalamala

Śrī Rāmānanda Rāya was a *mahā-bhāgavata* and thus full of *prema*. His mind could not be covered by Śrī Kṛṣṇa's illusory potency, *māyā*. Furthermore, he knew the inner identity of Mahāprabhu. Despite this, because Mahāprabhu's desire was so strong, his mind became restless.

Although Rāmānanda Rāya plainly realized and acknowledged the fact apparent that the form of Śrī Caitanya Mahāprabhu present before him was none other than Bhagavān, nonetheless, by the influence of Caitanya Mahāprabhu's intense desire, he forgot this fact. Śrī Rāmānanda Rāya then answered His question. It was the strong desire of Mahāprabhu that Śrī Rāmānanda Rāya should give a comprehensive presentation of every *tattva*.

8.131–132

rāya kahe,—"āmi—naṭa, tumi—sūtra-dhāra
yei mata nācāo, sei mata cāhi nācibāra

mora jihvā—vīṇā-yantra, tumi—vīṇā-dhārī
tomāra mane yei uṭhe, tāhāi uccāri

Śrī Rāmānanda Rāya said, "I am only a puppet, and You are the puppeteer pulling the strings. I will dance as You make me. My tongue is like a *vīṇā*, and You are the musician playing the *vīṇā*. Whatever Your mind desires to hear, I speak.

Kṛṣṇa-tattva

8.133–135

parama īśvara kṛṣṇa—svayaṁ bhagavān
sarva-avatārī, sarva-kāraṇa-pradhāna

ananta vaikuṇṭha, āra ananta avatāra
ananta brahmāṇḍa ihāṅ,—sabāra ādhāra

sac-cid-ānanda-tanu, vrajendra-nandana
sarvaiśvarya-sarvaśakti-sarvarasa-pūrṇa

"Śrī Kṛṣṇa is the Supreme Controller and He is Svayam Bhagavān, the original Supreme Person; He is both the source of all other incarnations and the principal cause of all causes. Śrī Kṛṣṇa is the root of unlimited Vaikuṇṭha planets, innumerable incarnations, and infinite universes. He is the actual form of eternality, knowledge, and bliss, yet still He is the son of Nanda Bābā, the king of Vraja. He is the eternal son of Nanda Mahārāja, even though factually He is unborn, being the primordial beginning of everything. Not only does Nanda Bābā feel "I am Kṛṣṇa's father," but Śrī Kṛṣṇa also maintains the eternal self-conception, "I am Nanda and Yaśodā's son." He is the definitive master of all opulences and all energies. Ultimately, He is *raso vai saḥ*, replete with all *rasas*, and *rasa-svarūpa*, the very embodiment of *rasa*.

8.136

īśvaraḥ paramaḥ kṛṣṇaḥ sac-cid-ānanda-vigrahaḥ
anādir ādir govindaḥ sarva-kāraṇa-kāraṇam

Śrī Brahmā-saṁhitā (5.1)

"'This same Śrī Kṛṣṇa, who is the very embodiment of eternality, knowledge, and bliss, is truly the supreme controller of all other controllers. He is the original two-handed form of Kṛṣṇa (*svayam-rūpa*). Furthermore, He is without beginning and He is the source of everything else. He is Govinda, the absolute cause of all causes.'

In the previous verse, Śrī Rāmānanda Rāya explained that Śrī Kṛṣṇa is the original Supreme Personality of Godhead, and now he gives evidence of this in this verse, wherein Śrī Kṛṣṇa is addressed as *īśvaraḥ paramaḥ*. This denotes that Śrī Kṛṣṇa is the Supreme Controller and the original Personality of Godhead, the source of all other forms of the Lord – *ete cāṁśa-kalāḥ puṁsaḥ kṛṣṇas tu bhagavān svayam* (*Śrīmad-Bhāgavatam* 1.3.28). Here "Kṛṣṇa" is the proper noun, and all the remaining terms are adjectives qualifying that noun. Śrī Brahmā said to Devarṣi Nārada, "O sinless one, I have described to you countless incarnations of the Lord, and I have counted Śrī Kṛṣṇa as one of these." However, no one should think that Śrī Kṛṣṇa is another incarnation of these three *puruṣa-avatāras*. Śrī Kṛṣṇa is the source of all other incarnations, including even Śrī Rāma and Śrī Nṛsiṁha. Therefore, it is clear that only Śrī Kṛṣṇa is Svayam Bhagavān, or the original Supreme Person. This is also confirmed in *Śrī Kṛṣṇa-sandarbha* (*Anuccheda* 82, text 36):

avatārā hy asaṅkhyātāḥ
kathitā me tavāgrataḥ
paraṁ samyak pravakṣyāmi
kṛṣṇas tu bhagavān svayam

"Now that I have described the innumerable incarnations of Godhead to you, I shall tell you that Śrī Kṛṣṇa is the original form of Bhagavān."

At the time of Śrī Kṛṣṇa's advent in this world, Śrī Gargācārya said, *kṛṣṇatāṁ gatāḥ*, meaning "Now all the other incarnations that appeared in the previous ages have appeared within this blackish complexioned child." In other words, all of the incarnations have entered into the body of Kṛṣṇa, and They have attained oneness within Him. According to the logic of *payasā kumbhaṁ pūrayati* (filling a clay pot with milk), or just as the pores of a clay pot becomes soaked with milk, the name "Śrī Kṛṣṇa" pervades the scriptures. He who is the supreme controller of all, the topmost reality and the nondual Absolute Truth, is known by the name Śrī Kṛṣṇa. In the conversation between Śrī Nārada and Kuśadhvaja that is included in the *Prabhāsa-khaṇḍa* [of the Mahābhārata] and the *Padma Purāṇa*, Śrī Bhagavān Himself declares: "*nāmnāṁ mukhyatamaṁ nāma kṛṣṇākhyaṁ me parantapa* – O Arjuna, subduer of enemies, of all My names, the most prominent is Kṛṣṇa."

Here in the verse under discussion (*īśvaraḥ paramaḥ kṛṣṇa*), Śrī Brahmā glorifies Śrī Kṛṣṇa by the name Govinda, who is none other than Śrī Kṛṣṇa Himself. He who maintains the cows, *gopas*, and *gopīs*, as well as all the other residents of Vraja is Śrī Govinda. His special characteristic is being the *indra*, or Lord, of the cows. In the context of the verse, the etymology of the word "Kṛṣṇa" is as follows:

kṛṣir bhū-vācakaḥ śabdo
ṇaś ca nirvṛtti-vācakaḥ
tayor aikyaṁ paraṁ brahma
kṛṣṇa ity abhidhīyate

Mahābhārata, Udyoga-parva (71.4)

This verse is related to Kṛṣṇa. The verbal root *kṛṣ* indicates all that exists (*bhū-* or *satta-vācaka*), and *ṇa* indicates His blissful nature (*ānanda-vācaka*), or He who generates an attraction towards Himself that negates attraction to everything else (*nirvṛtti-vācaka*).

Regarding the worship of Śrī Kṛṣṇa, the *Gautamīya-tantra*, one of the *sāttvata-tantras* (Vaiṣṇava scriptures) says:

kṛṣi-śabdasya sattārtho
ṇaś cānanda-svarūpakaḥ
sukha-rūpo bhaved ātmā
bhavānandamayas tataḥ

"The word *kṛṣi* indicates existence, or truth, and *ṇa* refers to the embodiment of natural bliss. The combined meaning is 'one whose existence is characterized by bliss' or 'one who attracts all and bestows bliss upon them.'"

He is Śrī Kṛṣṇa, the embodiment of happiness and He who is full of the topmost bliss.

Sadaiva saumya idamagramāsīt. This means, "O *saumya*, O gentle one, before the creation was manifest, there was only *sat-svarūpa* Bhagavān (He whose form is eternal)." He is a storehouse of total bliss. The *Vāsudeva Upaniṣad* also tells us: "*devakī-nandano nikhilam ānandayet* – The son of Devakī, Śrī Kṛṣṇa, makes all moving and nonmoving living entities blissful." Śrī Kṛṣṇa alone is Parabrahman, the Absolute Truth.

Śrīmad-Bhāgavatam (7.10.48) states that Śrī Kṛṣṇa is the Absolute Truth appearing under cover as a human being – *gūḍhaṁ paraṁ brahma manuṣya-liṅgam*. The *Gopāla-tāpanī Upaniṣad* also states "*yo 'sau paraṁ brahma* – Lord Gopāla is the Supreme Truth." Śrī Kṛṣṇa Himself says:

brahmaṇo hi pratiṣṭhāham
amṛtasyāvyayasya ca
śāśvatasya ca dharmasya
sukhasyaikāntikasya ca

Śrīmad Bhagavad-gītā (14.27)

"I, Śrī Kṛṣṇa, am *nirguṇa-saviśeṣa-tattva-svarūpa* – My form is possessed of all transcendental qualities, while devoid of even a scent of matter. It is I who am the shelter or source of the *brahmajyoti* (Brahman effulgence), which is the topmost goal of the impersonalists."

Immortality, immutability, eternality, *nitya-dharma* (*prema*), and *vraja-rasa*, the mellow of Vraja that bestows exclusive happiness – all these rest upon Śrī Kṛṣṇa's transcendental form, which is devoid of material qualities (*nirguṇa*) and full of all varieties of transcendental qualities (*sa-viśeṣa*). "*Kṛṣṇo vai paramaṁ daivatam* – Kṛṣṇa is the Supreme Personality of Godhead" (*Gopāla-tāpanī Upaniṣad* 1.2). As Śrī Kṛṣṇa is the Supreme Person (*parama-puruṣa*), He is also the Original Person (*ādi-puruṣa*):

śrutvā 'jitaṁ jarāsandhaṁ
nṛpater dhyāyato hariḥ
āhopāyaṁ tam evādya
uddhavo yam uvāca ha

Śrīmad-Bhāgavatam (10.72.15)

"After conquering all directions, Mahārāja Yudhiṣṭhira was contemplating how to defeat Jarāsandha, who seemed invincible. At that moment Bhagavān Śrī Kṛṣṇa, indeed the original personality, suggested a method that He had heard from Uddhava."

From this evidence, it is determined that Śrī Kṛṣṇa is the original Śrī Hari – this is certain. It is not only because He is the source of all *avatāras* that He has the quality of being the original cause; it is also because He is *anādi*, He has no beginning. He is the *sat-cit-ānanda-vigraha*, or the very form of eternality, knowledge, and bliss. His body is His soul, and His soul is indeed His body. "*Ānandaṁ brahmaṇo rūpam* – the form of the Supreme Person is *ānanda* (bliss)" (*Taittirīya Upaniṣad* 2.4.1).

In Vraja during His pastimes as a baby, a child, and a youth, He was called Vrajendra-nandana or Govinda. Śrī Sūta Gosvāmī says:

śrī-kṛṣṇa kṛṣṇa-sakha vṛṣṇy-ṛṣabhāvani-dhrug-
rājanya-vaṁśa-dahanānapavarga-vīrya
govinda gopa-vanitā-vraja-bhṛtya-gīta
tīrtha-śravaḥ śravaṇa-maṅgala pāhi bhṛtyān

Śrīmad-Bhāgavatam (12.11.25)

"O Kṛṣṇa! O friend of Arjuna! O best of the Vṛṣṇi dynasty! O destroyer of the royal dynasties who are ravishing the Earth! O You whose splendors bestow auspiciousness upon all who hear about them! O You whose sacred glories are sung by the cowherd men and women of Vraja! O Govinda! O Śrī Kṛṣṇa, please protect us, Your servants."

The Tenth Canto of *Śrīmad-Bhāgavatam* (10.27.20) states that while ceremonially bathing Śrī Kṛṣṇa, the Surabhī cow addressed Him as Govinda and said: "*tvaṁ na indro jagat-pate* – O You who are endowed with powerful, inconceivable energies! O You, the Supersoul of the entire universe! O Acyuta, who never fall from Your position! O Śrī Kṛṣṇa! O Jagatpati, Lord of the universe! You alone are our worshipful Lord. You, not Indra, are the maintainer of the universe." Śrī Kṛṣṇa received the name "Śrī Govinda" after His bathing ceremony was completed. *Śrīmad-Bhāgavatam* (10.27.23) states: "*govinda iti cābhyadhāt* – Indra named the Lord 'Govinda'."

In his prayers at the end of this subject in *Śrīmad-Bhāgavatam* (10.26.25), Śrī Śukadeva Gosvāmī also invokes the name Govinda: "*prīyān na indro gavām* – O *indra* of the cows (Govinda), be pleased with us." In the *Gautamīya Tantra*, there is the following description:

gopīṁ tu prakṛtiṁ vidyāj janas tattva-samūhakaḥ
anayor āśrayo vyāptyā kāraṇatvena ceśvaraḥ
sāndrānandaṁ paraṁ jyotir vallabhatvena ca kathyate
athavā gopī prakṛtir janas tad-aṁśa-maṇḍalam
anayor vallabhaḥ proktaḥ svāmī kṛṣṇāś ca īśvaraḥ
kārya-kāraṇayor īśaḥ śrutibhis tena gīyate
aneka-janma-siddhānāṁ gopīnāṁ patir eva vā
nanda-nandana ity uktas trailokyānanda-vardhanaḥ

"He who is famous amongst the cows, the Earth, and the Vedas, and, who is the shelter of all of these is Śrī Govinda-deva. He who is surrounded by the cows and is full of unparalleled opulence and sweetness is expert at manifesting His unlimited pastimes freely. He who is famous in all the worlds and in the Vedas, who always stays in Śrī Nanda-Gokula, and whose dark complexion is the color of fresh rain clouds, enchants the minds of the residents of Vraja. He expands His supremely sweet pastimes, and His sweet activities are sung loudly by the Vedas throughout all the worlds. That moon of Gokula, Śrī Kṛṣṇacandra, who wears the dress of a cowherd boy, is indeed called 'Govinda'."

It is clear that to the extent of the increase of *prema-rasa* in Lord Brahmā's heart, his greed to obtain the sweet form of Govinda increases to that same degree. Initially, he began to surrender himself unto the *svarūpa* of Govinda within Śrī Kṛṣṇa, that is, to Gopāla, a cowherd boy who is the son of Śrī Nanda Mahārāja, the king of Vraja, and who is the life and soul of Mother Yaśodā.

When that *prema-rasa* matured and filled the *rasika* heart of Brahmā, he became exceedingly restless to attain the supremely beautiful, dark complexioned Śyāmasundara, who is an ever-fresh youth (*nava-kiśora*), who is the greatest dancer (*naṭavara*), and whose beauty bewilders even Cupid himself (*madana-mohana*), especially when He is surrounded by the lotus-eyed *vraja-gopīs*. Furthermore, he offered himself unto *gopī-jana-vallabha* (the beloved of the *gopīs*) within Kṛṣṇa. Brahmā's heart was restless to taste the nectar of *gopī-prema*; thus he was not satisfied simply by chanting *kṛṣṇāya svāhā* (I offer myself to Kṛṣṇa) or *kṛṣṇāya govindāya svāhā* (I offer myself to Kṛṣṇa who is Govinda). His satisfaction came by only chanting *kṛṣṇāya govindāya gopī-jana-vallabhāya svāhā* (I offer myself to Kṛṣṇa who is Govinda and the beloved of the *gopīs*).

From the verbal root *gupa* comes the word *gopī*, which means "to protect and to maintain." In this case, the meaning refers to the special *śakti* that bestows *prema* and maintains the devotees – that energy is the *hlādinī-śakti*, which is embodied in Rādhā. The phrase *gopī-jana* consists of the words *gopī*, or *rādhā*, and *jana*, which indicates the associates who are Her expansions. Therefore, the phrase applies to the circle of Rādhā's associates, who are Her direct bodily expansions. One should understand the word *gopī-jana* to indicate Śrī Rādhā and Her *kāya-vyūha* expansions such as Lalitā and Viśākhā. Their *vallabha*, or most beloved, is Śrī Kṛṣṇa. Thus, *gopī-jana-vallabha* means "that form of Śrī Kṛṣṇa whom Śrī Rādhā embraces eternally." Therefore, the use of *gopī-jana-vallabha* naturally signifies the Divine Couple, Śrī Rādhā-Kṛṣṇa.

8.137–138

vṛndāvane 'aprākṛta navīna madana'
kāma-gāyatrī, kāma-bīje yāṅra upāsana

puruṣa, yoṣit, kibā sthāvara-jaṅgama
sarva-cittākarṣaka, sākṣāt manmatha-madana

"In Vṛndāvana, Śrī Kṛṣṇa is the ever-fresh transcendental Cupid. He is worshiped by the *kāma-gāyatrī* and the *kāma-bīja*, the seed sound vibration *klīṁ*. He attracts the hearts of all living entities – male and female, moving and non-moving alike – and He is directly the very attractor of Cupid himself.

Rasika-śekhara Nanda-nandana Śrī Kṛṣṇa is present in Vṛndāvana as Madana-mohana, the very enchanter of Cupid, with Śrī Rādhikā, who is surrounded by the ever-fresh, beautiful, lotus-eyed young *gopīs*. Even after attaining Him, one's greed to be with Him simply goes on increasing more and more. His beauty and sweetness are realized every second in eternally new ways. For this reason, He is the transcendental ever-fresh Cupid (*aprākṛta-navīna-madana*). In the hearts of those who worship Him as Cupid, a very powerful, spiritual amorous love (*kāma*) awakens, and a type of madness ensues. His ever-fresh Madana form is beyond material nature. The ordinary Cupid only operates in this material world, inciting attraction towards the flesh. This is simply lust, which is grossly materialistic and quite detestable. Those in the bodily conception of life are bound by this material Cupid and forced to submit to material lust.

Knowledge of one's relationship with Śrī Kṛṣṇa marks the onset of the *jīva* being situated in the transcendental position. This spiritual position is of two kinds: *svarūpa-gata* and *vastu-gata*. In the beginning stage, the *sādhaka* does not gain liberation from his relationship with matter. Only partial spiritualization arises in him at that point. Although he may come to live in Vṛndāvana, he is not a factual resident. This is *svarūpa-gata*. Once the materialistic tendency of the gross and subtle bodies is destroyed, the practitioner gradually achieves his factual position in Vṛndāvana by Kṛṣṇa's desire. At this point, during the stage of *sādhana* (spiritual practice), the *jīva* worships Śrī Kṛṣṇa by the *kāma-gāyatrī* and the transcendental *kāma-bīja*. "*Gāyantaṁ trāyate yasmāt gāyatrī tvaṁ tataḥ smṛtaḥ* – that which delivers the chanter is known as *gāyatrī*." The *kāma-gāyatrī* bestows appreciation of the form of the ever-fresh, transcendental Cupid, Śrī Kṛṣṇa, and reciting it makes that form manifest in the heart. Furthermore, by evoking a momentary glimpse of that form, it gives that person who meditates upon it an intense desire to obtain Him completely.

As revealed in *Hayaśīrṣa-pañcarātra*, those who are well-versed in understanding of fundamental truths have explained that the ultimate object – the Lord who is signified by His *mantra* – the reciter, the presiding deity, and the *mantra* itself are all non-different. The *kāma-bīja*, or the seed syllable of the *kāma-gāyatrī*, is *klīṁ*. Just as the *kāma-gāyatrī* is the *rasātmaka-svarūpa* (the form that is full of *rasa*) of the ordinary Vedic *gāyatrī*, the *kāma-bīja* is likewise the *rasātmaka-svarūpa* of the original sound vibration, *praṇava*, or *oṁkāra*. The *kāma-bīja* – *klīṁ* – consists of the four letters *ka*, *la*, *ī*, *bindu*, and *anusvāra*. The *Bṛhad-gautamīya-tantra* states:

ka-kāraḥ puruṣaḥ kṛṣṇaḥ sac-cid-ānanda-vigrahaḥ
ī-kāraḥ prakṛtī rādhā nitya vṛndāvaneśvarī
laścānandātmakaṁ premasukhaṁ tayośca kīrttitam
cumbana-ānanda-mādhuryaṁ nādabinduḥ samīritaḥ

The letter *ka* means Śrī Kṛṣṇa, the Supreme Person, whose body is composed of eternality, knowledge, and bliss. The letter *ī* designates the supreme power and the eternal presiding Goddess of Vṛndāvana (Vṛndāvaneśvarī) Śrī Rādhā. The letter *la* indicates the bliss of Śrī Rādhā-Kṛṣṇa, and the *nāda-bindu* suggests the *mādhurya* that comes from the happiness of Their kissing each other. Thus, the *kāma-gāyatrī*, composed of twenty-four and a half syllables, is the very form of Śrī Kṛṣṇa. This *mantra* makes the whole universe restless to attain love for Śrī Kṛṣṇa. From the verbal root *kam* (to desire), the word *kāma* is derived. *Kāma* is the object that one desires. Kāmadeva is the name of Madana-mohana Śrī Kṛṣṇa, the ever-fresh transcendental Cupid, who is endowed with beauty, sweetness, and all divine qualities such as *vaidagdhya* (cleverness). As the emperor and the very embodiment of amorous love, He attracts the minds of all.

There are twenty-five syllables of the *kāma-gāyatrī*: *kā*, *ma*, *de*, *vā*, *ya*, *vi*, *dma*, *he*, *pu*, *ṣpa*, *bā*, *ṇā*, *ya*, *dhī*, *ma*, *hi*, *ta*, *nno*, *na*, *ṅgaḥ*, *pra*, *co*, *da*, *yā*, and *t*. The syllable *ya* of the word *kāma-devāya* (the last syllable) is considered a half-syllable. Four aspects of Kṛṣṇa – the holy name, the *mantra*, His body (or deity form), and His *svarūpa* (nature) – are non-different from Him and from each other. Every syllable of the *kāma-gāyatrī* represents one of the "moons" within His form. One of these twenty-four moons is manifest upon every one of His limbs. His ten fingernails and ten toenails are twenty of these moons, two are His cheeks, one whole moon corresponds to His entire face, another is the drop of musk decorating His chin, and the half-moon is Śrī Kṛṣṇa's forehead.

Moved by a feeling of doubt and unable to discover the half-syllable of the *kāma-gāyatrī*, Śrī Viśvanātha Cakravartī Ṭhākura went to the bank of Rādhā-kuṇḍa to give up his life; but Śrī Rādhā revealed to him in a dream: *vi-kārānta-ya-kāreṇa (ca cārddhākṣaraṁ) praklrttitam*. The *Varṇāgama-bhāsvata*, which is a Sanskrit grammar book, also gives the same conclusion. Śrīmatī Rādhikā explained that when the letter *ya* precedes the letter *vi*, then *ya* is considered a half-syllable. It is stated in this book that except for the letter *ya* that precedes the letter *vi*, all other syllables are complete and are considered full-moons: "*vyanta ya-kāro 'rdhākṣam lalāṭe 'rdha-candra-bimbaḥ, tad-itaraṁ purṇākṣaraṁ purṇa-candraḥ iti* – The forehead of Śrī Kṛṣṇa is the half-moon, the half-syllable."

Śrī Śyāmasundara, who churns even the mind of Cupid, attracts the hearts of the entire world with His astonishingly beautiful attire:

madhuraṁ madhuraṁ vapur asya vibhor
madhuraṁ madhuraṁ vadanaṁ madhuram
madhu-gandhi mṛdu-smitam etad aho
madhuraṁ madhuraṁ madhuraṁ madhuram

Śrī Kṛṣṇa-karṇāmṛta (92)

The composer of *Śrī Kṛṣṇa-karṇāmṛta*, Śrī Bilvamaṅgala Ṭhākura, says, "Ah! The body of unlimited Śrī Kṛṣṇa is exceedingly sweet. Atop this body, His moon-like face is even sweeter still. Upon His face, His soft and mild smile and fragrant breath are even sweeter than the sweetest. Everything about Śrī Kṛṣṇa is sweet, sweet, sweet. This person, who is the ultimate extent of sweetness, completely blossoms when He is with Śrī Rādhā."

When Śrī Kṛṣṇa disappeared from the *rāsa-līlā*, leaving the *gopīs* behind, they became distressed in separation and lamented. Śrī Śukadeva Gosvāmī achieved oneness of mood (*tādātmya*) with these *gopīs* and said:

8.139

tāsām āvirabhūc chauriḥ
smayamāna-mukhāmbujaḥ
pītāmbara-dharaḥ sragvī
sākṣān manmatha-manmathaḥ

Śrīmad-Bhāgavatam (10.32.2)

"'When Śrī Kṛṣṇa again appeared before the beautiful ladies of Vraja, He was wearing a yellow cloth. He was also wearing a garland made of blossoming forest flowers, and upon His lotus face was a sweet smile. Indeed, the beauty of such a form bewilders the mind of even Cupid, who agitates the minds of all beings.'

The god of love (Kāmadeva), who is in the *svarūpa* of both Śrī Kṛṣṇa and the *gopīs*, was himself situated there in order to achieve Śrī Kṛṣṇa in the mood of the *gopīs*. Encountering such beauty and elegance, Kāmadeva himself fainted, being wounded by the arrows of love.

8.140

nānā-bhaktera rasāmṛta nānā-vidha haya
sei saba rasāmṛtera 'viṣaya' 'āśraya'

"The previously mentioned five types of devotees (*śānta*, *dāsya*, etc.) have various moods of worship. According to their devotional sentiments, they experience varieties of *rasa*. Both the worshipable object and shelter of all of these different *rasas* is Śrī Kṛṣṇa Himself.

It is stated in *Bhakti-rasāmṛta-sindhu* that there are twelve *rasas*. There are five *mukhya*, or primary *rasas*, namely, *śānta*, *dāsya*, *sakhya*, *vātsalya*, and *mādhurya*; and the *gauṇa*, or secondary *rasas*, are seven in number, namely, laughter (*hāsya*), compassion (*karuṇa*), chivalry (*vīra*), fear (*bhayānaka*), disgust (*vībhatsa*), and astonishment (*adbhuta*). The object (*viṣaya*) and the receptacle (*āśraya*), or the object of relish (*āsvādya*) and the relisher (*āsvādaka*), of all of these *rasas* is Śrī Kṛṣṇa Himself.

A description of the two aspects of *sakhya-rasa* is given as an example here. Upon His defeat, Śrī Kṛṣṇa carried His friends upon His shoulders. At this time He becomes the *āśraya* of *sakhya-rasa*; and when He is victorious and climbs upon the shoulders of His friends, He becomes the *viṣaya*, or the taster of *sakhya-rasa*.

8.141

akhila-rasāmṛta-mūrtiḥ
prasṛmara-ruci-ruddha-tārakā-pāliḥ
kalita-śyāmā-lalito
rādhā-preyān vidhur jayati

Bhakti-rasāmṛta-sindhu (1.1.1)

"'All glories to Him, all glories to Him, the complete embodiment of all nectarean loving mellows (*rasas*), who by the diffusion of His bodily effulgence, kept both the *gopīs* named Tārakā and Pālī most subjugated, who also controlled Lalitā and Śyāmā Sakhī, and who is the most beloved of Śrī Rādhā.'

This verse presents three adjectives establishing that Śrī Kṛṣṇa is the sole object of all *rasas*. Śrī Kṛṣṇa, the epitome of all nectarean *rasa*, is the only one who tastes the *rasa* of Śrī Rādhā, She who surpasses everyone in qualities, sweetness, and cleverness. Furthermore, He is the supreme and exclusive enjoyer of all the *gopīs*, who are the receptacles of love. He controls them all, including *sva-pakṣā* Lalitā, *vi-pakṣā* Tārakā or Candrāvalī, *suhṛt-pakṣā* Śyāmala, and *taṭasthā-pakṣā* Bhadrā (Pāli).

In *rāsa-līlā*, when Śrī Kṛṣṇa once more came before the *gopīs*, wearing a garland that was placed around His neck by a beloved in a solitary place, then Śrī Rādhā, who was full of loving anger, launched Her crooked glances at Him. Chastising Him She said, "O crest jewel of magicians, the use of Your loving poison on us was successful. You took the life out of our bodies. Have You come back to burn us on the funeral pyre?" Śrīmatī Rādhikā is the crest jewel of all of Śrī Kṛṣṇa's beloveds. She is full of crookedness that arises from Her honey-sweet affection for Śrī Kṛṣṇa (*madhu-sneha*), thus She is full of the feeling that "Śrī Kṛṣṇa is Mine." Situated on the next level beneath Rādhā in loving affairs are Śyāmā and Lalitā, while Tārakā and other *gopīs* such as Pālikā are on the third level.

8.142

śṛṅgāra-rasarāja-maya-mūrti-dhara
ataeva ātma-paryanta-sarva-citta-hara

"Of all the various *rasas*, the amorous mellow (*śṛṅgāra-rasa*) is the topmost. This *rasa* is the emperor of all transcendental mellows and Śrī Kṛṣṇa is the embodiment and the king of this mellow. This form of Śrī Kṛṣṇa is all-attractive, even to Himself.

8.143

viśveṣām anurañjanena janayann ānandam indīvara-
śreṇī-śyāmala-komalair upanayann aṅgair anaṅgotsavam
svacchandaṁ vraja-sundarībhir abhitaḥ praty-aṅgam āliṅgitaḥ
śṛṅgāraḥ sakhī mūrtimān iva madhau mugdho hariḥ krīḍati

Śrī Gītā-govinda (1.48)

"'O *sakhī*, in this spring season, Śrī Hari has become amorous love incarnate and intoxicated by this *rasa* is enjoying loving pastimes. With the limbs of His body, which are softer, darker, and more beautiful than a blue lotus, He begins the festival of love. With ever-increasing ardor, He is satisfying the *gopīs*' unbridled passion far in excess of their expectations, and having taken on an aggressive mood, the beautiful Vraja maidens are fully and unrestrainedly embracing each and every limb of His body.'

This verse establishes that Śrī Kṛṣṇa is the very personification of the amorous mellow, or *śṛṅgāra-rasa*.

8.144

lakṣmī-kāntādi avatārera hare mana
lakṣmī-ādi nārī-gaṇera kare ākarṣaṇa

"Śrī Nārāyaṇa, who is the beloved of Lakṣmī, and all the incarnations of Bhagavān, as well as Lakṣmī and all the other female energies of these incarnations – all are attracted to Śrī Kṛṣṇa.

Śrī Kṛṣṇa attracts the hearts of Bhūmā-puruṣa (Mahā-Viṣṇu), *puruṣa-avatāras*, Śrī Nārāyaṇa, Lakṣmī, and all others.

8.145

dvijātmajā me yuvayor didṛkṣuṇā
mayopanītā bhuvi dharma-guptaye
kalāvatīrṇāv avaner bharāsurān
hatveha bhūyas tvarayetam anti me

Śrīmad-Bhāgavatam (10.89.58)

"The Bhūmā-puruṣa (Lord Mahā-Viṣṇu) said to Śrī Kṛṣṇa, 'O Śrī Kṛṣṇa, who possesses all potencies! O Arjuna! Only to see both of you did I bring the sons of the *brāhmaṇa* to My abode. You have appeared with Your plenary portion to take away the burden of the Earth and to protect religion. After removing the burden of the Earth by killing the demons, please quickly return.'

Discussed here is an event that occurred in Dvārakā when a *brāhmaṇa's* new-born son died as soon as that child touched the Earth. Taking up his son's dead body, the *brāhmaṇa* placed it on the doorway of the royal palace and said, "Without a doubt, because of the bad behavior of this greedy, licentious, materialistic king, who is envious of the *brāhmaṇas*, my son has died. A king who is coarse and violent and whose senses are uncontrolled ensures that his subjects will always remain poor and unhappy."

The eight sons of the *brāhmaṇa* died successively in the same manner. The *brāhmaṇa* placed all the bodies of his dead sons at the palace gate. When the ninth of his sons died, Arjuna, who was standing near Bhagavān Śrī Kṛṣṇa, said, "O *brāhmaṇa*, is there no *kṣatriya* here in Dvārakā who carries a bow? This time I will protect your son." The *brāhmaṇa* replied, "If my sons could not be protected by Bhagavān Śrī Kṛṣṇa and Balarāma, then what can you do?" Arjuna said, "My name is Arjuna, and the name of my bow is Gāṇḍīva. After I fight with Yamarāja, the god of death, I will protect your son."

When the time came for the *brāhmaṇa's* wife to have their next son, the *brāhmaṇa* sent word to Arjuna, who arrived there and by his barrage of arrows formed a complete cage around the maternity house. At the time of birth, the *brāhmaṇa's* son cried and cried until suddenly, the child completely disappeared from the maternity room.

By the strength of his mystic power, Arjuna went to many planets, looking for the child. When he could not find him anywhere, he prepared to give up his life by entering fire and immolating himself. Witnessing this, Bhagavān said to Arjuna, "Come with Me. I will show you all the sons of the *brāhmaṇa*." Both Arjuna and Śrī Kṛṣṇa mounted the chariot and crossed the seven islands and seven mountain ranges of this universe. As they approached Lokāloka Mountain, such a dense darkness came upon them that even the four horses pulling Bhagavān's chariot, namely, Śaibya, Sugrīva, Meghapuṣpa, and Balāhaka, became bewildered and could no longer discern the correct path. Then Śrī Kṛṣṇa ordered His Sudarśana *cakra* to proceed ahead of the chariot to show the way. Moving onwards, Arjuna and Śrī Kṛṣṇa entered Mahākāla-purī, the city of Bhūmā-puruṣa (Śeṣa-nāga). That Śrī Bhūmā-puruṣa rests on the Causal Ocean. He is the Lord of the spiritual sky and non-different from Śrī Nārāyaṇa. That Bhūmā-puruṣa spoke this verse to Śrī Kṛṣṇa and Arjuna.

Thus, it is clear that Śrī Kṛṣṇa captures the hearts of Bhūmā-puruṣa, or Nārāyaṇa, and indeed of all of Bhagavān's incarnations. This verse gives evidence of Śrī Kṛṣṇa's all-attractiveness. The next verse presents further evidence of this:

8.146

kasyānubhāvo 'sya na deva vidmahe
tavāṅghri-reṇu-sparaśādhikāraḥ
yad-vāñchayā śrīr lalanācarat tapo
vihāya kāmān su-ciraṁ dhṛta-vratā

Śrīmad-Bhāgavatam (10.16.35)

"The wives of the serpent Kāliya said, 'O Bhagavān, we cannot understand which *sādhana* this Kāliya serpent has performed that rewarded him with the qualification to receive the dust of Your lotus feet on his head. To attain the dust of Your feet is so rare that even Lakṣmī, who is Your wife, performed severe austerities, in a very regulated manner, giving up all types of pleasures for a very long time.'

In essence, Lakṣmī was so attracted by the beauty of Śrī Kṛṣṇa that she left behind the enjoyment of intimate association with her husband, Śrī Nārāyaṇa, in favor of performing very severe austerities to avail herself of Śrī Kṛṣṇa's association. Yet even so, she still did not achieve the qualification to touch His lotus feet. She could only attain a faint glimmer, or shadow, of His association by becoming a fine golden line upon Śrī Śyāmasundara's chest.

By contrast, what pious activities did the serpent Kāliya perform that Śrī Kṛṣṇa bestowed His causeless mercy upon him by dancing upon his hoods, while Lakṣmī, to this day, is still performing severe austerities?

When Śrī Kṛṣṇa inquired from Lakṣmī the reason behind her austerities, she replied, "I want to sport in Vṛndāvana with You just like the *gopīs* do, and receive a form like theirs." Bhagavān Śrī Kṛṣṇa said, "Lakṣmī, it will be most difficult for you to attain that." From this it is clear that the beauty and sweetness of Śrī Kṛṣṇa stole the mind of even the wife of Śrī Nārāyaṇa.

8.147

āpana-mādhurye hare āpanāra mana
āpanā āpani cāhe karite āliṅgana

"The sweetness of Śrī Śyāmasundara is so unparalleled that it enchants His own mind. Becoming bewildered, He even wants to embrace Himself.

8.148

aparikalita-pūrvaḥ kaś camatkāra-kārī
sphurati mama garīyān eṣa mādhurya-pūraḥ
ayam aham api hanta prekṣya yaṁ lubdha-cetāḥ
sa-rabhasam upabhoktuṁ kāmaye rādhikeva

Lalita-mādhava (8.34)

"Seeing His own sweetness reflected in a bejeweled pillar, Śrī Kṛṣṇa said, 'How wonderful! How astonishing and indescribable is My profound beauty, which is the cause of great wonderment. I am enchanted by this beauty, which is arousing the eager desire to embrace and enjoy Myself, exactly like Śrīmatī Rādhikā does.'"

Rādhā-tattva

8.149–151

ei ta' saṅkṣepe kahila kṛṣṇera svarūpa
ebe saṅkṣepe kahi rādhā-tattva-rūpa

kṛṣṇera ananta-śakti, tāte tina—pradhāna
'cic-chakti', 'māyā-śakti', 'jīva-śakti'-nāma

'antaraṅgā', 'bahiraṅgā', 'taṭasthā' kahi yāre
antaraṅgā 'svarūpa-śakti'—sabāra upare

Śrī Rāmānanda Rāya then said, "I have thus briefly explained the fundamentals of Śrī Kṛṣṇa's original form. Now please hear as I give a brief description of Śrī Rādhā. Śrī Kṛṣṇa has unlimited potencies, of which three are prominent. These are the spiritual potency (*cit-śakti*), the material potency (*māyā-śakti*), and the marginal potency (*jīva-śakti*), which is otherwise known as the living entities. These are also known respectively as the internal potency (*antaraṅgā-śakti*), the external potency (*bahiraṅgā-śakti*), and the marginal potency (*taṭasthā-śakti*); but the internal potency, or *svarūpa-śakti*, predominates.

The Supersoul (Parabrahman) does not perform any material activities since He does not have material hands or feet. He performs His transcendental pastimes without any material cause. By His transcendental body, He resides everywhere in the whole universe at the same time. There is mention of this *cit-śakti* (spiritual potency) in the Upaniṣads:

te dhyāna-yogānugatā apaśyan
devātma-śaktiṁ sva-guṇair nigūḍhām
yaḥ kāraṇāni nikhilāni tāni
kālātma-yuktāny adhitiṣṭhaty ekaḥ

Śvetāśvatara Upaniṣad (1.3)

"Those *brahmavādī ṛṣis* who know the fundamental truths are firmly situated in the trance of *samādhi-yoga* and are empowered by the qualities of Parabrahman. While rapt in meditation, they have seen, by the influence of the Lord's energies, the exceedingly confidential divine potency born from His very form. He is the cause of all other causes, and the sole predominant and presiding deity of the living entities, of time, of material nature, and of activity."

Māyā-śakti is described in the following verse:

chandāṁsi yajñā kratavo vratāni
bhūtaṁ bhāvyaṁ yac ca vedā vadanti
asmān mayi sṛjate viśvam etat
tasmiṁś cānyo māyayā sanniruddhaḥ

Śvetāśvatara Upaniṣad (4.9)

"Paramātmā, who is the master of the deluding material nature, has created all the teachings of the Vedas. He has also created special *yajñas*, such as *jyotiṣṭoma*, that are performed with *ghee*; various types of *vrata* (fasts, sacrifices, penances); and everything else in existence in the past, present, and future. In other words, He has created the entire world, the description of which is found in the Vedas. The master of *māyā* has created all of this, and the ignorant *jīvas* are bound by His *māyā*."

It is possible to find further descriptions of this *māyā-śakti* in the other Upaniṣads:

ajām ekāṁ lohita-śukla-kṛṣṇāṁ bahvīḥ prajāḥ sṛjamānāṁ sarūpāḥ
ajo hy eko juṣamāṇo 'nuśete jahāty enāṁ bhukta-bhogām ajo 'nyaḥ

Śvetāśvatara Upaniṣad (4.5)

"There are two types of unborn *jīvas*. *Jīvas* of the first type are ignorant and worship Bhagavān's material potency called *prakṛti*. That *prakṛti*, whose modes are red, white, and black (*raja*, *sattva*, and *tama*), is also unborn like Bhagavān. However, unborn *jīvas* of the second type of are knowledgeable. They have overcome ignorance, and therefore have completely renounced that material energy which the others strive to enjoy."

There are two types of *jīvas*: one type is knowledgeable (*jñānīs*). They worship the Supreme Soul, completely renouncing the material energy that others are striving to enjoy. The other type of *jīvas* remains ignorant, engaging in the service of the material energy (*māyā*).

Although non-different from His own inconceivable internal potency, Bhagavān's desires are independent. That Supreme Person has an eternal, transcendental form whose glories are self-manifesting. The Supreme and Absolute Truth is eternally self-manifested. The following Vedic *mantra* provides another account of the three energies of that self-manifesting Truth:

sa viśva-kṛd viśva-vid ātma-yoniḥ
jñaḥ kāla-kālo guṇī sarva-vid yaḥ
pradhāna-kṣetrajña-patir guṇeśaḥ
saṁsāra-mokṣa-sthiti-bandha-hetuḥ

Śvetāśvatara Upaniṣad (6.16)

"That Paramātmā is omniscient and the creator of the universe. He is self-born, the controller of time (*kāla*), the knower of all, the Lord of the material energy (*pradhāna*), and the controller of all *jīvas*. He is full of all transcendental qualities and beyond all material qualities, yet He is their master. He binds the *jīvas* in the repeated cycle of birth and death, places them in their respective situations, and also liberates them from that cycle."

This *mantra* mentions the following three divisions of the internal energy of Bhagavān:

(1) *pradhāna* – the total manifestation of the three modes of material nature. This indicates *māyā-śakti*, or the illusory energy.
(2) *kṣetra-jñā* – the knower of the body. This indicates *jīva-śakti*, the individual souls.
(3) *kṣetra-pati* – the internal potency, or *cit-śakti*.

There is an axiom of logic that states, "*śakti-śaktimator abhedaḥ* – Bhagavān is non-different from His own multifarious potencies; *śakti* (potency) and *śaktimāna* (the possessor of potencies) are non-different." In accordance with this logical principle, we may understand that this world is the work of the external potency known as *māyā-śakti*; the manifestation of the countless individual souls is the work of the *jīva-śakti*; and the manifestation of the spiritual world is the work of the internal potency known as *cit-śakti*.

By the same logic we may appreciate that despite all the work performed by His energy, Bhagavān Himself remains unaffected and immutable at all times. *Māyā-śakti* is the shadow of *cit-śakti*. This can be understood by the example of someone's reflection in a large mirror. At first glance the person and his reflection might appear to be identical, but upon a more thorough examination it becomes apparent that both are, in fact, diametrically opposite each other. One is the person himself and the other is simply his reflection. In a similar fashion, the varieties within the spiritual and material world might at first appear to be alike, but a more careful examination would in fact reveal them to be quite opposite.

Śrīmatī Rādhikā is said to be *svarūpa-śakti*. Just as musk and its fragrance or fire and its potency to burn are inseparable from one another, similarly, Śrīmatī Rādhikā and Śrī Kṛṣṇa are always inseparable, even though They are eternally distinct in the matter of relishing nectarean *līlā*. *Svarūpa-śakti* performs three kinds of functions: manifesting the internal potency (*cit-śakti*), *māyā-śakti*, and *jīva-śakti*.

An alternative name of *cit-śakti* is *antaraṅgā-śakti* (the internal potency), another name of *māyā-śakti* is *bahiraṅgā-śakti* (the external potency), and lastly, another name for *jīva-śakti* is *taṭasthā-śakti* (the marginal potency). Śrī Kṛṣṇa is the root cause and the shelter of limitless incarnations of Bhagavān, and infinite abodes of those incarnations, as well as unlimited universes. Yet despite personally being the limitless ocean of *rasa* who attracts the hearts of all, and despite directly being the very attractor of Cupid himself, still He is controlled by the *prema* of Śrī Rādhā.

8.152

viṣṇu-śaktiḥ parā proktā
kṣetra-jñākhyā tathā parā
avidyā-karma-saṁjñānyā
tṛtīyā śaktir iṣyate

Viṣṇu Purāṇa (6.7.61)

"'Śrī Viṣṇu has three energies: the internal potency (*parā-śakti*), the living entity (*kṣetrajñā*), and the illusory energy (*avidyā-śakti*). The internal potency of Viṣṇu is known as *svarūpa-śakti*, or *cit-śakti*; the living entity potency is also known as *taṭasthā-śakti*; or *jīva-śakti*; and the illusory potency is also known as *māyā-śakti*, or the external material energy.'

8.153–154

sac-cid-ānanda-maya kṛṣṇera svarūpa
ataeva svarūpa-śakti haya tina rūpa

ānandāṁśe 'hlādinī', sad-aṁśe 'sandhinī'
cid-aṁśe 'saṁvit', yāre jñāna kari' māni

"Śrī Kṛṣṇa's transcendental form is composed of eternity, bliss, and knowledge (*sac-cid-ānanda-maya*); therefore His internal potency also has three different forms. From His aspect of eternality, or existence, comes *sandhinī*, from His aspect of bliss comes *hlādinī*, and from His aspect of knowledge comes *saṁvit*. The cognizance portion of the internal potency has been accepted as real *jñāna* (knowledge).

8.155

hlādinī sandhinī samvit
tvay ekā sarva-saṁsthitau
hlāda-tāpa-karī miśrā
tvayi no guṇa-varjite

Viṣṇu Purāṇa (1.12.69)

"'O Bhagavān! You are the shelter of everything. Your three spiritual potencies – *hlādinī*, *sandhinī*, and *saṁvit* – are always present within You. When the material energy acts upon the conditioned soul, he experiences happiness, misery, and a mixture of the two. None of these, however, are able to touch You, as the material energy has no influence upon You.'

The meaning here is that the three potencies – *hlādinī*, *sandhinī*, and *saṁvit* – exists within Śrī Kṛṣṇa's own form, so they are always within Him, but they are never fully within the *jīvas*. Bhagavān is beyond the influence of the material energy, which consists of the modes of goodness, passion, and ignorance. Thus it is never possible for the potency of the mode of goodness, which gives material happiness to the mind; the potency of the mode of ignorance, which gives suffering; and the potency of the mode of passion, which gives a mixture of both; to touch Śrī Kṛṣṇa. But when the individual soul, who is a minute particle of consciousness, is controlled by the material energy, he obtains the three different results when he takes shelter of the three modes of the material energy.

Bhagavān, who is beyond the modes of materal nature, and His *svarūpa-śakti* are always one. She is always present in a supremely pure state devoid of any touch of the material qualities. Thus, the internal potency is always separate from these three modes of nature. Furthermore, Bhagavān Śrī Kṛṣṇa is the presiding deity of these three modes of material nature, headed by the mode of goodness. These material energies permanently reside under the shelter of the Lord, as do the bliss and other potencies. The difference is that the three varieties of *svarūpa-śakti* (*hlādinī*, *sandhinī*, and *saṁvit*) are always non-different from the actual *svarūpa* of Śrī Kṛṣṇa. Goodness, passion, and ignorance are functions of His external, illusory potency, and they are not in the category of His internal energy. Thus, even though He is the presiding deity of the external potency, which is endowed with the three modes of nature, still He always remains untouched by them.

8.156–157

kṛṣṇake āhlāde, tā'te nāma—'āhlādinī'
sei śakti-dvāre sukha āsvāde āpani

sukha-rūpa kṛṣṇa kare sukha āsvādana
bhakta-gaṇe sukha dite 'hlādinī'—kāraṇa

"The potency that gives Bhagavān Śrī Kṛṣṇa transcendental pleasure is called *hlādinī*. By this pleasure potency, Śrī Kṛṣṇa personally tastes all spiritual pleasure, even though He is the very embodiment of bliss. This potency also gives happiness to the devotees.

Every one of the eternal symptoms of *svarūpa-śakti* is present in full in *cit-śakti*, minutely present in *jīva-śakti*, and present in a distorted manner in the external energy, *māyā-śakti*. As mentioned above, *hlādinī*, *sandhinī*, and *saṁvit* are three functions of *svarūpa-śakti*. In *Daśa-mūla-śikṣā* [instruction on the ten fundamental principles] by Śrīla Bhaktivinoda Ṭhākura, we find this explanation:

sa vai hlādinyāś ca praṇaya-vikṛter hlādana-ratas
tathā samvic-chakti-prakaṭita-raho-bhāva-rasitaḥ
tayā śrī-sandhinyā kṛta-viśada tad-dhāma-nicaye
rasāmbhodhau magno vraja-rasa-vilāsī vijayate

Daśa-mūla (4)

"There are three functions of *svarūpa-śakti*. Śrī Kṛṣṇa remains perpetually immersed in the ecstatic transformations of the bliss potency (*hlādinī-śakti*). By manifesting the internal and confidential devotional sentiments through knowledge potency (*saṁvit-śakti*), He is always enjoying the mellows of loving exchanges. And by the existence potency (*sandhinī-śakti*), the pure abode of Vṛndāvana is manifested, where Śrī Kṛṣṇa, who always performs blissful pastimes, eternally sinks by His own volition in the ocean of *vraja-rasa*."

In summary, the influence of the three aspects of *svarūpa-śakti* – *hlādinī*, *sandhinī*, and *saṁvit* – is seen throughout all the activities of the cognizence potency, the marginal potency, and the external potency. The daughter of Śrī Vṛṣabhānu Mahārāja, Śrīmatī Rādhikā, is the personification of the the pleasure function of *svarūpa-śakti* and She always bestows complete transcendental happiness upon Śrī Kṛṣṇa. Śrīmatī Rādhikā is made of *mahābhāva* and She is always giving all varieties of bliss to Him. Her non-different expansions (*kāya-vyūha-svarūpa*), in the form of the eight principal *gopīs*, are Her eight different *bhāvas*; and Her four moods of service eternally manifest as the four types of *sakhīs*, namely, *priya-sakhī*, *prāṇa-sakhī*, *narma-sakhī*, and *parama-preṣṭha-sakhī*. All of them are eternally perfected *sakhīs* (*nitya-siddha sakhīs*) present in the Vṛndāvana of the spiritual realm. The cognizance (*saṁvit*) function of *svarūpa-śakti* manifests all of the different relationships in Vraja.

The existence function (*sandhinī-vṛtti*) manifests the transcendental land, bodies of water, villages, primary and subsidiary forests, mountains like Śrī Giri-Govardhana, and other scenic places where Śrī Kṛṣṇa and His associates perform their pastimes. Moreover, the *sandhinī-vṛtti* gives rise to the transcendental forms of Śrī Kṛṣṇa, Śrī Rādhā, the *sakhās* and *sakhīs*, cows, and every other servant and maidservant of Vraja, as well as all of the completely spiritual paraphernalia used in their pastimes. Śrī Kṛṣṇa forever remains immersed in the supreme bliss of the loving transformations of the pleasure function (*hlādinī-vṛtti*), while the full variety of *bhāvas* generated by the cognizance function (*saṁvit-vṛtti*) provides Him with the tastes of loving mellows, or *rasa*. Śrī Kṛṣṇa expands such pastimes as attracting the *gopīs* by playing His flute, cow grazing, *rāsa-līlā*, and other such pastimes by the agency of the cognizance function of His internal energy (*parā-śakti*). Vraja-vilāsī Śrī Kṛṣṇa, He who eternally enjoys pastimes in Vṛndāvana, always remains absorbed in the divine abode, manifested by the existence function (*sandhinī-vṛtti*).

The *jīva-śakti* is a minute potency that is reliant upon *svarūpa-śakti*. The three tendencies of *svarūpa-śakti* are only present minutely in the *jīva-śakti*. In the *jīva*, the bliss function (*hlādinī-vṛtti*) is present in the form of *brahmānanda* (the bliss achieved through realization of the formless Brahman); the cognizance function (*saṁvit-vṛtti*) is present as knowledge of that impersonal Brahman; and the existence function (*sandhinī-vṛtti*) is always present as minute individual consciousness.

Likewise, the three functions of *svarūpa-śakti* are present in *māyā-śakti*. The bliss function is present in the form of material happiness, the cognizance function is present as material knowledge, and the existence function takes the form of the entire material creation, including this universe composed of fourteen planetary systems and the material bodies of the *jīvas*.

Māyā-śakti is a perverted or reflected form of the superior, internal energy of Bhagavān. In fact, *māyā-śakti* is only a name for the transformation of Bhagavān's *parā-śakti* and is its shadow. It is not a separate, independent power. *Māyā* is the sole cause of the *jīva's* bondage and also his liberation. When the *jīva*'s orientation is opposed to Śrī Kṛṣṇa, *māyā* at once places him in bondage and punishes him. And when the *jīva* turns towards Śrī Kṛṣṇa, *māyā* bestows knowledge of Śrī Kṛṣṇa upon the *jīva* by manifesting the material mode of goodness (*sattva-guṇa*) and liberates him from the ocean of birth and death, thus making him qualified for *kṛṣṇa-prema*. Bound by *māyā* in the form of the three modes of material nature, the *jīva* is unable to understand that the pure form of *māyā* is the *svarūpa-śakti* of Bhagavān and instead considers the shadow known as *māyā* to be the prominent potency.

8.158–159

hlādinīra sāra aṁśa, tāra 'prema' nāma
ānanda-cinmaya-rūpa rasera ākhyāna

premera parama-sāra 'mahābhāva' jāni
sei mahābhāva-rūpā rādhā-ṭhākurāṇī

"The most essential part of this pleasure potency, or *hlādinī-śakti*, is called *prema*, also known as *ānanda-cinmaya-rasa*, the mellow of transcendental bliss. This mellow can only be tasted by *prema*. The essence of *prema* is called *mahābhāva*, which is personified in Śrī Rādhā Ṭhākurānī.

8.160

tayor apy ubhayor madhye
rādhikā sarvathādhikā
mahābhāva-svarūpeyaṁ
guṇair ativarīyasī

Ujjvala-nīlamaṇi (4.3)

"'Between the two *gopīs* [Rādhikā and Candrāvalī], Śrī Rādhikā is superior in every respect, because Her very form is composed of the highest expressions of love (*mahābhāva*). By qualities, She far outshines all the other beautiful damsels of Vraja.'

Tāpanī-śrutis call Śrī Rādhā "Gāndharvā." The fundamental truths about Śrī Rādhā are unprecedented and astonishing.

8.161

premera 'svarūpa-deha'—premera bhāvita
'kṛṣṇera preyasī-śreṣṭha' jagate vidita

"Śrī Rādhā's nature (*svarūpa*) is comprised of *prema* and Her body is also made of *prema*. She is the most excellent of all of Śrī Kṛṣṇa's beloveds. This fundamental truth is known throughout the entire creation.

8.162

ānanda-cinmaya-rasa-pratibhāvitābhis
tābhir ya eva nija-rūpatayā kalābhiḥ
goloka eva nivasaty akhilātma-bhūto
govindam ādi-puruṣaṁ tam ahaṁ bhajāmi

Brahma-saṁhitā (5.37)

"'Śrī Govinda, who is all-pervading and who exists within the hearts of all, resides in His Goloka-dhāma along with Śrī Rādhā, who is the embodiment of His pleasure potency and the counterpart of His own spiritual form. She is the epitome of transcendental *rasa*, and is expert in sixty-four arts. They are also accompanied by the *sakhīs*, who are expansions of Śrī Rādhā's own transcendental body, and who are infused with blissful, spiritual *rasa*. I worship that original personality, Śrī Govinda.'

Śrīla Jīva Gosvāmī identifies the planet of the *gopīs* as none other than Goloka-dhāma. Śrī Kṛṣṇa only resides where the *gopīs* reside. The phrase *nija-rūpatayā kalābhiḥ* means that the *gopī* beloveds of Śrī Kṛṣṇa are actually His parts, non-different from Himself, and the very embodiment of the essential function of *hlādinī-śakti*. They are expansions of *unnatojjvala-rasa*, or the amorous mellow, and because of their complete immersion in transcendental ecstasy, they are certainly Śrī Kṛṣṇa's dear-most beloveds. The word *pratibhāvita* indicates those *gopīs* who have immersed themselves completely in the *prema-rasa* for the king of mellows, Śrī Kṛṣṇa. Moreover, it indicates those *gopīs* whose hearts, being inundated by a deluge of this loving affection, have themselves been loved by Him. By offering Him such wonderful and expert affection, the *gopīs* bestowed upon Śrī Kṛṣṇa a greatly beneficial gift.

The functions (*vṛtti*) of the pleasure potency (*hlādinī-śakti*) are all manifested in the form of different arts. The arts number sixty-four: (1) *nṛtya* – dancing, (2) *gīta* – singing, (3) *vādya* – playing on musical instruments, (4) *nāṭya* – performing theater, (5) *ālekhya* – painting, (6) *viśeṣakacchedya* – painting the face and body with colored unguents and cosmetics, (7) *taṇḍula-kusuma-balī-vikāra* – preparing offerings from rice and flowers, (8) *puṣpāstaraṇa* – making coverings of flowers for a bed, (9) *daśana-vasanāṅga-rāga* – applying preparations for cleansing the teeth and coloring the cloth and body, (10) *maṇi-bhūmikā-karma* – making a groundwork of jewels, (11) *śayyā-racana* – preparing the pastime bed, (12) *udaka-vādya* – playing music on the water or *udaka-ghāta* – splashing with water, (13) *citra-yoga* – painting, (14) *mālya-grathana-vikalpa* – designing varieties of garlands, (15) *śekharāpīḍa-yojana* – setting a crown upon the head, (16) *nepathya-yoga* – dressing in the retiring room, (17) *karṇapātra-bhaṅga* – decorating the ears, (18) *sugandha-yukti* – applying scents, (19) *bhūṣaṇa-yojana* – applying or setting ornaments, (20) *aindra-jāla* – performing jugglery, (21) *kaucumāra-yoga* – engaging in decorative art, (22) *hasta-lāghava* – tricking others with sleight of hand, (23) *citra-śākā-pūpa-bhakṣya-vikāra-kriyā* – preparing varieties of salad, bread, cake and delicious edibles, (24) *pānaka-rasa-rāgāsava-yojana* – preparing palatable drinks and tingeing drinks with a red color, (25) *sūcī-vāya-karma* – doing needlework and weaving, (26) *sūtra-krīḍā* – playing with thread, (27) *vīṇā-ḍamarūka-vādya* – playing on the lute and small x-shaped drum, (28) *prahelikā* – posing and solving riddles, (29) *pratimālā* – reciting a verse as a trial of memory or skill, (30) *durvacaka-yoga* – speaking in a way that is difficult to understand, (31) *pustaka-vācana* – reciting books, (32) *nāṭikākhyāyikā-darśana* – enacting short plays and anecdotes, (33) *kāvya-samasyā-pūraṇa* – resolving unfathomable statements, verses, or poetry, (34) *paṭṭikā-vetra-bāṇa-vikalpa* – designing shields, canes, and arrows, (35) *tarku-karma* – spinning, (36) *takṣaṇa* – doing carpentry, (37) *vāstu-vidyā* – engineering, (38) *rūpya-ratna-parīkṣā* – testing silver and jewels, (39) *dhātu-vāda* – practicing metallurgy, (40) *maṇi-rāga-jñāna* – coloring jewels, (41) *ākara-jñāna* – practicing mineralogy, (42) *vṛkṣāyurveda-yoga* – practicing medical treatment by herbs, (43) *meṣa-kukkuṭa-śāvaka-yuddha-vidhi* – training rams, cocks, and birds to fight, (44) *śuka-sārikā-pralāpana* – training male and female parrots to converse, and also understanding their conversations, (45) *utsādana* – using perfumes to heal or cleanse a person, (46) *keśa-mārjana-kauśala* – combing and decorating hair, (47) *akṣara-muṣṭikā-kathana* – talking with letters and fingers, (48) *mlecchita-kutarka-vikalpa* – fabricating barbarous philosophies or foreign sophistry, (49) *deśa-bhāṣā-jñāna* – knowing provincial dialects, (50) *puṣpa-śakaṭikā-nirmiti-jñāna* – preparing of toy carts using flowers, (51) *yantra-mātṛkā* – knowing the art of designing *yantras*, (52) *dhāraṇa-mātṛkā* – wearing and using *yantras*, (53) *samvācya* – conversing, (54) *mānasī-kāvya-kriyā* – composing verses mentally, (55) *kriyā-vikalpa* – designing a literary work or a medical remedy, (56) *chalitaka-yoga* – juggling words to defeat another, (57) *abhidhāna-koṣa-cchando-jñāna* – using lexicography and meters, (58) *vastra-gopana* – concealing cloths, (59) *dyūta-viśeṣa* – specific gambling, (60) *ākarṣa-krīḍā* – playing with dice by using magnets, (61) *bālaka-krīḍanaka* – using children's toys, (62) *vaināyikī vidyā* – enforcing discipline, (63) *vaijayikī vidyā* – gaining victory, and (64) *vaitālikī vidyā* – awakening one's master with music at dawn.

All of these artistic abilities are eternally present in their personified forms in Goloka-dhāma. By the help of His beloved friend – the flute – Śrī Govinda, the hero of Goloka, accepts the self-conception of being the unmarried lover (*upapati*) of the *gopīs*, and enacts His pastimes such as *rāsa-līlā*. There, too, the *gopīs*, since time without beginning, retain the feeling that they are His beloveds, while married to another man. Śrī Kṛṣṇa tastes this mood in one form in the spiritual realm (Goloka), and in another form in the Vṛndāvana of this world (Gokula).

8.163–180

seī mahābhāva haya 'cintāmaṇi-sāra'
kṛṣṇa-vāñchā pūrṇa kare ei kārya tāṅra

'mahābhāva-cintāmaṇi' rādhāra svarūpa
lalitādi sakhī—tāṅra kāya-vyūha-rūpa

rādhā-prati kṛṣṇa-sneha—sugandhi udvartana
tā'te ati sugandhi deha—ujjvala-varaṇa

kāruṇyāmṛta-dhārāya snāna prathama
tāruṇyāmṛta-dhārāya snāna madhyama

lāvaṇyāmṛta-dhārāya tad-upari snāna
nija-lajjā-śyāma-paṭṭasāṭi-paridhāna

kṛṣṇa-anurāga—dvitīya aruṇa-vasana
praṇaya-māna-kañculikāya vakṣa ācchādana

saundarya—kuṅkuma, sakhī-praṇaya—candana
smita-kānti—karpūra, tine—aṅge vilepana

kṛṣṇera ujjvala-rasa—mṛgamada-bhara
sei mṛgamade vicitra kalevara

pracchanna-māna-vāmya—dhammilla-vinyāsa
'dhīrādhīrātmaka' guṇa—aṅge paṭa-vāsa

rāga-tāmbūla-rāge adhara ujjvala
prema-kauṭilya—netra-yugale kajjala

'sūddīpta-sāttvika' bhāva, harṣādi 'sañcārī'
ei saba bhāva-bhūṣaṇa saba aṅge bhari'

'kila-kiñcitādi'-bhāva-viṁśati-bhūṣita
guṇa-śreṇī-puṣpamālā sarvāṅge pūrita

saubhāgya-tilaka cāru-lalāṭe ujjvala
prema-vaicittya—ratna, hṛdaya—tarala

madhya-vayasa, sakhī-skandhe kara-nyāsa
kṛṣṇalīlā-manovṛtti-sakhī āśa-pāśa

nijāṅga-saurabhālaye garva-paryaṅka
tā'te vasi' āche, sadā cinte kṛṣṇa-saṅga

kṛṣṇa-nāma-guṇa-yaśa—avataṁsa kāṇe
kṛṣṇa-nāma-guṇa-yaśa-pravāha-vacane

kṛṣṇake karāya śyāma-rasa-madhu pāna
nirantara pūrṇa kare kṛṣṇera sarva-kāma

kṛṣṇera viśuddha-prema-ratnera ākara
anupama-guṇagaṇa-pūrṇa kalevara

"*Mahābhāva* is the essence of all perfection and is like a wish fulfilling desire stone; its only business is to fulfill all of Śrī Kṛṣṇa's desires. Śrī Rādhā is the topmost spiritual gem, and the other *gopīs* such as Śrī Lalitā are Her direct expansions (*kāya-vyūha*). Śrī Kṛṣṇa's affection for Her is like a perfumed massage, which makes Śrī Rādhā's transcendental body brilliantly lustrous and fragrant.

"Śrī Rādhā takes Her first bath in the shower of the nectar of compassion, and She takes Her second bath at mid-day in the nectar waves of fresh youth. Later on, Rādhārāṇī takes Her third and last bath in the nectar-ocean of bodily luster. She wears the garment of shyness, in the form of a very fine, dark blue silk *sārī*.

"Śrīmatī Rādhārāṇī's affection for Kṛṣṇa is Her upper cloth, which is reddish in color. She then covers Her breasts with a bodice comprised of overwhelming affection (*praṇaya*) and jealous anger (*māna*) for Kṛṣṇa. Śrīmatī Rādhārāṇī's personal beauty is the reddish vermilion (saffron) powder known as *kuṅkuma* placed upon Her body. Her affection for Her *sakhīs* is sandalwood pulp, and the sweetness of Her gentle smile is camphor. These three combined – camphor, sandalwood pulp, and *kuṅkuma* – are smeared over Her body.

"Amorous love for Kṛṣṇa is the fragrance of musk, and special decorative pictures drawn with that musk nicely decorate Her entire divine body. Concealed sulkiness and Her unsubmissive leftist mood constitute Her hair style. The quality of *dhīrādhīra* – an indignant heroine who greets her faithless beau sometimes with wry politeness while rebuffing him with ambiguous words, and sometimes with harshness, caustically rejecting him – is the silk garment covering Her body. Her attachment for Kṛṣṇa is the reddish stain from betel nuts upon Her lips, which causes them to shine brilliantly. Her crookedness in loving affairs is the decorative black mascara around Her eyes. The ornaments on Her body are the forms of Her eight types of fully blazing devotional ecstatic transformations (*sāttvika-bhāvas*) and the other *sañcārī-bhāvas* (thirty-three transitory emotions that swell from the ocean of *sthāyi-bhāva*) headed by jubilation. All these ecstasies are like the decorations that beautifully embellish Her body.

"These bodily ornaments constitute twenty kinds of ecstatic symptoms, beginning with *kila-kiñcita-bhāva* (a mixture of seven moods – pride, desire, crying, laughing, malice, fear, and anger – that manifest simultaneously). Her transcendental qualities such as sweetness are the flower garland hanging upon Her whole body. A supremely beautiful *tilaka* of good fortune adorns Her forehead. Her various loving moods such as *prema-vaicittya* are the various gems from which Her necklace is composed, and Her heart is the locket of Her affection, which nicely decorates Her.

"She rests Her hands on the shoulder of a *sakhī*, who represents eternal, fresh adolescence. Rādhā's *sakhīs*, who always stay close by Her, are the forms of Her various mental activities, which all dwell upon the pastimes of Śrī Kṛṣṇa. Within Śrīmatī Rādhārāṇī's palace, which represents Her bodily beauty, is Her bedstead composed of pride itself; She is always seated there thinking of Śrī Kṛṣṇa's intimate association.

"Śrī Kṛṣṇa's name, fame, and qualities decorate Her ears, and His name and fame flow continually from Her speech. Śrī Rādhā induces Kṛṣṇa to drink the honey of amorous pleasure, and She completely satisfies all of His desires. Her body is exactly like the valuable jewel of completely pure *prema*, the only object of which is Śrī Kṛṣṇa. These unparalleled spiritual qualities always decorate Śrī Rādhā's transcendental body.

Śrī Rādhā is *mahābhāva-cintāmaṇi-svarūpa* – She is the embodiment of *mahābhāva* and is just like a wish fulfilling spiritual jewel. As a *cintāmaṇi* fulfills all of one's desires, so Śrī Rādhā fulfills all of the desires of Vrajendra-nandana Śrī Kṛṣṇa, who is the hero of unlimited universes and the crest-jewel of those who taste ecstatic devotional mellows. If Śrī Kṛṣṇa has any desire to taste the *rasa* of associating with the *gopīs* who are opposed to Śrī Rādhā (the *vipakṣa gopīs*), then Śrī Rādhā manifests Herself as Candrāvalī, and in that form fulfills Her beloved's desire. All of the *vraja-gopīs* are personifications of the different moods of Śrī Rādhā. In harmony with Śrī Kṛṣṇa's particular desire, She presents Herself accordingly.

The queens of Dvārakā and the different incarnations of Lakṣmī are all Śrī Rādhā's pastime expansions (*vaibhava-vilāsa*). Some are *aṁśa* (parts), and some are *kalā* (part of a part). Śrī Rādhā has assumed all of these various forms, thus they are Her non-different bodily expansions, known as *kāya-vyūha*. Each of these forms is always happy and alert to fulfill each of Śrī Kṛṣṇa's desires, but only *cintāmaṇi-svarūpā* Śrī Rādhā can satisfy all of His desires.

The term *kāya-vyūha* signifies the multiple distinct forms that are manifest simultaneously in order to perform a variety of different activities. Each *kāya-vyūha* body is similar to the original one.

Śrī Rādhā's *sakhīs* increase the wonder and astonishment of the love-filled pastimes. Śrī Kṛṣṇa's affection for Śrī Rādhā is such that it is extremely fragrant. When Śrī Rādhā recalls Śrī Kṛṣṇa's astonishing love, Her entire body becomes supremely fragrant and brilliantly radiant. She is the confluence, or meeting place, of the three currents known as *kāruṇya-amṛta* (the nectar of mercy), *tāruṇya-amṛta* (the nectar of youth), and *lāvaṇya-amṛta* (the nectar of beauty).

Bhakti-rasāmṛta-sindhu (2.1.64) states: "*para-duḥkhāsaho yas tu karuṇaḥ sa nigadyate* – One who cannot tolerate the unhappiness of others is called merciful." When an adjective is formed, the noun "mercy" becomes "merciful." In addition, the nectar of mercy, or *kāruṇya-amṛta*, is a wave upon the current of *prema*, and it is in this nectar of mercy that Śrī Rādhā takes Her first bath. It is very auspicious to bathe in the early morning in a river, as it makes the body extremely smooth, glistening, and soft. For this reason, Śrī Rādhā takes bath in the waves of the nectar of compassion, first thing in the morning. "Early morning" indicates Śrī Rādhā's age, known as *vayasa-sandhi* (the conjunction of two ages) and at this time, all the restlessness of infancy (*bālya*) and childhood (*paugaṇḍa*) disappear.

At midday, Śrī Rādhā takes Her second bath in *tāruṇya-amṛta*, or the nectar flow of just-rising youthfulness. Upon completing Her morning bath, Śrī Rādhā goes to Śrī Nanda Bābā's palace, and after preparing edibles for Her treasured Śrī Kṛṣṇa, She goes to Śrī Rādhā-kuṇḍa to bathe. Making some excuse to get away from His friends, Śrī Śyāmasundara joins Her there. As soon as Śrī Rādhā catches sight of Him, His body automatically blossoms with ever-fresh youthfulness. Now They very expertly perform boating pastimes, water-sports, and other water pastimes (*jala-vihāra*), and lastly They take an ecstatic bath in Śrī Rādhā-kuṇḍa together. This bath is full of wondrous, mutual loving sentiments. After this midday bath the waves of youthful nectar cover Them both, and Śrī Rādhā's natural youthfulness becomes fully blazing:

muktāphaleṣu chāyāyās taralatvam ivāntarā
pratibhāti yad aṅgeṣu lāvaṇyaṁ tad ihocyate

Ujjvala-nīlamaṇi (10.28)

"Just as one can perceive the luster of a pearl from any direction, similarly one can see the heartfelt devotional sentiments radiating from within the body of Śrī Rādhā."

These *bhāvas* make Śrīmatī Rādhikā's beauty shine even more brightly. When She goes to meet with Śrī Kṛṣṇa in the night at the appointed meeting place, Her budding youth and exceeding beauty manifest fully. It is by this *lāvaṇya-amṛta* (nectar of Her beauty) that She fulfills all the desires of Her most beloved, giving Him the topmost happiness. It is in this flow of *lāvaṇya-amṛta* in the evening that She takes Her third bath.

Therefore, Śrī Rādhā is the root cause and shelter of all mercy, youthfulness, and beauty. As She approaches Her budding, fresh youth, Her body takes on a sense of gravity, and very naturally, shyness starts to make its appearance in Her. To cover Her femininity, She wears a dark blue *sārī*, which is the actualized form of the amorous mellow, or *śṛṅgāra-rasa*. It appears as if Her shyness has wrapped Her entire body with this blue cloth.

Over Her *sārī* She wears a veil the color of the rising sun that represents Her attraction for Śrī Kṛṣṇa:

> *sadānubhūtam api yaḥ kuryyān nava-navaṁ priyam*
> *rāgo bhavan nava-navaḥ so 'nurāga itīryate*
>
> *Ujjvala-nīlamaṇi* (14.146)

"That ever fresh, all-consuming attraction (*rāga*) which itself causes one to realize one's beloved in a novel manner every moment, is called *anurāga*."

Since Śrī Rādhā wishes to remain constantly absorbed in this *anurāga*, She always covers Her upper torso with red cloth.

At all times She is beautifully decorated with sixteen decorative items (*ṣoḍaśa-śṛṅgāra*): a bath, a shining bejeweled nose-piece, blue cloth, an ornamented belt around Her waist, a braid, swaying earrings, an ointment of camphor, musk, and sandalwood smeared on Her body, flowers decorating Her hair, a garland about Her neck, a pastime lotus in Her hand, *tāmbūla* in Her mouth, a spot of musk on Her chin, *kajjala* (black mascara) on Her eyes, *tilaka* on Her forehead, dolphins (*makarī* – the aquatic animals on the flag of Cupid) drawn in musk on Her pinkish cheeks, and Her feet tinted with red dye.

Twelve more ornaments (*dvādaśa-ābharaṇa*) beautifully decorate Śrīmatī Rādhikā's body: an effulgent jeweled crown, large golden earrings, a golden waist sash, a silver necklace, small golden ear studs and hair pin, rings on Her fingers, a neck ornament, and bangles on Her wrist. Upon Her chest is a glittering chain, upon Her arm are amulets, and on Her ankles and toes are jeweled ankle bells and toe rings.

The following transcendental qualities are always within Śrīmatī Rādhikā's possession: She is wonderfully beautiful to behold, She is situated in the prime of fresh youth, She has restless eyes and casts sidelong glances, She is always adorned with a mild, sweet smile, and the soles of Her feet are marked with enchanting lines indicating unlimited auspiciousness. Her bodily fragrance maddens Kṛṣṇa, Her singing of the fifth note equals the sweetness of a cuckoo, and She is expert in the science of singing with music. She speaks sweetly, She is expert at joking, She is humble, merciful, extremely clever, and expert in all activities. She is shy and follows proper etiquette. Thus She shows respectful behavior to Her superiors. (This respectful behavior is of three types: inborn, learned from others, and deemed proper by Her own deliberation.) She is patient, grave, expert in knowing appropriate rhythm and tune, and possessed of ecstatic symptoms such as *hāva* and *bhāva*. She demonstrates the highest form of love called *mahābhāva*. Seeing Her, the hearts of all the residents of Gokula flood with *prema*. Her fame is spread throughout the universe, She is most beloved of Her superiors, She is controlled by the love of Her girlfriends, She is the most prominent of Śrī Kṛṣṇa's beloveds, and Śrī Kṛṣṇa always obeys Her orders.

Prema-tattva

8.181

kā kṛṣṇasya praṇaya-jani-bhūḥ śrīmatī rādhikaikā
kāsya preyasy anupama-guṇā rādhikaikā na cānyā
jaihmyaṁ keśe dṛśi taralatā niṣṭhuratvaṁ kuce 'syā
vāñchā-pūrtyai prabhavati hare rādhikaikā na cānyā

Śrī Govinda-līlāmṛta (11.112)

"'Who is the source of love for Śrī Kṛṣṇa? The answer is it is Śrī Rādhā only. Who is Śrī Kṛṣṇa's most beloved? The answer is Śrī Rādhā, the repository of all transcendental qualities, and no one else. Her hair is very curly, Her eyes are always darting back and forth, and Her breasts are firm. Thus, Śrī Rādhā alone is able to fulfill all of Kṛṣṇa's desires, no one else.'

8.182–184

yāṅra saubhāgya-guṇa vāñche satyabhāmā
yāṅra ṭhāñi kalā-vilāsa śikhe vraja-rāmā

yāṅra saundaryādi-guṇa vāñche lakṣmī-pārvatī
yāṅra pativratā-dharma vāñche arundhatī

yāṅra sadguṇa-gaṇane kṛṣṇa nā pāya pāra
tāṅra guṇa gaṇibe kemane jīva chāra"

"Satyabhāmā and Śrī Kṛṣṇa's other queens eternally long for the good fortune and excellent qualities of Śrīmatī Rādhikā, from whom all the *gopīs* have learned the various arts. Even the goddess of fortune, Lakṣmī, and Lord Śiva's wife Pārvatī yearn for Her standard of beauty. The respected Arundhatī also, the celebrated chaste wife of Vasiṣṭha, desires to rise to the level of Her chastity and religious observance. Even Śrī Kṛṣṇa Himself cannot fully enumerate Śrīmatī Rādhārāṇī's transcendental qualities. How, then, could an insignificant living entity possibly estimate them?"

Vilāsa-tattva

8.185–186

prabhu kahe,—"jāniluṅ kṛṣṇa-rādhā-prema-tattva
śunite cāhiye duṅhāra vilāsa-mahattva"

rāya kahe,—"kṛṣṇa haya 'dhīra-lalita'
nirantara kāma-krīḍā—yāṅhāra carita

After hearing these descriptions of *kṛṣṇa-tattva*, *rādhā-tattva*, and *prema-tattva* from Śrī Rāya Rāmānanda, Śrīman Mahāprabhu replied, "O Rāya, I have come to understand the truths about Śrī Kṛṣṇa, Śrī Rādhā, and *prema* itself. Now I wish to hear the glories of Their playful loving exchanges."

Śrī Rāya Rāmānanda replied, "Lord Kṛṣṇa is *dhīra-lalita-nāyaka*, and He is ever devoted to lusty affairs (*kāma-krīḍā*).

Expert in relishing loving exchanges, ever youthful, clever at joking, and always carefree – these are the qualities of the *dhīra-lalita-nāyaka*, a hero controlled by his beloved. When the hero is symptomized as being completely favorable to the heroine and unable to remain apart from her, he is called *dhīra-lalita-anukūla-nāyaka*. In his *Bhakti-rasāmṛta-sindhu*, Śrī Rūpa Gosvāmī says:

8.187

vidagdho nava-tāruṇyaḥ
parihāsa-viśāradaḥ
niścinto dhīra-lalitaḥ
syāt prāyaḥ preyasī-vaśaḥ

Bhakti-rasāmṛta-sindhu (2.1.230)

"'He who is expert in the art of love, ever youthful, clever at joking, happy-go-lucky, and subjugated by the love of his sweethearts is called a *dhīra-lalita-nāyaka*.'

Śrī Paurṇamāsī said to Nāndīmukhī: "O Nāndīmukhī, because of their indescribable, compelling love for Śrī Kṛṣṇa, Śrī Nanda and Yaśodā never burden their son with any specific responsibility. Thus, being fully carefree, Śrī Kṛṣṇa continuously plays with Śrī Rādhā on the banks of the Yamunā River, decorating the *kuñjas* there with His very presence."

8.188

rātri-dina kuñje krīḍā kare rādhā-saṅge
kaiśora-vayasa saphala kaila krīḍā-raṅge

"Day and night Śrī Kṛṣṇa continuously sports, jokes, and enjoys in various ways with Śrī Rādhā in the *kuñjas*. In this way, through His amorous diversions He makes His youth successful.

The meaning of amorous play (*krīḍā-raṅga*) in the present context is *prema-līlā*, pastimes of love, which are ongoing, meaning "whenever the opportunity arises." If the meaning were taken as "every moment," then the sequence in the flow of the *līlās* would be disrupted, giving no chance for Kṛṣṇa to perform His cow-grazing and other pastimes. These other *līlās* are essential limbs of the principle pastimes of meeting with the *vraja-gopīs*, and all of the *līlās* have their own appropriate timings.

8.189

vācā sūcita-śarvarī-rati-kalā-prāgalbhyayā rādhikām
vrīḍā-kuñcita-locanāṁ viracayann agre sakhīnām asau
tad-vakṣoruha-citra-keli-makarī-pāṇḍitya-pāraṁ gataḥ
kaiśoraṁ saphalī-karoti kalayan kuñje vihāraṁ hariḥ

Bhakti-rasāmṛta-sindhu (2.1.231)

"'Śrī Kṛṣṇa impudently boasted of His amorous escapades of the previous night in front of the *sakhīs*, making Śrī Rādhā close Her eyes out of embarrassment. At that moment, He painted some charming, playful *makarī* [Cupid's dolphin carrier] upon Her breasts, and thus manifested the pinnacle of cleverness. By such loving pastimes in the *kuñjas*, Śrī Hari made His youth successful.'"

8.190–192

prabhu kahe,—"eho haya, āge kaha āra"
rāya kahe,—"ihā vai buddhi-gati nāhi āra

yebā 'prema-vilāsa-vivarta' eka haya
tāhā śuni' tomāra sukha haya, ki nā haya"

eta bali' āpana-kṛta gīta eka gāhila
preme prabhu sva-haste tāṅra mukha ācchādila

Śrīman Mahāprabhu said, "Whatever you have said regarding the loving exchanges between Śrī Rādhā and Kṛṣṇa is all right, but please say something more." Śrī Rāya Rāmānanda replied, "O Lord, my intelligence cannot penetrate this subject any further, but there is another stage called *prema-vilāsa-vivarta*. However I do not know if such a description will be to Your satisfaction or not." Saying this, Śrī Rāmānanda Rāya began to sing his own composition, but Śrī Caitanya Mahāprabhu immediately covered Rāmānanda's mouth with His lotus hand.

According to Śrīla Bhaktivinoda Ṭhākura, in the present verse, it is Śrīman Mahāprabhu's intention here to confirm that in Śrī Rāmānanda Rāya's deliberation on the goal of human life, he has described the *prema* between Śrī Rādhā and Śrī Kṛṣṇa, and illuminated the greatness of Their pastimes when Śrī Kṛṣṇa manifests His *dhīra-lalita-nāyaka* form. This deliberation describes the glories of the amorous pastimes between Śrī Rādhā and Śrī Kṛṣṇa – Rādhā who is the source or sum total of all *rasa* (*akhaṇḍa-rasa-vallabhā*), the embodiment of *mahābhāva*, and the personification of *kāntā-prema*, and Kṛṣṇa who is the unlimited ocean of all *rasas* (*akhila-rasāmṛta-sindhu*), the personification of *śṛṅgāra-rasa*, amorous love, the king of all mellows, and the direct attracter of even Cupid himself.

Yet Śrīman Mahāprabhu asked, "Can you explain more than this?"

Śrī Rāmānanda replied, "Since such topics are beyond material intelligence, it is extremely rare to find anyone qualified enough to hear or speak on them. However, there is one topic, namely *prema-vilāsa-vivarta*, that I shall describe, but I do not know whether this will make You happy or not. This is my doubt.

"*Prema-vilāsa* is of two types. One is meeting (*sambhoga*) and the other is separation (*vipralambha*). Without separation, there is no joy or sustenance in meeting. In the stage of *adhirūḍha-mahābhāva*, this condition of bewilderment, or illusion, (*vivarta*) causes feelings of separation even within meeting. Meeting for the duration of a day of Brahmā seems to last only for a moment. Even though Śrī Kṛṣṇa is happy, one iota of difficulty for Him still causes great unhappiness [for the devotee]. Although the devotee is beyond illusion, when he is in separation from Kṛṣṇa, he automatically forgets everything and considers even a moment to be like millions upon millions of years.

The words *prema-vilāsa* mean "the loving, playful pastimes that are generated from *prema*," and *vivarta* means "mistaking one thing for something else." It also means "opposite, bewildered, and completely ripened." During *prema-vilāsa-vivarta* there is cause for some pastimes to flow in a seemingly contradictory manner. This stage is most astonishing and the ultimate expression of loving exchanges. Thus we find the statement:

advaitād girijāṁ harārdha-vapuṣaṁ sakhyāt priyoraḥ-sthitāṁ,
lakṣmīm acyuta-citta-bhṛṅga-nalinīṁ satyāṁ ca saubhāgyataḥ
mādhuryān madhureśa-jīvita-sakhīṁ candrāvalīṁ ca kṣipan,
paśyāruddha hariṁ prasārya laharīṁ rādhānurāgāmbudhiḥ

Ujjvala-nīlamaṇi (14.178)

"The waves of the great ocean of Śrī Rādhā's compelling love now completely cover Śrī Kṛṣṇa with their waters because She actually identifies as Him. Thus She defeats all other goddesses, including Pārvatī, who, being non-different from Lord Śiva, is his wife; Lakṣmī, who, because of intimate friendship with Śrī Nārāyaṇa, reclines on His chest; Satyabhāmā, who because of her great good fortune, is like a lotus flower that attracts the bumble-bee of Śrī Kṛṣṇa's mind; and also Candrāvalī, who, because of her sweetness, is the life and soul of Madhureśa (the Lord of all sweetness)."

Prema-vilāsa means "loving pastimes," and *vivarta* indicates *prema-vaicittya*, which is the topmost level of *prema*. In this stage of the performance of loving exchanges, the knowledge of the difference between the lover and his beloved is annihilated. Everything else apart from the joy of meeting, including their own existence, is forgotten. Their heart and mind melt to such a degree that both of them become one, and they do not recognize any difference between each other. In this profusion of *prema*, absorption in oneness reaches its highest stage. The knowledge "I am the heroine (beloved) and you are the hero (lover)" becomes covered due to a delusion that arises in the course of amorous exchanges. In this stage, sometimes Śrī Rādhā mistakenly considers Herself to be the hero (*ramaṇa*), and Śrī Kṛṣṇa thinks Himself to be the heroine (*ramaṇī*). This is *viparīta-bhāva*, in which roles are reversed.

When Madhumaṅgala says, "O Rādhā, Madhusūdana has gone away," Śrī Rādhā begins to lament in separation from Him, even though Śrī Kṛṣṇa is right next to Her. This is *prema-vilāsa-vivarta*.

The following song was composed by Śrī Rāya Rāmānanda:

8.193

"pahilehi rāga nayana-bhaṅge bhela
anudina bāḍhala, avadhi nā gela

nā so ramaṇa, nā hāma ramaṇī
duṅhu-mana manobhava peṣala jāni'

e sakhī, se-saba prema-kāhinī
kānu-ṭhāme kahabi vichurala jāni'

nā khoṅjaluṅ dūtī, nā khoṅjaluṅ ān
duṅhuko milane madhya ta pāṅca-bāṇa

ab sohi virāga, tuṅhu bheli dūtī
su-purukha-premaki aichana rīti"

"Lamenting in separation, Śrīmatī Rādhikā says, 'Alas, before We ever met, We first experienced an initial attachment to each other instigated by an exchange of glances. In just a blink of the eyelid, without a moment's delay, an emotion named *rāga* (driving attachment) immediately arose between Us. This compelling love grew day by day, and in no time at all, in just a few days, it developed so much that there was no limit to it. That attachment flowed without stop and continued to increase.'

rādhā-premā vibhu—yāra bāḍīte nāhi ṭhāñi
tathāpi se kṣaṇe kṣaṇe bāḍaye sadai

Śrī Caitanya-caritāmṛta, Ādi-līlā (4.128)

"Śrī Rādhā's love extends everywhere, leaving no space for it to expand any further. Still it continuously increases every second."

Śrī Kṛṣṇa also says:

man-mādhurya, rādhāra prema—doṅhe hoḍa kari'
kṣaṇe kṣaṇe bāḍe doṅhe, keha nāhi hāri

Śrī Caitanya-caritāmṛta, Ādi-līlā (4.142)

"My sweetness and Rādhā's *prema* increase every moment, and neither knows defeat."

"That *rāga*, or attraction, arises naturally in both of Us." It is Śrī Rādhā's desire to give happiness to Śrī Kṛṣṇa continuously, and Śrī Kṛṣṇa desires to do the same for Śrī Rādhā. Neither Śrī Kṛṣṇa, the lover par excellence, nor Śrī Rādhā, the pre-eminent beloved, is the cause of this spontaneous attraction, but it awakens just from seeing each other and turns into Cupid, who grinding or melting Their minds together, makes them one. Their hearts and minds, desiring only to give happiness to one another, become non-different from each other. At that time, They become obsessed with desire to engage in loving pastimes and They forget all else except meeting together. In essence, at that time, Śrī Kṛṣṇa forgets that He is a hero, or lover, and Śrī Rādhā also loses the feeling that She is a heroine, or beloved. "*Se-saba prema-kāhinī* – these are all topics of *prema*."

"O *sakhī*! If you think that, due to Our separation from each other, Śrī Kṛṣṇa has forgotten all of Our previous loving affairs, please tell Him that the influence of Mathurā is such that it causes everyone who goes there to forget their previous existence. If you go, then kindly remind Him that at the time of Our first meeting there was no messenger between Us, nor did I request anyone to arrange Our meeting. Indeed, only Our great mutual eagerness to meet one another, or Cupid's five arrows, were Our via media and the one and only cause."

This demonstrates Śrī Rādhā's feminine virtue of dedication (*lalanā-niṣṭha*)[16] to meet Śrī Kṛṣṇa, known as *mañjiṣṭhā*[17]*-rāga*[18].

Furthermore, one can see that this special attraction (*rāga*) in Her heart is completely pure, free from material designations and independent of everything else. No helper, messenger, or other intermediary was required to facilitate Śrī Rādhā-Kṛṣṇa's meeting.

Sohi. "O *sakhī*, now Kṛṣṇa has lost His intense attraction for Me. Due to the powerful influence of this *anurāga*, He came to Me on His own, without the intervention of anyone else, but now He has forgotten all this." At this time of separation, the attachment (*rāga*) of meeting has transformed into an exceptional attachment (*vi-rāga* or *viccheda-gata-rāga*, a very special, unbroken and unlimited attraction

16 *Lalanā-niṣṭha-svarūpa* is a self-manifest *rati* that is expressed as an involuntary impulse towards Śrī Kṛṣṇa, even when one has not seen Him or heard about His beauty and qualities.

17 *Mañjiṣṭhā* is a plant, Indian madder, which produces a very bright and long-lasting red dye.

18 *Mañjiṣṭhā-rāga* is the *rāga* that is self-manifest; that is, it is not dependent on others; it is never destroyed; it is always steadfast; and it is never dulled. Such *rāga* is found in Śrīmatī Rādhikā and Śrī Kṛṣṇa.

felt in separation), otherwise named *adhirūḍha-bhāva* – highly elevated ecstatic love. Here, this *virāga*, or *adhirūḍha-bhāva*, is addressed as a female friend (*sakhī*) and asked to become a messenger to Kṛṣṇa: "*Tuṅhu bheli dūtī.* O *sakhī*! You should act as My envoy. I am sending you to Him with a message. *Su-purukha-premaki aichana rīti* – you should go and ask Him, 'Is it the conduct of an expert lover, a cultured gentleman, to first establish *prema* and then sometime later forget it?'" Here Śrī Rādhā is speaking in jest. The purport is, "It is completely improper for a skilled suitor like You to display such a profusion of intense love and later on, just drop it."

All of this essentially means that at the time of meeting, *rāga*, or attraction, remains as an emissary in the form of Cupid. Then, during separation, that *rāga* awakens up to the stage of *adhirūḍha-bhāva* and ultimately becomes *prema-vilāsa-vivarta*. Moreover, while experiencing feelings of separation, if one has a vision within the heart (*sphūrti*) of meeting, then that vision takes the form of a female messenger. Śrī Rādhā addresses this messenger as *sakhī* (dear friend), and then speaks with her. The happiness that one experiences in this state of meeting in *prema-vilāsa*, is, in truth, also experienced in separation. Similarly, because one becomes so absorbed in Śrī Kṛṣṇa when parted from Him, the mood of service reaches to the topmost peak. This variety of *vivarta* gives rise to *adhirūḍha-mahābhāva*. This is a type of meeting in which, for example, Śrī Rādhā, mistakes a blackish *tamāla* tree for Śrī Kṛṣṇa, and runs to embrace it.

Upon hearing a portion of Śrī Rāmānanda Rāya's song, Śrīman Mahāprabhu became maddened in *prema*. Arising, Mahāprabhu covered Śrī Rāmānanda's mouth with His own hand. In this song, Śrī Rāmānanda Rāya reveals Śrī Rādhā's visions in Her states of separation. The *rāga* described is the embodiment of Śrī Rādhā-Kṛṣṇa's very nature. Neither Śrī Kṛṣṇa, the lover par excellence, nor Śrī Rādhā, the pre-eminent beloved, is the cause of this *rāga*; rather, this *rāga* is self-propelling, and ascends to the stage of *mādanākhya-mahābhāva*. In this stage, all the *bhāvas* manifest in a fully jubilant state. This condition is unprecedented and indescribable because within it one directly and simultaneously experiences all of the countless types of happiness and distress that are experienced both in meeting and in separation respectively. The words *nā so ramaṇa, nā hāma ramaṇī* indicate all the *bhāvas* experienced in the fully ripened stage of meeting in *prema-vilāsa*, while the words *ab sohi virāga* indicate mutual feelings of separation.

In the commentary on such verses as "*vakāre sumukhi nava-vivartaḥ* – O enemy of Bakāsura, this beautiful faced maiden is manifesting a new type of transformation of love towards You," (*Ujjvala-nīlamaṇi*). Śrīla Jīva Gosvāmī writes *vivartaḥ paripākaḥ*. He defines the word *vivarta* as *paripāka*, or completely matured, meaning that the state of *vivarta* is a manifestation of fully matured passion. In the first act of the drama *Śrī Lalita-mādhava*, in the commentary on the line *paurṇa putri māyāvivattau 'yaṁ*, there is a discussion about *prema-vilāsa-vivarta. Anya dharma tyāyatrāropo vivarttaḥ.* When a foreign quality is superimposed upon something, it is called *vivarta*. The meaning of *prema* is "desire," the meaning of *vilāsa* is "pastimes," and the meaning of *vivarta* is "a reversal." Thus, *prema-vivarta* means "the culmination of loving pastimes in which the hero and heroine exchange roles, or *viparīta-kāma-krīḍā*." Instead of Śrī Kṛṣṇa leading the amorous sports, Śrī Rādhikā assumes the dominant role in Their love-play. This pastime of enacting opposite roles (*viparīta-vilāsa*) is exceedingly high-class and pure, and no other enjoyment is more exalted. It is in this fully matured condition of loving pastimes that Śrī Rādhā said, "*Nā so ramaṇa, nā hāma ramaṇī*." After that the intolerable state of separation described by the words *ab sohi virāga* appeared in Her life. Therefore, to prevent this being spoken out loud, Śrīman Mahāprabhu covered Śrī Rāmānanda Rāya's mouth.

Śacīnandana Śrī Gaurasundara is the combined form of *rasa-rāja* Śrī Kṛṣṇa and *mahābhāva-svarūpiṇī* Śrī Rādhā. "*Rādhā-bhāva-dyuti-suvalitaṁ naumi kṛṣṇa-svarūpam* – I bow down to that Śrī Gaurasundara who has manifested Himself with the moods and luster of Śrī Rādhā although He is Śrī Kṛṣṇa Himself" (*Śrī Caitanya-caritāmṛta, Ādi-līlā* 4.55). However, Śrī Gaurahari wished to conceal His nature as being Śrī Kṛṣṇa internally, covered by a golden complexion. He did not want Śrī Rāmānanda Rāya to reveal His identity, so He covered Rāmānanda's mouth before he could utter this fact.

Jagad-guru Śrīla Bhaktisiddhānta Sarasvatī Ṭhākura Prabhupāda says that there is also another reason why Śrīman Mahāprabhu covered Śrī Rāmānanda Rāya's mouth: it remains completely impossible for members of the *sampradāya* of the mundane *prākṛta-sahajiyās* to follow the conception of *vilāsa-vivarta* (reversal of roles during the pastimes) and *vilāsa-vaicitrya* (variegatedness within the pastimes) of the different types of *adhirūḍha-mahābhāva* such as *mādana* (meeting) and *mohana* (separation), which Śrī Rāmānanda Rāya had explained. To reveal such highly and extraordinarily confidential, indescribable, and unprecedented subject matter about the path of devotional service to dull-headed philosophical speculators is always improper. For this very reason, Śrīman Mahāprabhu covered Śrī Rāmānanda Rāya's mouth to prevent him from speaking further.

Śrī Kavi Karṇapūra elaborates on this in his drama *Śrī Caitanya-candrodaya-nāṭaka* (7.87): "*nirupādhi hi prema kathañcid apy upādhiṁ na sahate iti pūrvārdha bhagavatoḥ rādhā-kṛṣṇayor anupādhi prema śrutvā tad eva puruṣārthī-kṛtaṁ, bhagavatā mukha-pidhānañcāsya tad-rahasyatva-prakāśakam* – The absolute love that Śrī Rādhā-Kṛṣṇa bear for one another is completely pure and free from any imperfection. Just by hearing about it, Śrī Caitanya-deva could understand that this prema was the ultimate spiritual attainment. After hearing the most confidential subject matter of *prema* as issued from the mouth of Śrī Rāmānanda Rāya, Śrīman Mahāprabhu immediately covered the speaker's mouth. The Lord did not want that the supremely confidential topics of Śrī Rādhā's extraordinary *prema-vilāsa* be broadcasted everywhere." In verse 83 of this same drama it states:

sakhi na sa ramaṇo nāṭaṁ
ramaṇīti bhidāvarovāste
prema-rasenobhaya ina
madano nidi peṣa balāt

and,

ahaṁ kāntā kāntas tvam iti na tadānīṁ matir abhūn
mano-vṛttir luptā tvam aham iti nau dhīr api hatā
bhavān bhartā bhāryāham iti yad idānīṁ vyavasitas
tathāpi prāṇānāṁ sthitir iti vicitraṁ kim aparam

Śrī Rādhā says, "I no longer think, 'I am Your beloved and You are My beloved.' For Us the conception of 'I' and 'You' is now destroyed. There is no longer any distinction between Us. It seems like Cupid has ground Our hearts together with great vigor, while sprinkling them with the ambrosia of perfect love.

"O friend, the feeling that He is My lover and I am His beloved has not come to My mind. My mind and intelligence have ceased to function. Now I am thinking He is My beloved, and I am His beloved, but when *prema* strongly manifests then Our beings melt together. When We are apart We think We are two, but when meeting We become one. How astonishing this is!"

The intent behind Śrī Rādhā's words is that right from childhood there was some *kāma*, or amorous desire, present in Her heart. The very first time Rādhā and Kṛṣṇa saw each other, lust sprouted; *rāga* awoke with Their first exchange of glances. They had not actually met yet. Śrīla Rūpa Gosvāmī calls this state *pūrva-rāga*. This *rāga* grew with each day until it became full-blown, bringing Śrī Rādhā to say: "*nā so ramaṇa, nā hāma ramaṇī* – Śrī Kṛṣṇa is not My lover, and I am not His mistress. Kandarpa (the transcendental Cupid) has melted both of Our hearts and made them one. The feeling no longer remains that Śrī Kṛṣṇa is the *ramaṇa*, the hero who initiates amorous attraction (*rati*), and I (Rādhā) am the *ramaṇī* or the heroine, the bestower of *rati*, or intimate enjoyment. In the absence of such feelings, Cupid has ground Our hearts together and made them one, and in the ensuing powder, the enjoyer (*ramaṇa*) or the enjoyed (*ramaṇī*) are not separate. Now, abandoned by Śrī Kṛṣṇa, this separation has herself become the female messenger. Respectable persons' dealings in love are not like this."

8.194

rādhāyā bhavataś ca citta-jatunī svedair vilāpya kramād
yuñjann adri-nikuñja-kuñjara-pate nirdhūta-bheda-bhramam
citrāya svayamambaraṁ jayad iha brahmāṇḍa-harmyodare
bhūyobhir nava-rāga-hiṅgula-bharaiḥ śṛṅgāra-kāruḥ kṛtī

Ujjvala-nīlamaṇi (14.155)

"'O King of mad elephants (Śrī Kṛṣṇa), who dallies in Govardhana's love bowers, there is an accomplished artist of the name *śṛṅgāra-rasa* (Kāmadeva) and upon the fire generated from the heat of the emotions coming from both You and Śrī Rādhā, he has slowly melted the shellac-like hearts of You both and made them one. Then mixing that with profuse quantities of the *kuṅkuma* of Your ever-fresh driving love, he is painting an astonishing picture upon the inner walls of the grand temple of the universe.'"

The topmost special manifestation of *mahābhāva* is called *mādanākhya*. When Śrīman Mahāprabhu asked the final question about *prema*, He covered Śrī Rāmānanda Rāya's mouth just when He received that most complete answer.

In the verse at hand, Śrī Vṛndā-devī describes the joyful sweetness of *mahābhāva*. Once, when Rādhā and Kṛṣṇa were tasting Their mutual sweetness, Their bodies became beautifully decorated with the fully blazing symptoms of rapture, or *uddīpta-sāttvika-bhāvas*. To paint a palace red, and wishing to delight everyone, an artist places shellac in a fire, and prepares an extraordinarily shining mixture by completely blending the melted shellac with a red dye. In just the same way, the artist of the personified amorous mellow places the shellac of Śrī Rādhā's and Śrī Kṛṣṇa's hearts, which are completely full of *mahābhāva*, into the fire of *prema* and slowly melts them into one. He then mixes this with the color of Their eternally ever-fresh *rāga*, or Their compelling attraction for each other, and by so doing, he creates an astonishingly wonderful mixture.

Adri-nikuñja-kuñjara-pate. Śrī Vṛndā-devī has addressed Śrī Kṛṣṇa as the master of the forest bowers at Govardhana. Just as an intoxicated king of elephants independently sports with many she-elephants, similarly Śrī Kṛṣṇa, intoxicated with *prema*, sports with Śrī Rādhā in Giri-Govardhana's secluded caves and bowers. By the heat of the fire of Their emotions – perspiration coming as a *sāttvika-bhāva* (ecstatic transformation) – Śrī Rādhā-Kṛṣṇa's shellac-like hearts have been melted.

Hiṅgula – fresh *rāga*, or attraction, with which the interior and exterior of Their hearts have been even more excessively colored. Just as shellac is red through and through, similarly *mañjiṣṭhā-rāga* thoroughly colors both of Their hearts. This indeed is the intrinsic nature of *mādanākhya-mahābhāva*.

Kṛtī. Here it means "expert in his activities." Being most adept, the artist of the personified amorous mellow has melted the shellac of Śrī Rādhā-Kṛṣṇa's hearts and, completely mixing them together, has added the color of Their ever-fresh, compelling mutual attraction (*rāga*). A skilled artist will paint the interior of a royal palace with wonderfully beautiful and variegated illustrations, which completely astonish the materialists. In the same way, the artist of the personified amorous mellow has painted a picture using Śrī Rādhā-Kṛṣṇa's hearts, which, by the influence of Their *prema*, have attained *mahābhāva*. Their hearts have become so completely amalgamated that one can no longer distinguish between them. The artist of the personified amorous mellow did so with a particular intention: all devotees throughout the world should be amazed upon realizing that, due to the agitation caused by *mahābhāva's* activities, Their hearts have been decorated and melted together.

Under the Guidance of the Sakhīs

8.195–204

prabhu kahe,—"sādhya-vastura avadhi' ei haya
tomāra prasāde ihā jāniluṅ niścaya

'sādhya-vastu' 'sādhana'-vinā keha nāhi pāya
kṛpā kari' kaha, rāya, pābāra upāya"

rāya kahe,—"yei kahāo, sei kahi vāṇī
ki kahiye bhāla-manda, kichui nā jāni

tribhuvana-madhye aiche haya kon dhīra
ye tomāra māyā-nāṭe ha-ibeka sthira

mora mukhe vaktā tumi, tumi hao śrotā
atyanta rahasya, śuna, sādhanera kathā

rādhā-kṛṣṇera līlā ei ati gūḍhatara
dāsya-vātsalyādi-bhāve nā haya gocara

sabe eka sakhī-gaṇera ihāṅ adhikāra
sakhī haite haya ei līlāra vistāra

sakhī binā ei līlā puṣṭa nāhi haya
sakhī līlā vistāriyā, sakhī āsvādaya

sakhī binā ei līlāya anyera nāhi gati
sakhī-bhāve ye tāṅre kare anugati

rādhā-kṛṣṇa-kuñjasevā sādhya sei pāya
sei sādhya pāite āra nāhika upāya

Having heard Śrī Rāmānanda Rāya singing his own composition, Śrīman Mahāprabhu said, "O Rāya, that is sufficient. You have described the topmost limit of *sādhya-vastu*, or the ultimate object of attainment. By your mercy (here Mahāprabhu reveals His humility), I have understood the different gradations of this subject matter. However without the appropriate *sādhana*, one cannot attain this rare *sādhya*. Therefore, please be kind enough to describe the method to achieve this goal."

Hearing this, Rāmānanda Rāya said in great meekness, "I am only speaking those instructions which You desire me to speak. Among my statements I cannot discern what is good or bad. Who within these three worlds is so forbearing that he is not shaken upon seeing the drama enacted by Your illusory potency? You are the one who speaks from within my mouth, and You have also become the audience. Please now hear the discussion of this most confidential *sādhana*. These pastimes of Śrī Rādhā-Kṛṣṇa are extremely private. They are beyond the understanding of those associates of the Lord who have taken shelter of *dāsya*, *sakhya*, and *vātsalya rasa*. Being inaccessible, they are extremely rare.

"These *līlās* come only within the jurisdiction of Śrīmatī Rādhikā's *sakhīs*, because *mahābhāva* is found exclusively within them. These pastimes develop only due to the *sakhīs*' participation; the *sakhīs* alone have the right to taste them. Apart from those situated in this *sakhī-bhāva*, no other associates may enter into these *līlās*. Only the *sādhakas* who remain under the guidance of those with this *sakhī-bhāva* may enter the domain of ultimate attainment – rendering service to Śrī Rādhā-Kṛṣṇa within the groves of Vṛndāvana. Apart from this method, there is no other means to achieve this goal.

Śrīla Bhaktivinoda Ṭhākura says that only when Mahāprabhu had heard everything in full, does He affirm that the topic of *sādhya* has been discussed comprehensively. Now Mahāprabhu inquires, "What is the *sādhana* of achieving this ultimate goal? Please speak about that." Śrī

Rāmānanda reviewed the premise that those *sādhakas* who worship in the moods of *dāsya*, *sakhya*, and *vātsalya* are unable to attain entrance into this most confidential subject matter. Only the *sakhīs* of Vraja are situated in *mahābhāva*; they alone have accepted this mood, and solely by the performance of *sādhana* under their guidance is it possible to attain the most brilliant, most confidential, most mysterious, and most intensely sweet goal – the *kuñja-sevā* of Śrī Rādhā-Kṛṣṇa. There is no other process to attain this goal.

No one except the *sakhīs* can enter this *līlā*. This infers that Lalitā, Viśākhā, and other *sakhīs* such as Śrī Rūpa Mañjarī are eternal associates of Śrī Rādhā-Kṛṣṇa's *kuñja-sevā*. It is thus essential to perform *sādhana* under their guidance (*ānugatya*).

Owing to a lack of association with pure saintly devotees, there remains present within the *jīvas* a wide variety of material desires such as a yearning for residence in the heavenly planets, the longing for liberation, and desires to attain the abodes of the other incarnations of Bhagavān. Śrī Bhagavān fulfills all of these desires, also. Śrī Kṛṣṇa Caitanya Mahāprabhu is the incarnation of *prema* (*premāvatārī*) and the combined form of *rasa-rāja* Śrī Kṛṣṇa and *mahābhāva-mayī* Śrī Rādhikā. It is He who distributed the glories of the pure *prema* of Vraja, and who tasted *unnata-ujjvala-prema*, especially the *mādanākhya-bhāva* of Śrī Rādhā. And it was He who, in order to bestow mercy upon the pure *sādhakas*, asked this topmost question, and also spoke these confidential and secretive truths from the mouth of Śrī Rāmānanda Rāya. Only by the mercy of Śrīman Mahāprabhu, and only by staying under the guidance of His devotees, can one understand the difference between loving sentiments for the Lord in awe and reverence (*aiśvarya-prema*) and sentiments for Śrī Kṛṣṇa predominated by feelings of sweetness and intimacy (*mādhurya-prema*).

This *mahābhāva* is not found within the sentiments of *dāsya*, *sakhya*, and *vātsalya*. And actually, the *mādhurya-rasa* or *śṛṅgāra-rasa* present in Vaikuṇṭha, Ayodhyā, Dvārakā, and Mathurā is called *svakīya* (when the hero and heroine are married), and is mixed with sentiments of awe and reverence (*aiśvarya*). Śrī Kṛṣṇa cannot be controlled completely by those moods. The fact that Śrī Lakṣmī-devī herself is performing austerities in Belvana (a forest within Vraja-maṇḍala) in order to achieve the transcendental amorous love of the *gopīs*, proves this. The *sakhīs* of Śrī Rādhā are the exclusive proprietors and presiding goddesses of this highest aspect of *bhāva* found in the *nikuñja-sevā*. Therefore, remaining under their guidance is the topmost *sādhana* for achieving service to Śrī Rādhā-Kṛṣṇa.

8.205

vibhur api sukha-rūpaḥ sva-prakāśo 'pi bhāvaḥ
kṣaṇam api na hi rādhā-kṛṣṇayor yā ṛte svāḥ
pravahati rasa-puṣṭiṁ cid-vibhūtīr iveśaḥ
śrayati na padam āsāṁ kaḥ sakhīnāṁ rasa-jñaḥ

Govinda-līlāmṛta (10.17)

"'Śrī Rādhā-Kṛṣṇa's *bhāvas* are self-manifest, unlimited, and composed of complete ecstasy. Even so, not even one iota of *rasa* can be experienced without the *sakhīs*, just as Iśvara, the Supreme Controller, is never manifested without His spiritual potencies or opulences. Therefore, what knower of *rasa* will try to enter these pastimes without taking the shelter and guidance of the lotus feet of the *sakhīs*?'

The *bhāvas* of Śrī Rādhā-Kṛṣṇa are exceedingly full of happiness; indeed, they are the very embodiment of the highest form of joy. A *sādhaka* of transcendental amorous love who is filled with this *prema* can automatically savor the sweetness of this *rasa*. By this sweetness he, also, is able to experience great happiness, just as a person automatically tastes the sweetness of sugar candy by keeping it within his mouth. However, without the grace of the *sakhīs*, the *prema* of Śrī Rādhā-Kṛṣṇa cannot reach its fullest state of blissful completeness.

The question may arise: if this is so, then what is the necessity of mentioning the self-manifesting and unlimited nature of the love of Śrī Rādhā-Kṛṣṇa? *Svarūpa-śakti* is unlimited, she is also completely spiritual (*brahma-vastu*), and her special play is *prema*, or *bhakti*. If *prema*, or *bhakti*, were not in fact unlimited, then how could she have brought the complete spiritual entity Bhagavān under her control? The Śrutis say, "*bhaktir eva garīyasī* – *bhakti* is indeed glorious" and "*bhakti-vaśaḥ puruṣaḥ* – the Supreme is controlled by *bhakti*."

The ocean is an immeasurable body of water, and by the force of the wind, waves rise up, making it appear as if the ocean is leaping. Similarly, even though the oceanic *prema* of Śrī Rādhā-Kṛṣṇa is self-manifesting, still it is supported and nourished by the assistance of the wave-like *sakhīs*. In the axiom about the love of Śrī Rādhā-Kṛṣṇa, the *sakhīs'* glories are extraordinary. Despite Himself being the unlimited, omnipresent, and self-manifesting Supreme Controller, His quality of being the controller is even further enhanced by the assistance of *cit-śakti*. Similarly, *śṛṅgāra-rasa* is even more deeply nurtured by the ministration of the *sakhīs*. *Prema* and the *sakhīs* are not separate entities; indeed, the development of *prema* hinges on their participation. The *sakhīs* are *prema-svarūpiṇī*, meaning that they are composed of *prema* and they are also embodiments of *prema*, as well as expansions of the bliss potency (*hlādinī-śakti*).

8.206–209

sakhīra svabhāva eka akathya-kathana
kṛṣṇa-saha nija-līlāya nāhi sakhīra mana

kṛṣṇa saha rādhikāra līlā ye karāya
nija-sukha haite tāte koṭi sukha pāya

rādhāra svarūpa—kṛṣṇa-prema-kalpalatā
sakhī-gaṇa haya tāra pallava-puṣpa-pātā

kṛṣṇa-līlāmṛta yadi latāke siñcaya
nija-sukha haite pallavādyera koṭi-sukha haya

"The nature of the *sakhīs* is unparalleled and indescribable. Never does the thought of finding their own happiness in an intimate meeting with Śrī Kṛṣṇa even appear within their minds. The happiness they experience by arranging the solitary meeting of Śrī Rādhikā with Śrī Kṛṣṇa, they accept as being millions of times greater than what they would experience by being with Śrī Kṛṣṇa directly. Śrī Rādhā is likened to the truly personified form of the wish-fulfilling vine of *prema* for Śrī Kṛṣṇa; and the various *sakhīs* are the leaves, twigs, and flowers that take shelter of this desire-fulfilling creeper. By sprinkling the creeper with the nectar of Śrī Kṛṣṇa's pastimes, the sprouts, flowers, and leaves become happier than if someone sprinkles them directly.

Śrīla Bhaktivinoda Ṭhākura confirms that Śrī Rādhā is the transcendental wish-fulfilling vine of *kṛṣṇa-prema*, and all the various *sakhīs* are its leaves, buds, and flowers. When this vine in the form of Śrī Rādhā is watered, then the flowers and buds, who have taken shelter of the vine, are automatically nurtured. In the same way, the *gopīs* do not directly enjoy the happiness of meeting with Śrī Kṛṣṇa; rather by arranging Śrī Rādhā's meeting with Śrī Kṛṣṇa they become joyful.

8.210

sakhyaḥ śrī-rādhikāyā vraja-kumuda-vidhor hlādinī-nāma-śakteḥ
sārāṁśa-prema-vallyāḥ kiśalaya-dala-puṣpādi-tulyāḥ sva-tulyāḥ
siktāyāḥ kṛṣṇa-līlāmṛta-rasa-nicayair ullasantyām amuṣyāṁ
jātollāsāṁ sva-sekāc chata-guṇam adhikaṁ santi yat tan na citram

Govinda-līlāmṛta (10.16)

"'The *sakhīs* of Vraja are similar to Śrī Rādhā. They are the essential parts of Vraja-kumuda-candra's[19] *hlādinī*, or pleasure potency, known as Śrī Rādhikā, who is the personification of His internal energy. She is the wish-fulfilling creeper of *prema* and the other *gopīs* are that vine's buds, leaves, and flowers. When the nectar of Kṛṣṇa's pastimes is showered on the supremely blissful Śrī Rādhikā, all the *gopīs* experience the pleasure a hundred times more than if they were showered themselves. This is not at all surprising.'

19 Śrī Kṛṣṇa, who is the moon that gives pleasures to the lotus-like inhabitants of Vrajabhūmi.

Vraja-kumuda-vidhoḥ. Here it refers to none other than Śrī Kṛṣṇa, who is just like the moon for the lotus-like *gopīs* of Vraja. The word *vidhoḥ* is given in the possessive case (*ṣaṣṭhī*, sixth conjunction indicating a relationship). Here *vidhoḥ* indicates Śrī Kṛṣṇa's energy known as *hlādinī*. This is confirmed by use of the words *prema-vallarī* (creeper of love), which signify the essential principle of this *hlādinī-śakti*. The *ṣaṣṭhī* is again used for the noun *sakhyaḥ-śrī-rādhikāyāḥ*, with reference to the *sakhīs* of Śrīmatī Rādhikā. The phrase *kisalaya-dala-puṣpādi-tulyāḥ* describes the *gopīs*, who are likened to new leaves, sprouts, and flowers. Here *sva-tulyāḥ* refers to those *gopīs* who look like Śrīmatī Rādhikā and who are Her non-different expansions (*kāya-vyūha-svarūpā*).

Just as the night lotus blossoms naturally upon the rising of the moon, similarly the residents of Vraja, who are like night lotuses, naturally blossom once they obtain *darśana* of the moon of Vraja, Śrī Kṛṣṇa. Of all the Vrajavāsīs, the *gopīs* especially become pleased. Thus Śrī Kṛṣṇa has been called *vraja-kumuda-vidhu*, or the moon for the lotuses of Vraja. The essence of Śrī Kṛṣṇa's internal potency, or pleasure potency, is *prema*, and the vine of this *prema* is Śrī Vṛṣabhānu-nandinī Herself, Śrī Rādhā. The various *gopīs* are the newly blossomed sprouts, flowers, and leaves of this vine. These *sakhīs* are the beauty of this wish-fulfilling vine of *prema*, Śrī Rādhā. Her happiness, indeed, constitutes the happiness of these *gopīs*. If water is supplied to the actual root of the vine then all of the flowers, leaves, and twigs are also nourished; there is no need to water each part separately. In a similar manner, all of the other *gopīs*, who are compared to the leaves, sprouts, and flowers, automatically reap supreme satisfaction from Śrī Rādhā's happiness.

8.211–214

yadyapi sakhīra kṛṣṇa-saṅgame nāhi mana
tathāpi rādhikā yatne karāna saṅgama

nānā-cchale kṛṣṇe preri' saṅgama karāya
ātma-sukha-saṅga haite koṭi-sukha pāya

anyonya viśuddha preme kare rasa puṣṭa
tāṅ-sabāra prema dekhi' kṛṣṇa haya tuṣṭa

sahaja gopīra prema,—nahe prākṛta kāma
kāma-krīḍā-sāmye tāra kahi 'kāma'-nāma

"Although the *sakhīs* do not possess even the slightest desire to enjoy themselves with Śrī Kṛṣṇa directly, still Rādhikā makes an active effort that enables them to meet with Him. She sends the *gopīs* to Kṛṣṇa, employing a great variety of clever ruses, as well as inspiring His heart with a desire to meet them. At such times, She enjoys a happiness ten million times greater than the happiness She experiences when directly meeting with Him. Since the internal consciousness of Śrī Rādhikā and the *gopīs* is pervaded by *viśuddha-sattva*, or pure spiritual existence, Śrīmati Rādhikā always remains engaged in continuously bestowing happiness upon the *gopīs*, and vice versa. They are ever absorbed in nourishing, or expanding, sentiments of *rasa*. Upon seeing their mutual exchanges, Śrī Kṛṣṇa becomes most satisfied. The *prema* of the *gopīs* is completely natural. There is not even the slightest scent of profane lust within them. Due to its resembling mundane lusty affairs, this *prema* is often called *kāma*, or lust.

Even though the *kāma* of the *gopīs* and the *kāma* of this material world bear a resemblance to each other, factually the difference between them is like that of heaven and hell. In this *aprākṛta-kāma*, or transcendental (non-material) lust, there is not even a trace of desire for one's own happiness; rather, the sole desire is an abiding, continuous thirst to bestow happiness upon one's beloved. Thus this *kāma* is *viśuddha* (transcendentally pure) *prema*. The *kāma* of the material world is self-centered, performed for one's own enjoyment, insignificant, detestable, and the path to hell.

Śrīla Bhaktivinoda Ṭhākura says that Śrī Rādhikā engages the *sakhīs* in the service of Śrī Kṛṣṇa, and the *sakhīs* find happiness in arranging for Her to meet with Him. People devoid of *rasa* and intelligence say that Śrī Rādhā and the *gopīs* desire to meet with Śrī Kṛṣṇa. Is this a form of material lust, in which they are seeking their own enjoyment, or not? Śrīla Bhaktivinoda Ṭhākura says, "No, no, it is not. Factually, intimately meeting with Śrī Kṛṣṇa or arranging for Śrī Kṛṣṇa to meet with others is performed only out of love for Him. Seeing Śrī Kṛṣṇa's pleasure, the *gopīs* also feel happiness, and they think that their lives have become successful, being engaged in His service. The people of this material world cannot conceive of even a shadow of this *prema*, what to speak of approach it. Thus, due to their polluted tendencies, people see this completely pure and sacred *prema* to be the same as insignificant, profane lust."

8.215

premaiva gopa-rāmāṇāṁ
kāma ity agamat prathām
ity uddhavādayo 'py etaṁ
vāñchanti bhāgavat-priyāḥ

Bhakti-rasāmṛta-sindhu (1.2.285–286)

"'The *prema* of the beautiful maidens of Vraja is known as *kāma*, or lust. However, by constitution that *prema* has no mundane lust in its makeup. It is for this reason that Uddhava and other devotees of the Lord also desire this *prema*.'

Although both iron and gold are categorized as metals, there is an enormous difference between them. Likewise, both material lust (*kāma*) and pure love (*prema*) appear somewhat similar, but they are in fact totally distinct. Lust is a function of the illusory potency known as *māyā*, while *prema* is a function of the all-spiritual *svarūpa-śakti*. Śrīla Bhaktivinoda Ṭhākura further says that there are various alluring desires presented in the Vedic scriptures such as the desire for elevation to higher worlds, the desire for progeny, especially sons, and the desire for material wealth and opulence.

These material desires give rise to worldly religiosity; the religious principles enunciated in the Vedas; the pursuance of religious principles according to one's birth and body; desires for self-happiness in the form of *mukti*, or liberation; adherence to the path of elevated society; the maintenance of affection for one's family members; performance of fruitive actions (*karma*); womanly shyness; patience; chastisement from family members and friends; and fear. All of these are self-seeking behaviors and forms of self-indulgence, performed for one's own sense enjoyment and to fulfill one's own desires. They are all material, and performed for one's personal pleasure and success.[20] There is a difference of heaven and hell between *prema* (love) and *kāma* (sacrilegious lust); the *kāma* of the *gopīs* is beyond material intelligence.

8.216–217

nijendriya-sukha-hetu kāmera tātparya
kṛṣṇa-sukha-tātparya gopī-bhāva-varya

nijendriya-sukha-vāñchā nāhi gopikāra
kṛṣṇe sukha dite kare saṅgama-vihāra

"*Kāma* is the desire to give pleasure to one's own senses. The topmost sentiment of the *gopīs* is called *prema*, and its only intention is to give pleasure to Śrī Kṛṣṇa. These *gopīs* never have any desire for their own enjoyment; all of their intimate meetings with Śrī Kṛṣṇa are only for the purpose of giving Him pleasure.

[20] *Śrī Caitanya-caritāmṛta, Ādi-līlā* (4.167–169) gives the evidence:

loka-dharma, veda-dharma, deha-dharma, karma
lajjā, dhairya, deha-sukha, ātma-sukha-marma

dustyaja ārya-patha, nija parijana
sva-jane karaye yata tāḍana-bhartsana

sarva-tyāga kari' kare kṛṣṇera bhajana
kṛṣṇa-sukha-hetu kare prema-sevana

"The *gopīs* have completley abandoned worldly social conventions, the injunctions of the Vedas, the demands of the body, the performance of work with a desire for the fruits, shyness, forbearance, bodily pleasures, personal satisfaction, and the path of *varṇāśrama-dharma*, all of which are difficult to give up. They have forsaken their families, and suffered punishment and admonishment from their relatives, all so that they can serve Śrī Kṛṣṇa. Indeed, only for His happiness do they serve Him with great love."

Śrīla Bhaktivinoda Ṭhākura explains that the tendency to perform the topmost service to Śrī Kṛṣṇa, who is Himself the very embodiment of pure and complete spiritual knowledge (*saṁvit-vigraha*), can never be said to be *kāma*, or mundane lust. Rather, abandoning Śrī Kṛṣṇa's happiness, to pursue other forms of enjoyment is called *kāma*. May one's life be dedicated to Śrī Kṛṣṇa, and may the service performed to Him be *prema-mayī*, or loving service, then Śrī Kṛṣṇa may be pleased. The *sakhīs* are entirely composed of these selfless desires, which are present within them to an unrestricted extent, and these *gopīs*, who are the embodiment of *prema*, remain committed to eagerly serve in this manner.

8.218

yat te sujāta-caraṇāmburuhaṁ staneṣu
bhītāḥ śanaiḥ priya dadhīmahi karkaśeṣu
tenāṭavīm aṭasi tad vyathate na kiṁ svit
kūrpādibhir bhramati dhīr bhāvad-āyuṣāṁ naḥ

Śrīmad-Bhāgavatam (10.31.19)

"The *gopīs*, afflicted by feelings of separation from Śrī Kṛṣṇa, lament, 'Your divine feet, even softer than a lotus, we place upon our hard breasts – very timidly and very carefully, lest we hurt them. Those same soft lotus feet carry You through the dark forest. Are they feeling any pain, being wounded by pebbles and stones? Simply the thought of this sets our heads spinning, causing us to fall in a swoon. O Śrī Kṛṣṇa! O Śyāmasundara! O Prāṇanātha, O possessor of our lives! We live only for Your sake; we are Yours, we are Yours.'

Śrīla Jīva Gosvāmīpāda explains that after this the *gopīs* began crying very loudly. They then became senseless and fell upon the ground. In this way, simply by the mere thought of the slightest pain to their beloved, the *gopīs* fell unconscious, whereupon Śrī Kṛṣṇa appeared amongst them. Thus seeing their *prāṇa-vallabha*, their dear-most beloved, Śrī Śyāmasundara, whose beauty defeats that of millions upon millions of Cupids, the Vraja *gopīs* again took possession of their life airs, which returned to their bodies. All together they stood up and with loving glances from their blossoming eyes they looked towards Him in a mood of great happiness.

8.219–222

sei gopi-bhāvāmṛte yāṅra lobha haya
veda-dharma-loka tyaji' se kṛṣṇke bhajaya

rāgānuga-mārge tāṅre bhaje yei jana
sei jana pāya vraje vrajendra-nandana

vraja-lokera kona bhāva lañā yei bhaje
bhāva-yogya deha pāñā kṛṣṇa pāya vraje

tāhāte dṛṣṭānta—upaniṣad śruti-gaṇa
rāga-mārge bhaji' pāila vrajendra-nandana

"One who has developed greed to attain the *gopīs'* nectarean *prema* completely abandons the regulative principles of Vedic life, such as the *varṇāśrama* system, as well as various materialistic goals such as attaining residence in the heavenly planets. Rather, the devotee completely surrenders unto Śrī Kṛṣṇa and performs exclusive *bhajana* to Him. Those devotees who are inclined towards the path of *rāgānuga-bhakti*, or spontaneous devotional service, adopt the sentiment of *ānugatya*, or remaining under guidance of superiors. They perform service to Śrī Kṛṣṇa, and in the holy abode of Śrī Vṛndāvana, they attain Śrī Vrajendra-nandana Śrī Kṛṣṇa. Whoever accepts one of the moods of the various eternal associates of Vraja-maṇḍala and performs *bhajana* following their moods of service to Śrī Kṛṣṇa, after receiving an appropriate spiritual body (*siddha-deha*), achieves the service of Śrī Kṛṣṇa in Vraja. The Upaniṣads and the Śrutis serve as testimony to those who achieved the service of Śrī Vrajendra-nandana by doing *bhajana* in the mood of *rāga-mārga*.

Śrīla Bhaktivinoda Ṭhākura says that the sixty-four limbs of *bhakti* are especially pertinent in *vaidhī-bhakti*. By performing these limbs of devotion with pure faith, or *śraddhā*, one receives the qualification to enter into *bhakti*. Sometimes, however, after appreciating the loving service combined with the natural *anurāga*, or deep attraction, that the residents of Vraja feel towards Śrī Kṛṣṇa, a greed may awaken in the hearts of some extremely fortunate persons to also achieve the same loving service towards Śrī Kṛṣṇa that the residents of Vraja have, and they will become fully dedicated to attaining that desire. This is the path of *rāgānuga-bhakti*. Greed to attain the nectarean moods of the *vraja-gopīs* bestows the qualification to enter the path of *rāgānuga-bhakti*. After entering the path of spontaneous devotion (*rāga-mārga*), and then performing this *bhajana*, attachment for the path of Vedic principles, such as the following of *varṇāśrama*, is automatically and easily dispelled.

Within the realm of Vraja are Śrī Kṛṣṇa's servants Raktaka and Patraka, His friends Śrīdāma and Subala, and His parents Nanda and Yaśodā. They naturally serve Him according to their particular moods. Although one may have great enthusiasm to perform this *vraja-rasa-bhajana* (devotional service in the mellow of Vraja), still one will have a special greed for a particular *rasa*. And it is in accordance with that particular greed that one will receive a completely spiritual body that is also compatible to one's mood. In this way, at the time of attaining perfection, one achieves Śrī Kṛṣṇa. The Upaniṣads and the Śrutis give evidence of this. The Śrutis have expounded that one cannot attain the qualification to perform *bhajana* of Vrajendra-nandana Śrī Kṛṣṇa in Vraja without being under the guidance of the *vraja-gopīs*. In this consideration, the Śrutis too accepted the supervision of the *vraja-gopīs*, and by following the path of *rāga-bhakti* in their spiritual forms as *gopīs*, the Śrutis served Vrajendra-nandana Śrī Kṛṣṇa.

Śrīla Bhaktivinoda Ṭhākura says that one should take shelter of the lotus feet of the *vraja-rasa-rasika* Vaiṣṇavas, who are expert in tasting the *rasa* of Vraja. Accepting both initiation (*dīkṣā*) and instructions (*śikṣā*) from such personalities, one should reside in Vṛndāvana under their guidance, and perform *bhajana* according to the principles of *rāgānuga-bhakti*. Additionally, in one's *bhajana* one should follow the guidance of a specific, eternally perfected associate of Śrī Kṛṣṇa. Thus, one should perform *mānasī-sevā* (service performed in the mind). More precisely, by serving internally with one's eternally perfect spiritual body (*siddha-deha*), one should thus follow the associates of Śrī Kṛṣṇa such as Śrī Rādhā, Lalitā, Viśākhā, and Śrī Rūpa Mañjarī. One should also serve as a *sādhaka* by one's physical body, following the example set by devotees such as Śrī Rūpa, Śrī Sanātana, and other residents of Vraja.

It is only in the Lord's absolutely perfected eternal associates (*nitya-siddha-parikaras*) that *rāgātmika-bhakti* is found. This pure devotion is always present within their hearts. Wholly perfect, absorption in one's desired object is called *rāga*. Those persons in whom this *rāga* naturally resides are called *rāgātmika* devotees. Śrī Rūpa Gosvāmī has explained all this:

iṣṭe svārasikī rāgaḥ
paramāviṣṭatā bhavet
tanmayī yā bhaved bhaktiḥ
sāt 'ra rāgātmikoditā

Bhakti-rasāmṛta-sindhu (1.2.272)

"*Rāga* is the unquenchable loving thirst for the object of one's affection, which gives rise to spontaneous and intense absorption in that object. *Rāgamayī-bhakti* is the performance of *sevā*, such as stringing garlands, with such intense *rāga*."

virājantīm abhivyaktāṁ
vraja-vāsi-janādiṣu
rāgātmikām anusṛtā
yā sā rāgānugocyate

Bhakti-rasāmṛta-sindhu (1.2.270)

"Devotional service imbued with spontaneous, profound love and attachment (*rāgātmika-bhakti*), is vividly expressed and manifested by the eternal residents of Vṛndāvana. Devotional service that follows their devotional mood is called *rāgānuga-bhakti*, or devotional service following in the wake of the *rāgātmika* associates of Śrī Rādhā-Kṛṣṇa in Vraja."

The following evidence shows that the personified Vedas performed *bhajana* in *rāga-mārga*:

8.223

nibhṛta-marun-mano 'kṣa-dṛḍha-yoga-yujo hṛdi yan
munaya upāsate tad arayo 'pi yayuḥ smaraṇāt
striya uragendra-bhoga-bhuja-daṇḍa-viṣakta-dhiyo
vayam api te samāḥ sama-dṛśo 'ṅghri-saroja-sudhāḥ

Śrīmad-Bhāgavatam (10.87.23)

"The personified Vedas are praying, 'O Lord! Greatly learned sages and *yogīs*, having conquered the life-airs, mind, and senses by strictly practicing the mystic *yoga* system and worshiping the impersonal Brahman effulgence, have ultimately achieved the position of *nirvāṇa*, or liberation. But even Your enemies have attained that position, simply by thinking of You in enmity and always desiring Your ruination.

'Śrī Rādhikā and Your other eternal beloveds place Your nectar-filled lotus feet on their firm breasts, being attracted and bound by the beauty of Your supremely soft, rounded, elongated, and nicely decorated arms, which are like the king of serpents. We have also tasted the nectar of Your lotus feet in exactly the same way as have Your eternal beloveds, the *gopīs*, by following in their footsteps.'

In this verse, the word *arayaḥ* indicates the enemies of Śrī Kṛṣṇa such as Kaṁsa, who always thought ill of Śrī Kṛṣṇa, or to be precise, who always thought of Him in fear. By remembering Him in this way, His enemies achieved liberation, or *brahma-sāyujya*, the very same destination achieved by *yogīs* and saints after millions of years of extremely difficult austerities. That is the first astonishing thing.

The second amazing point is that the same destination is achieved by both saintly personalities through their constant meditation upon Bhagavān and those demons who also think incessantly of Bhagavān.

Third, saintly persons who faithfully worship Bhagavān with full devotion and knowledge achieve the same destination as the enemies of the Lord who consider Him to be an ordinary human and even harbor feelings of hatred and violence towards Him. There is another utterly remarkable concept in the words "*uragendra-bhoga-bhuja-daṇḍa-viṣakta-dhiyaḥ* – the hearts of Śrī Kṛṣṇa's beloveds were attracted by His charming arms which, being soft, rounded, and elongated, resembled the body of the king of snakes." Those *gopīs* who were embraced by His arms, and who considered the all-pervading Śrī Kṛṣṇa to be limited, clasped His soft lotus feet to their breasts. Śrī Kṛṣṇa's heart, burning with the fire of lust, thus became supremely cool.

In this context *samā* refers to following the *gopīs*, and by so doing, the personified Vedas achieved the bodies of *gopīs*, and received the nectar of Śrī Kṛṣṇa's lotus feet. Here is one more point that merits deeper thought – the eternally perfected *gopīs* considered Śrī Kṛṣṇa as their *upapati*, or unwedded lover, and they also regarded His form to be localized, or limited. The Śrutis, however, considered Śrī Kṛṣṇa to be the Supreme Truth and therefore they accepted Śrī Kṛṣṇa as all-pervading and unlimited. Hence the Śrutis offered prayers and attained the bodies of *gopīs*, the accomplishment of which is extremely hard. Only by virtue of being under the guidance of the *gopīs* did it become possible.

It is also worth bearing in mind that the *gopīs* are Śrī Kṛṣṇa's eternal beloveds; therefore it is completely natural for them to hold His lotus feet to their breasts. The Śrutis, however, are not Śrī Rādhā's *kāyavyūha-rūpā* (bodily expansions) and not His eternal beloveds; still they, too, held Śrī Kṛṣṇa's lotus feet upon their breasts, which is very rarely attained. The *Bṛhad-Vāmana Purāṇa* testifies that the Śrutis had been praying unto Bhagavān for a long time. This pleased Bhagavān, and when He asked them to choose a benediction they replied, "We want to perform loving service to Śrī Kṛṣṇa as the *vraja-gopīs* do." Bhagavān said, "O goddesses, this desire of yours is very difficult to fulfill, however your desire shall certainly come to pass." At that very moment, by the mercy of Bhagavān, the Śrutis achieved birth as *gopīs* in Vraja, and attained the service of Śrī Kṛṣṇa in the mood of *aupapatya-bhāva*, or unwedded relationship.

8.224–225

'sama-dṛśaḥ'-śabde kahe 'sei bhāve anugati'
'samāḥ'-śabde kahe śrutira gopī-deha-prāpti

'aṅghri-padma-sudhā'ya kahe 'kṛṣṇa-saṅgānanda'
vidhi-mārge nā pāiye vraje kṛṣṇacandra

"The phrase *sama-dṛśaḥ* means to accept the *ānugatya* (guidance) of the *vraja-gopīs* and to perform *bhajana* following their moods. Thus these words signify the acceptance of *aupapatya-bhāva*, or the mood of the *gopīs* as being in an unwedded relationship with Śrī Kṛṣṇa. Use of the word *samāḥ* specifies that by *bhajana* the Śrutis attained beautiful bodies just like those of the *vraja-gopīs*, thus they are called *samāḥ*, which means 'the same,' or 'equal.' The words *aṅghri-padma-sudhā* mean 'the nectar emanating from the lotus feet of Śrī Kṛṣṇa' or 'the happiness generated by the service or the intimate association with Him.' The Śrutis accepted the guidance of the *vraja-gopīs*, and did *bhajana*, taking on the *gopīs' bhāva* towards Śrī Kṛṣṇa. They received accordingly the bodies of *gopīs* in Vraja and it was in these bodies that they obtained the intimate association of Śrī Kṛṣṇa and the ecstasy of His service. By contrast, one cannot attain Vrajendra-nandana Śrī Kṛṣṇa by practicing *vidhi-mārga*, the path of devotion according to regulative principles. Only those who practice *rāgānuga-bhakti*, or spontaneous devotional service, like the personified Vedas, can achieve that.

In support of this, the following verse is quoted:

8.226

nāyaṁ sukhāpo bhagavān dehināṁ gopikā-sutaḥ
jñānināṁ cātma-bhūtānāṁ yathā bhakti-matām iha

Śrīmad-Bhāgavatam (10.9.21)

"Śrī Śukadeva Gosvāmī is saying to Parīkṣit Mahārāja, 'Bhagavān Śrī Kṛṣṇa, the son of Mother Yaśodā, is easily attained by those devotees engaged in spontaneous loving service, but He is not as easily accessible to the performers of severe austerities who remain attached to the body, or to the mental speculators, the *jñānīs*, who are striving for self-realization, or to the seers of the self.'

Bhagavān Śrī Kṛṣṇa allowed Mother Yaśodā to experience indescribable joy in considering Him to be an ordinary child, as she witnessed His childish restlessness and bound Him with a rope. This joy is not possible for anyone other than those in Śrī Yaśodā's own group. Such inexplicable joy is unavailable to those who perform great austerities, all the while identifying with the body. The performer of austerities may receive some minute realization of Śrī Kṛṣṇa if any *mahā-bhāgavata* bestows mercy upon him and then offers those endeavors to Śrī Kṛṣṇa.

Again, by the mercy of association with devotees, both he who is *ātma-bhūta*, meaning "free from identifying the body as the self," and he who considers himself to be non-different from the Supreme, may also partially realize the *svarūpa* of Śrī Kṛṣṇa as the formless impersonal Brahman. The performers of austerities and the *jñānīs* never directly realize Śrī Kṛṣṇa's *saviśeṣa* feature, full of all transcendental attributes. Without following the *vraja-gopīs*, even Brahmā, Śiva, and Lakṣmī herself are unable to achieve the service of Śrī Kṛṣṇa, the son of the King of Vraja. In this way, Śrī Śukadeva Gosvāmī has glorified to Parīkṣit Mahārāja the transcendental, natural quality of the *rāgātmika-bhakti* of Mother Yaśodā and the other ladies of Vraja, with which they can easily bring Śrī Kṛṣṇa under their control.

8.227–230

ataeva gopī-bhāva kari' aṅgīkāra
rātri-dina cinte rādhā-kṛṣṇera vihāra

siddha-dehe cinti' kare tāṅhāñi sevana
sakhī-bhāve pāya rādhā-kṛṣṇera caraṇa

gopī-ānugatya vinā aiśvarya-jñāne
bhajileha nāhi pāya vrajendra-nandane

tāhāte dṛṣṭānta—lakṣmī karila bhajana
tathāpi nā pāila vraje vrajendra-nandana

"Only on the path of *rāgānuga-bhakti*, or spontaneous devotional service, does one achieve the service of Vrajendra-nandana Śrī Kṛṣṇa in Vraja. That same achievement is not possible on the path of *vaidhī-bhakti*, or regulative devotional service. Therefore the *sādhaka* should submit himself to the mood of the *gopīs*, and day and night always think of Śrī Rādhā-Kṛṣṇa's pastimes that occur at that time of the day. Holding in mind the spiritual body that one has received from the spiritual master, and being endowed with the moods of the *sakhīs*, one should perform service via the appropriate, internally conceived spiritual form (*mānasī-sevā*) to the feet of Śrī Rādhā-Kṛṣṇa, according to the appropriate place and time that their pastimes are being performed.

"One can only attain service to the Divine Couple's lotus feet by adopting the mood of the *sakhīs*. Without accepting the guidance of the *vraja-gopīs*, and being endowed with the moods of awe and reverence instead, despite being engaged in devotional service, a person will be overcome by knowledge of the Lord's opulence and will not be able to attain the *prema-mayī sevā* of Śrī Rādhā-Kṛṣṇa. The goddess of fortune, Lakṣmī-devī, who worships the Lord in the mood of awe and reverence, could not, despite performing very severe austerities and worship, achieve loving service to Vrajendra-nandana Śrī Kṛṣṇa like that of the *gopīs* of Vraja, without becoming subservient to them.

By the *mantra* and *bhāva*[21] received from the *guru* who is expert in tasting the mellows of Vraja, and by following the appropriate sentiments

21 Here *bhāvas* refers to *ekādaśa bhāvas* – the eleven integral parts of one's spiritual form as a resident of the transcendental Vraja-dhāma, and *pañca-daśā* – five stages of development in one's spiritual absorption, culminating in *samādhi*.

of one's particular relationship with Śrī Kṛṣṇa, one should become absorbed day and night in the remembrance of Śrī Rādhā-Kṛṣṇa's *aṣṭa-kālīya-līlā*, Their eternal pastimes performed throughout the day.

Externally, by the *sādhaka-deha*, one should follow the limbs of *bhakti* such as singing *kīrtana*, chanting a fixed number of holy names daily, and offering prostrated obeisances [to the deities, the Vaiṣṇavas, and to the Lord's *dhāmas*, associates, and pastime places]. Internally however, in one's mentally conceived spiritual body, one should remain absorbed in the eight-fold daily pastimes of Śrī Rādhā-Kṛṣṇa so that one may achieve perfection. If one does not accept the *ānugatya* of the mood of the *gopīs*, and remains fixed in the concept of awe and reverence, thinking, "Śrī Kṛṣṇa is Svayam Bhagavān, the Supreme controller, the Lord of unlimited universes, and I am a most insignificant *jīva*," then even despite performing *bhajana*, one can never achieve Vrajendra-nandana. Being attracted by that service rendered by the Vrajavāsīs, particularly by the *gopīs*, even Lakṣmī-devī, who is worshipful for everyone, came to Vraja to serve Śrī Vrajendra-nandana; yet because of her knowledge of Śrī Kṛṣṇa's opulence (*aiśvarya-jñāna*) and because of her not coming under the guidance of the *vraja-gopīs*, she remains cheated of that service to this very day.

In his commentary on *Śrī Caitanya-caritāmṛta* called *Śrī Anubhāṣya*, Śrīla Bhaktisiddhānta Sarasvatī Prabhupāda has stated that beyond the present gross and subtle material bodies exists the spiritual body appropriate for the service of Śrī Rādhā-Kṛṣṇa, which is called the *siddha-deha*. As a result of mundane fruitive activities, the *jīva* receives a material body, which due to desires for gross material enjoyment, eventually transforms into the attainment of yet another material body. The *jīva* becomes covered by a subtle body, the mind, by desiring to enjoy materially, and then uses the mind to accomplish this; thereafter, upon death, he achieves another gross body.

In this way, under the influence of his lusty material desires, the pure spirit soul accepts birth in this material world, temporarily taking on both gross and subtle bodies. However, when the nature of his desires changes, the happiness of Śrī Kṛṣṇa becomes everything to him, and he receives an eternal spiritual body in Vaikuṇṭha or Goloka-dhāma, in which he performs transcendental service to Śrī Rādhā-Kṛṣṇa. For the subtle material body, it is impossible to comprehend an object that is beyond either matter or the purview of its own enjoyment. Therefore, only the devotee who is beyond the influence of the three modes of material nature, being attracted by Śrī Kṛṣṇa's transcendental qualities, becomes situated in his own appropriate spiritual body. Assisted by his transcendental senses, he contemplates that object, which is non-material. He performs transcendental service under the guidance of the transcendental moods of the *sakhīs* to achieve, at last, transcendental service unto the lotus feet of Śrī Rādhā-Kṛṣṇa.

Without the *ānugatya* of the *vraja-gopīs*, one does not achieve the service of Vrajendra-nandana Śrī Kṛṣṇa, despite performing *bhajana* with a mood of great awe and reverence. The verse mentioned below from *Śrīmad-Bhāgavatam* proves this:

8.231

nāyaṁ śriyo 'ṅga u nitānta-rateḥ prasādaḥ
sa-yoṣitāṁ nalina-gandha-rucāṁ kuto 'nyāḥ
rāsotsave 'sya bhuja-daṇḍa-gṛhīta-kaṇṭha-
labdhāśiṣāṁ ya udagād vraja-sundarīṇām

Śrīmad-Bhāgavatam (10.47.60)

"'At the time of the festival of *rāsa-līlā*, Bhagavān Śrī Kṛṣṇa enfolded His arms around the necks of the *gopīs* of Vraja and fulfilled all of their desires. The mercy and *prema* that He bestowed upon those *gopīs* was never enjoyed even by the goddess of fortune, Lakṣmī-devī, who is the eternal loving consort of Bhagavān and who always resides on His chest. Nor was such a boon achieved by the most beautiful heavenly damsels, whose bodily luster and aroma are like a lotus flower, what to speak of the beautiful women of this world.'"

The *vraja-gopīs* are glorified everywhere because of their above mentioned *adhirūḍha-bhāva*, yet for Śrī Lakṣmī-devī, who always resides upon the chest of the Lord of Vaikuṇṭha, Śrī Nārāyaṇa, there is no such example of this exalted good fortune. In the same way, despite being the source of all incarnations, Śrī Kṛṣṇa performed actions which society and the common man regard as low-class, such as cow-grazing, eating with monkeys and cowherd boys, stealing butter and yoghurt, and clutching at and stealing the clothes of young girls. Yet, still, He is glorified everywhere and has achieved the utmost limit of exaltedness. Likewise, although the *vraja-gopīs* are non-different from Bhagavān's own self, being the crown jewel of His pleasure giving potency (*hlādinī-śakti*), they are renowned as ladies of the forest-dwelling cowherd community who decorate their bodies with the harsh words used against them by society, which [because they gave up their marriage vows] regards them as being of low character.

Even so, the good fortune that the *vraja-gopīs* have attained is still far more exalted than that of Lakṣmī and other beloveds of Bhagavān. Despite being the one and only beloved of Śrī Nārāyaṇa, and always situated upon His chest, Lakṣmī is still not able to receive the good fortune of the *vraja-gopīs*. If even Lakṣmī cannot achieve such good fortune, then what to speak of the wives of other incarnations of Bhagavān, such Śrī Upendra, who have attained great beauty and good fortune, and whose bodily fragrance and luster are just like those of the lotus flower? In the *rāsa-līlā* festival, the *vraja-gopīs*, when embraced by the arms of Bhagavān Śrī Kṛṣṇa, became exclusive recipients of the utmost limit of exalted and merciful good fortune.

8.232–243

eta śuni' prabhu tāṅre kaila āliṅgana
dui jane galāgali karena krandana

ei-mata premāveśe rātri goṅāilā
prātaḥ-kāle nija-nija-kārye duṅhe gelā

vidāya-samaye prabhura caraṇe dhariyā
rāmānanda rāya kahe vinati kariyā

"more kṛpā karite tomāra ihāṅ āgamana
dina daśa rahi' śodha mora duṣṭa mana

tomā vinā anya nāhi jīva uddhārite
tomā vinā anya nāhi kṛṣṇa-prema dite"

prabhu kahe,—"āilāṅa śuni' tomāra guṇa
kṛṣṇa-kathā śuni, śuddha karāite mana

yaiche śuniluṅ, taiche dekhiluṅ tomāra mahimā
rādhā-kṛṣṇa-premarasa-jñānera tumi sīmā

daśa dinera kā-kathā, yāvat āmi jība'
tāvat tomāra saṅga chāḍite nāriba

nīlācale tumi-āmi thākiba eka-saṅge
sukhe goṅāiba kāla kṛṣṇa-kathā-raṅge"

eta bali' duṅhe nija-nija kārye gelā
sandhyā-kāle rāya punaḥ āsiyā mililā

anyonye mili' duṅhe nibhṛte vasiyā
praśnottara-goṣṭhī kahe ānandita hañā

prabhu puche, rāmānanda karena uttara
ei mata sei rātre kathā paraspara

After hearing this most unprecedented *rasa-siddhānta*, Śrī Caitanya Mahāprabhu became overjoyed and embraced Śrī Rāmānanda Rāya. Each embraced the neck of the other, and both of them began to weep. They passed the entire night in this manner, absorbed in discussions and overwhelmed by ecstatic *prema*. In the morning they departed, so as to tend to their respective duties.

When it became time to part from Śrī Caitanya Mahāprabhu, Śrīman Rāmānanda Rāya caught hold of the Lord's lotus feet and spoke with extreme humility, saying, "O Lord, You have come here just to bestow Your mercy upon me. Therefore, please stay here for at least ten days and purify my polluted mind. Other than You, there is no one who can deliver this *jīva*, and You alone can give love of Kṛṣṇa."

Upon hearing Śrī Rāmānanda Rāya's humble and love-filled words, Śrīman Mahāprabhu said, "Having heard about your good qualities from the mouth of Śrī Sārvabhauma Bhaṭṭācārya, I have come here to hear about Kṛṣṇa from you and thus purify My mind. Now I am seeing your glories, which before I had only heard about. You are the most learned in the *tattvas* of Śrī Rādhā, Śrī Kṛṣṇa, *prema*, and *rasa*. What to speak of ten days, I will not be able to leave you throughout My whole life. We will remain together in Jagannātha Purī, where we shall spend our time happily, completely delighted by speaking *kṛṣṇa-kathā*."

Speaking thus, they both went away to perform their respective duties, and again at dusk, Śrī Rāmānanda Rāya came to meet with Śrīman Mahāprabhu. After greeting each other, they went to a solitary place and sat down. With great happiness, they began to ask each other questions and receive the answers. Śrīman Mahāprabhu asked the questions, and Śrī Rāmānanda Rāya answered them. In this way the entire night passed in discussion.

When the passage explains that they were weeping, it actually means that both were affected by *sāttvika-bhāvas*. For that reason their throats were choked, and because their discussions were full of *prema*, both of them began to cry. Here *goṣṭhī*, or meeting, particularly refers to the conversation between them.

Questions and Answers

What is the topmost knowledge?

8.244

prabhu kahe,—"kon vidyā vidyā-madhye sāra?"
rāya kahe,—"kṛṣṇa-bhakti vinā vidyā nāhi āra"

Śrīman Mahāprabhu asked, "Of all types of knowledge, which is the most important?" Rāmānanda Rāya replied, "*Kṛṣṇa-bhakti* is the essence of all knowledge. Apart from this there is no other type of knowledge."

Śrīla Bhaktivinoda Ṭhākura has explained that in the first line Mahāprabhu asks a question, and in the second line, Śrī Rāmānanda Rāya gives the answer. Mahāprabhu asked, "Which type of knowledge is the topmost?" and Rāya replied, "Apart from knowledge of *kṛṣṇa-bhakti*, there is no other knowledge." This means that, although the *jīva* is an eternal servant of Śrī Kṛṣṇa, because of Śrī Kṛṣṇa's external, or illusionary, potency, the *jīva* forgets his constitutional position and considers his temporary gross body to be his eternal identity.

The knowledge about how to become situated in one's pure eternal form from such a condition, and to realize one's nature as being a servant of Kṛṣṇa – this constitutes *sādhana*, specifically the performance of *bhakti* to Śrī Kṛṣṇa. By this knowledge one can understand *jīva-tattva*, *māyā-tattva*, *bhāgavat-tattva*, and all other *tattvas* progressively. Ultimately, the unconquerable Śrī Kṛṣṇa is controlled by the *śuddha-bhakti* of a devotee. That knowledge, or *vidyā*, which is above all others, is knowledge of the nature of devotion to Śrī Kṛṣṇa. Material knowledge (*jaḍa-vidyā*) leads to material enjoyment, but that *vidyā* which gives knowledge of *viṣṇu-bhakti* is far superior to even knowledge of the impersonal Brahman (*brahma-vidyā*), which is beyond any material knowledge. However, even superior to knowledge of *viṣṇu-bhakti* is knowledge of *kṛṣṇa-bhakti.*

Śrīmad-Bhāgavatam supports this *siddhānta* in so many places:

tat karma hari-toṣaṁ yat
sā vidyā tan-matir yayā

Śrīmad-Bhāgavatam (4.29.49)

"Factual work, or *karma*, is that by which one can satisfy Śrī Hari. Factual *vidyā*, or knowledge, is that by which one's mind is absorbed in Bhagavān."

śravaṇaṁ kīrtanaṁ viṣṇoḥ
smaraṇaṁ pāda-sevanam
arcanaṁ vandanaṁ dāsyaṁ
sakhyam ātma-nivedanam
iti puṁsārpitā viṣṇau
bhaktiś cen nava-lakṣaṇā
kriyeta bhāgavaty addhā
tan manye 'dhītam uttamam

Śrīmad-Bhāgavatam (7.5.23–24)

Śrī Prahlāda Mahārāja says, "The *bhakti* of Bhagavān Viṣṇu has nine limbs: hearing and chanting about the transcendental holy name, form, qualities, and pastimes of Lord Viṣṇu; remembering them; serving His lotus feet; offering the Lord respectful worship; offering prayers to the Lord; becoming His servant; becoming His friend; and surrendering everything unto Him. If one performs these nine limbs of devotion with a mood of surrender, then we should know this to be the topmost knowledge of the scriptures. His cultivation of the scriptures is successful."

And it is also described here:

idaṁ hi puṁsas tapasaḥ śrutasya vā
sviṣṭasya sūktasya ca buddhi-dattayoḥ
avicyuto 'rthaḥ kavibhir nirūpito
yad-uttamaśloka-guṇānuvarṇanam

Śrīmad-Bhāgavatam (1.5.22)

"Learned persons accept as the pinnacle of knowledge the very best verses, which describe Śrī Kṛṣṇa's qualities and activities."

In the following verses spoken between Śrīman Mahāprabhu and Śrī Rāmānanda Rāya, there is a gradation and comparison between the relative worth of material objects and transcendental objects, as well as a discussion of subject matter affiliated with Goloka and Śrī Kṛṣṇa's unmotivated devotional service. The material conception is thus defeated and the worth of transcendence is established.

What is the most glorious act?

8.245

'kīrti-gaṇa-madhye jīvera kon baḍa kīrti?'
'kṛṣṇa-bhakta baliyā yāṅhāra haya khyāti'

Śrī Caitanya Mahāprabhu then asked, "Out of all glorious activities of the *jīva*, which is the greatest?" Śrī Rāmānanda Rāya replied, "To be called a devotee of Lord Kṛṣṇa is the topmost glory of the *jīva*."

In the material world there are many, many glories that may be attributed to a *jīva*, like wealth, wonderful qualities, intelligence, or fame. However, all such reputation is related to this material body. Upon the body's demise, this fame is destroyed along with it. The greatest form of fame in this world is therefore to become a *premī-bhakta*, because such fame is directly related to the soul. The soul is unending and eternal. Factually, it is composed of eternality, knowledge, and bliss (*sac-cid-*

ānanda-maya). Since the soul is never destroyed, the devotees of Śrī Kṛṣṇa are likewise never destroyed. Devotees of Kṛṣṇa are just like a boat, and one cannot know how many *jīvas* they shelter and ferry across the ocean of birth and death. The devotees alone secure the qualification to serve their worshipful Lord. Performing such service, they successfully dispel lamentation, illusion, and attachment forever.

Śrīmad-Bhāgavatam (11.19.40) says, "*vidyātmani bhidā-bādhaḥ* – knowledge of the soul nullifies duality." To be known as a devotee of Śrī Kṛṣṇa is the greatest fame. It is the *jīva's* considered opinion, due to his greed for material objects of sense enjoyment, that service to inert matter constitutes the greatest fame. Actually, the best position is to be known as a *viṣṇu-bhakta*, which is superior even to the topmost fame within this material world. This means to be afforded the position of a knower of Brahman. Yet, greater than the glory of being a devotee of Śrī Viṣṇu is to be renowned as a devotee of Śrī Kṛṣṇa. Indra states in *Garuḍa Purāṇa*:

kalau bhāgavataṁ nāma
durlabhaṁ naiva labhyate
brahma-rudra-padotkṛṣṭaṁ
guruṇā kathitaṁ mama

"In this Age of Kali, it is extremely rare to find one who is celebrated as an excellent devotee, or a *bhāgavata*. However, such a position is superior to that of the major demigods like Brahmā and Mahādeva."

In *Itihāsa-samuccaya*, in the conversation between Śrī Nārada and Puṇḍarīka, Śrī Nārada says:

janmāntara-sahasreṣu
yasya syād buddhir īdṛśī
dāso 'haṁ vāsudevasya
sarvān lokān samuddharet

"'I am Bhagavān Vāsudeva's servant.' A person who realizes this after thousands and thousands of births can deliver the entire universe."

In the conversation between Śrī Kṛṣṇa and Arjuna, as recorded in the *Ādi Purāṇa* it states: "*bhaktānām anugacchanti muktayaḥ śrutibhiḥ saha* – The liberated souls (*mukta-puruṣas*) and the Vedic literatures follow the footsteps of the devotees of the Lord."

In *Bṛhad-nāradīya Purāṇa*, it is further stated:

adyāpi ca muni-śreṣṭhā brahmādyā api devatāḥ
prabhāvaṁ na vijānanti viṣṇu-bhakti-ratātmanām

"Until today, even the great sages and demigods such as Brahmā did not know the influence of a devotee absorbed in *viṣṇu-bhakti*."

The *Garuḍa Purāṇa* similarly states:

brāhmaṇānāṁ sahasrebhyaḥ satra-yājī viśiṣyate
satra-yāji-sahasrebhyaḥ sarva-vedānta-pāragaḥ
sarva-vedānta-vit-koṭyā viṣṇu-bhakto viśiṣyate
vaiṣṇavānāṁ sahasrebhya ekānty eko viśiṣyate
ekāntinastu puruṣā gacchanti parama padam

"Out of thousands of *brāhmaṇas*, one who is qualified to perform sacrifices is the best, and out of many thousands of such qualified *brāhmaṇas*, one who is learned in the Vedānta is considered the best among all. Out of thousands of such knowledgeable *brāhmaṇas*, one who is a devotee of Lord Viṣṇu is the best, and out of many thousands of devotees of Viṣṇu, one who is a one-pointed Vaiṣṇava is the best. Indeed, such an unalloyed Vaiṣṇava certainly attains the supreme destination."

In *Śrīmad-Bhāgavatam* (3.13.4), it is stated:

śrutasya puṁsāṁ sucira-śramasya
nanv añjasā sūribhir īḍito 'rthaḥ
tat-tad-guṇānuśravaṇaṁ mukunda-
pādāravindaṁ hṛdayeṣu yeṣām

"O *muni*, hearing the qualities of a devotee in whose heart the lotus feet of Śrī Mukunda are always present is the main fruit of one who has undergone long, hard endeavor in the study of the scriptures. This is the opinion of learned persons."

In *Nārāyaṇa-vyūha-stava* it is said:

nāhaṁ brahmāpi bhūyāsaṁ
tvad-bhakti-rahito hare
tvayi bhaktas tu kīṭo 'pi
bhūyāsaṁ janma-janmasu

"I do not aspire to take birth as a Brahmā, if I am to be a Brahmā devoid of devotion. I am praying to get the association of Your devotees, even if I have to take thousands of births as an insect."

sva-dharma-niṣṭhaḥ śata-janmabhiḥ pumān
viriñcatām eti tataḥ paraṁ hi mām
avyākṛtaṁ bhāgavato 'tha vaiṣṇavaṁ
padaṁ yathāhaṁ vibudhāḥ kalātyaye

Śrīmad-Bhāgavatam (4.24.29)

Śrī Mahādeva says to Śrī Maitreya, "A person who properly executes his occupational duty, or *varṇāśrama-dharma*, for one hundred births becomes qualified to occupy the post of Brahmā, and if he becomes even more pious, he can approach me (Lord Śiva). A person who is an unalloyed devotee of Śrī Viṣṇu is immediately promoted after death to the supreme destination, which is completely beyond the material universe. I myself in my Rudra form, as well as other ruling demigods, attain these planets only after the destruction of this material world and our positions within it."

śriyam anucaratīṁ tad-arthinaś ca
dvipada-patīn vibudhāṁś ca yat sva-pūrṇaḥ
na bhajati nija-bhṛtya-varga-tantraḥ
katham amum udvisṛjet pumān kṛta-jñaḥ

Śrīmad-Bhāgavatam (4.31.22)

"By nature Bhagavān is completely full of bliss. He does not care for the goddess of fortune, Lakṣmī, who always remains engaged in His service, or for the kings who perform everything to attain her favor, or for the other demigods. Despite this, He becomes dependent on His devotees. *Aho!* How could a person who is actually grateful, be able to leave Śrī Hari, who is such an ocean of mercy, even for a moment?"

In the words of Śrī Brahmā:

tad astu me nātha sa bhūri-bhāgo
bhave 'tra vānyatra tu vā tiraścām
yenāham eko 'pi bhāvaj-janānāṁ
bhūtvā niṣeve tava pāda-pallavam

Śrīmad-Bhāgavatam (10.14.30)

"Therefore, O Bhagavān, I pray to be so fortunate that in this life or the next, whether I take birth as any kind of bird or beast, I may be a servant of any of Your servants, and again be able to engage in devotional service to Your lotus feet."

In regard to Śrī Prahlāda being the best of all the devotees, Śrī Rudra says:

bhakta eva hi tattvena
kṛṣṇaṁ jānāti na tv aham
sarveṣu hari-bhakteṣu
prahlādo 'ti-mahattamaḥ

Skanda Purāṇa

"A devotee is one who understands Kṛṣṇa in truth. I am not among them. Amongst all of Śrī Hari's devotees, Prahlāda Mahārāja is the best."

In addition:

kvāhaṁ rajaḥ-prabhāva īśa tamo 'dhike 'smin,
jātaḥ suretara-kule kva tavānukampā
na brahmaṇo na tu bhavasya na vai ramāyā,
yan me 'rpitaḥ śirasi padma-karaḥ prasādaḥ

Śrīmad-Bhāgavatam (7.9.26)

Prahlāda Mahārāja is saying, "O my Lord, just look at my position. I was born in a demonic family full of the hellish material qualities of passion and ignorance. What is to be said of Your causeless mercy? You are glorious! You offered Your supreme mercy and kept Your lotus hand on my head. This is the topmost reward and fully removes material miseries. You never did this for Lord Brahmā, Lord Śiva, or even for Lakṣmī."

bhāvanti puruṣā loke
mad-bhaktās tvām anuvratāḥ
bhavān me khalu bhaktānāṁ
sarveṣāṁ pratirūpa-dhṛk

Śrīmad-Bhāgavatam (7.10.21)

Bhagavān Śrī Nṛsiṁha-deva is saying, "O My son Prahlāda! The people in this material world who will follow your example will become My devotees. You are an ideal for all of My devotees."

The Pāṇḍavas are far superior, even to *bhakta* Prahlāda:

yūyaṁ nṛ-loke bata bhūri-bhāgā
lokaṁ punānā munayo 'bhiyanti
yeṣāṁ gṛhān āvasatīti sākṣād
gūḍhaṁ paraṁ brahma manuṣya-liṅgam
sa vā ayaṁ brahma mahad-vimṛgya-
kaivalya-nirvāṇa-sukhānubhūtiḥ
priyaḥ suhṛd vaḥ khalu mātuleya
ātmārhaṇīyo vidhi-kṛd guruś ca

Śrīmad-Bhāgavatam (7.10.48–49)

The spiritual master of the demigods, Śrī Nārada Muni, said to the Pāṇḍavas: "O Yudhiṣṭhira, of all the people on this Earth planet, your good fortune is exceedingly glorious, because the Absolute Truth, Parabrahman, the all-pervading Supersoul, has taken a human form and secretly lives in your palace. Great saintly persons, who purify the entire creation, again and again visit you and your palace for His *darśana*.

"Great saintly persons continually search for Him, the Paramātmā, the Parabrahman, and the all peaceful embodiment of topmost ecstasy, who is completely devoid of even the slightest trace of *māyā*. That same Śrī Kṛṣṇa for whom they search is your beloved friend, well-wisher, your maternal cousin, worshipful deity, obedient servant, and spiritual master. Indeed, He is like your very own self."

Superior to the Pāṇḍavas are the Yādavas:

aho bhoja-pate yūyaṁ
janma-bhājo nṛṇām iha
yat paśyathāsakṛt kṛṣṇaṁ
durdarśam api yoginām

Śrīmad-Bhāgavatam (10.82.28)

At the time of the solar eclipse at Kurukṣetra, the assembled earthly kings said, "O King of the Bhojas, Ugrasena, among all the men of this world, only the lives of you Yadus are truly successful. You are glorious! You are greatly blessed, because you continuously behold Śrī Kṛṣṇa, who is rarely visible even to great *yogīs*."

tad-darśana-sparśanānupatha-prajalpa-
śayyāsanāśana-sayauna-sapiṇḍa-bandhaḥ
yeṣāṁ gṛhe niraya-vartmani vartatāṁ vaḥ
svargāpavarga-viramaḥ svayam āsa viṣṇuḥ

Śrīmad-Bhāgavatam (10.82.30)

"O Ugrasena, you have marital and blood relationships with Śrī Kṛṣṇa. Not only that, you constantly see and touch Him, and you walk, talk, sleep, sit, and dine with Him. You are caught in the net of family affairs, which is the path to hell, but in your palace the all-pervading Lord Viṣṇu, the mere *darśana* of whom makes one forget about residence in heaven and liberation, has taken one form and resides there with you."

Uddhava is superior to the Yadus:

na tathā me priyatama
ātma-yonir na śaṅkaraḥ
na ca saṅkarṣaṇo na śrīr
naivātmā ca yathā bhavān

Śrīmad-Bhāgavatam (11.14.15)

"O Uddhava, as a *premī-bhakta* you are more dear to Me than My son, Brahmā; than Śaṅkara; than My real brother Balarāma; and than Lakṣmī, who is My wife. You are more dear to Me than My own self."

In *Śrīmad-Bhāgavatam* (11.16.29), Śrī Kṛṣṇa says, "*tvaṁ tu bhāgavateṣv aham* – O Uddhava, you represent Me amongst My *premī-bhaktas*; indeed, you are Me," and also again in *Śrīmad-Bhāgavatam* (3.4.31), "*noddhavo 'ṇv api man-nyūno* – Uddhava, you are not even fractionally less than Me."

Superior to Śrī Uddhava are the *gopīs* of Vraja:

etāḥ paraṁ tanu-bhṛto bhuvi gopa-vadhvo
govinda eva nikhilātmani rūḍha-bhāvāḥ
vāñchanti yad bhāva-bhiyo munayo vayaṁ ca
kiṁ brahma-janmabhir ananta-kathā-rasasya

Śrīmad-Bhāgavatam (10.47.58)

Śrī Uddhava prayed, "Of all embodied beings upon this earth, these *gopīs* are certainly the best and they alone are successful, because they have the utmost divine ecstasy named *mahābhāva* for the soul of all souls, Bhagavān Śrī Kṛṣṇa. Their most exalted loving position is coveted not only by those who are desirous of liberation due to being afraid of material existence, nor only by greats saints and liberated *mukta-puruṣas*, but also by devotees such as myself. However we are unable to achieve it. If one cannot achieve the *rasa* emanating from topics of the *kathā* of Bhagavān, then what is the benefit of taking birth again and again as Lord Brahmā and having a life span of millions of years?"

In *Bṛhad-vāmana Purāṇa*, Śrī Brahmā says to Bhṛgu and the other *ṛṣis*:

śaṣṭi-varśa-sahasrāṇi mayā taptaṁ tapaḥ purā
nanda-gopa-vraja-strīṇāṁ pāda-reṇūpalabdhaye
tathāpi na mayā prāptās tāsāṁ vai pāda-reṇavaḥ
nāhaṁ śivaśca śeṣaśca śrīśca tābhiḥ samāḥ kvacit

"Although I performed severe austerities for sixty thousand years to attain the dust from the *vraja-gopīs'* lotus feet, I was unable to attain it. You should clearly understand that I (Brahmā), Śaṅkara, Śeṣa, and Lakṣmī are not equal to the *vraja-gopīs*."

In the *Ādi Purāṇa*, Śrī Bhagavān says:

na tathā me priyatamo brahmā rudraś ca pārthiva
na ca lakṣmīr na cātmā ca yathā gopī-jano mama

"O Pārtha (Arjuna), not even Brahmā, Śiva, Lakṣmī-devī, or even My own self is as dear to Me as the *gopīs* of Vraja."

Among the *vraja-gopīs*, Śrīmatī Rādhikā is the most excellent, and Śrī Kṛṣṇa is indeed Her dear-most beloved. Taking Her mood and complexion He came as Śrī Gaurāṅga, whose topmost confidential servitor is Śrīla Rūpa Gosvāmīpāda. Śrī Rūpa's single-pointed followers are widely celebrated as *rūpānugas*, and he is described thus in *Caitanya-candrāmṛta*:

āstāṁ vairāgya-koṭir bhavatu śama-dama-kṣānti-maitry-ādi-koṭis
tattvānudhyāna-koṭir bhavatu bhavatu vā vaiṣṇavī-bhakti-koṭiḥ
koṭy-aṁśo 'py asya na syāt tad api guṇa-gaṇo yaḥ svataḥ-siddha āste
śrīmac-caitanya-candra-priya-caraṇa-nakha-jyotir-āmoda-bhājām

"Persons who are receiving the bliss coming from the rays of the effulgent toe nails of the lotus feet of Śrī Caitanya Mahāprabhu's beloved devotees are fully qualified with all transcendental qualities. The unlimited good qualities that are found in the devotees of Viṣṇu, such as strong renunciation, equanimity, sense control, forgiveness, and friendship with all living entities, even if multiplied millions of times, cannot be compared to a fraction of the transcendental attributes of those who are the recipients of the mercy of the devotees of Śrī Caitanya Mahāprabhu."

What is the greatest treasure?

8.246

'sampattira madhye jīvera kon sampatti gaṇi?'
'rādhā-kṛṣṇe prema yāṅra, sei baḍa dhanī'

Śrīman Mahāprabhu asked, "Of all the different varieties of riches, what is the greatest treasure of the *jīva*?" Śrī Rāmānanda Rāya replied, "Whoever possesses the wealth of *prema* to Śrī Rādhā-Kṛṣṇa is the wealthiest."

In this world, the *jīvas* possess many sorts of wealth, but these material riches are destructible. From the ancient past till now they have they not given anyone any real happiness, nor shall they ever do so in the future. Never mind the ordinary *jīvas*, Indra's opulences and Lord Brahmā's own planet are destructible and thus are merely fleeting. Such wealth may be destroyed at any moment. Yet, whoever possesses the wealth of *prema* to Śrī Rādhā-Kṛṣṇa is truly the wealthiest person. Even Svayam Bhagavān Śrī Kṛṣṇa, who is the wealth of the wealthy, personally runs behind such a person. In actual fact, such a *premī-bhakta* is able to bestow his incalculable wealth of *prema* upon another and make him completely happy forever.

The suffering *jīva* is full of material desires to enjoy, and is totally addicted to matter. He pursues sense gratification and so considers the attainment of material wealth to be his primary duty. But if one comprehensively deliberates upon the various categories of wealth, with subtle spiritual discrimination, then factually no other wealth can compare with the wealth of *prema* for Śrī Rādhā-Kṛṣṇa.

kim alabhyaṁ bhāgavati
prasanne śrī-niketane

tathāpi tat-parā rājan
na hi vāñchanti kiñcana

Śrīmad-Bhāgavatam (10.39.2)

"O Parīkṣit, is there anything unattainable for those devotees who have pleased Śrī Kṛṣṇa, who is the shelter of Lakṣmī, the goddess of fortune? Such devotees can obtain whatever they may fancy, even though they do not desire anything."

What is the greatest distress?

8.247

'duḥkha-madhye kona duḥkha haya gurutara?'
'kṛṣṇa-bhakta viraha vinā duḥkha nāhi dekhi para'

Śrīman Mahāprabhu asked, "Of all kinds of unhappiness, which is the most distressful?" Śrī Rāmānanda Rāya replied, "Separation from the devotee of Śrī Kṛṣṇa is truly the greatest misery. There is no suffering worse than this."

Only they who know the essence of *bhakti* can really know the glories of the devotees of Śrī Kṛṣṇa, and they alone can appreciate the association of a devotee as being the supreme gain. No one else can understand this. It has been said:

sva-jīvanādhika-prārthya-śrī-viṣṇu-jana-saṅgateḥ
vicchedena kṣaṇañ cātra na sukhāṁśaṁ labhāmahe

Bṛhad-bhāgavatāmṛta (1.5.54)

Mahārāja Śrī Yudhiṣṭhira said: "In fact, the association of devotees of Bhagavān Śrī Viṣṇu is more precious to us than our own life. On the other hand, due to separation from those very devotees in this world, we cannot get even a moment of happiness now."

Kṛṣṇa says elsewhere:

mām anārādhya duḥkhārtaḥ
kuṭumbāsakta-mānasaḥ
sat-saṅga-rahito martyo
vṛddha-sevā-paricyutaḥ

"One who fails to worship Me, who is overly absorbed in material life, who does not stick to the path of devotional service, who does not affiliate with saintly personalities, and who does not serve his elders, is a most unhappy fellow."

Who is truly liberated?

8.248

'mukta-madhye kon jīva mukta kari' māni?'
'kṛṣṇa-prema yāṅra, sei mukta-śiromaṇi'

Śrīman Mahāprabhu then said, "Out of all liberated persons, which *jīva* should be accepted as truly liberated?" Rāmānanda Rāya replied, "He who has *prema* for Śrī Kṛṣṇa is the crown jewel of all liberated persons."

The real meaning of *mukta*, or liberated soul, is one who is freed from material bondage. Those fortunate persons in whom *kṛṣṇa-prema* is present are factually the crown jewels among liberated personalities. Parīkṣit Mahārāja has said:

muktānām api siddhānāṁ
nārāyaṇa-parāyaṇaḥ
su-durlabhaḥ praśāntātmā
kotiṣv api mahā-mune

Śrīmad-Bhāgavatam (6.14.5)

"O great sage, even out of many millions of perfected and liberated persons, it is very difficult to meet a *mahā-puruṣa* who is completely and exclusively dedicated to Bhagavān. Such a *premī-bhakta* day and night remains immersed in the pure nectar of *kṛṣṇa-prema* and by continually savoring that indescribable nectar, he becomes forgetful of his own body."

jāya prema bhayo mana-mohana se
vānai choḍa diyā sabaro ghara bārā
bhāva-vibhora rahe niśi-dina
aura nayana bahata avirala dhārā

masta rahe, alamasta rahe
bāke pīche ḍolata nanda ko lālā
'sundara' aise bhakta ke hita
bauhe pasārata madana gopālā

"Those who have love and affection for Madana-mohana Śrī Kṛṣṇa, leave everything for Him, including wife, children, relatives, and home. They are always sinking in love and affection for Him, and due to that love, tears continually flow from their eyes. Such devotees are always blissful, and Śrī Kṛṣṇa always follows behind them wherever they may go. Madana-mohana Śrī Kṛṣṇa waits to embrace such devotees with arms wide open."

A *kṛṣṇa-premī-bhakta* is factually liberated in the above manner.

What is the greatest song?

8.249

'gāna-madhye kona gāna—jīvera nija dharma?'
'rādhā-kṛṣṇera prema-keli'—yei gītera marma'

Śrīman Mahāprabhu asked, "Among many songs, which one is the natural activity of the living entity?" Śrī Rāmānanda Rāya replied, "Songs that describe Śrī Rādhā-Kṛṣṇa's love-filled pastimes (*prema-keli-līlā*) are the vital core of all."

Without intrinsic *dharma*, nothing can exist; without the intrinisic *dharma* of the soul, the soul cannot exist. Every question asked by Śrīman Mahāprabhu referred to the soul; He never inquired using the words "human beings" or "mankind." For the benefit of the *jīvas*, Śrīman Mahāprabhu asked about duties pertaining to the intrinsic activity (*svarūpa-dharma*) of the *jīva*. Therefore, it is the constitutional position of the living being to perform *saṅkīrtana*, or congregational chanting, of the loving pastimes of Śrī Rādhā-Kṛṣṇa. Owing to the great ecstasy of *prema* inherent within Their amorous pastimes, simply hearing such songs creates an awakening within one's internal consciousness. Thus, a song that intrinsically consists of such glorification is the real essence of all songs. Those songs that are found in *Śrīmad-Bhāgavatam* – such as *Veṇu-gīta*, *Gopī-gīta*, *Bhramara-gīta*, and *Yugala-gīta* – are classified as being *svarūpa-dharma*, or the constitutional function of the spirit soul. *Sāma Veda* is a body of prayers that are also accepted as songs. By nature the *jīva* is the eternal servant of Śrī Kṛṣṇa. It is, therefore, his factual religion to sing about the pastimes of his worshipful deity.

anugrahāya bhaktānāṁ
mānuṣaṁ deham āsthitaḥ
bhajate tādṛśīḥ krīḍa
yāḥ śrutvā tat-paro bhavet

Śrīmad-Bhāgavatam (10.33.36)

In order to bestow His mercy upon the *jīvas*, Śrī Bhagavān manifests His human-like form and performs such pastimes that induce anyone who hears about them to become devoted to Him. The living beings, now dedicated to the Lord, become ecstatic in *prema* and begin to sing of His pastimes.

The best of saints, Śrī Śukadeva Gosvāmī, has said that when Śrī Kṛṣṇa goes to the forest for cow-grazing, He gets tired from walking so far. Using a friend's lap as a pillow, He falls asleep. Some friends massage His feet, while others fan Him very slowly. To please Him while He rests happily, the animals and birds sing of His amorous pastimes with Śrī Rādhā.

What is the most beneficial activity?

8.250

'śreyo-madhye kona śreyaḥ jīvera haya sāra?'
'kṛṣṇa-bhakta-saṅga vinā śreyaḥ nāhi āra'

Śrīman Mahāprabhu asked, "Out of all beneficial activities, which is the most favorable for the living entities?" Rāmānanda Rāya replied, "There is no pursuit more auspicious than to associate with Śrī Kṛṣṇa's devotees."

Śreya means "auspicious." The result of affiliating with Śrī Kṛṣṇa's devotees is that one is able to obtain *kṛṣṇa-prema*. Therefore, the association of these devotees is the ultimate form of good fortune. Having forgotten his *svarūpa* as the eternal servant of Śrī Kṛṣṇa, the *jīva* instead becomes the servant of the illusory potency (*māyā*), and as he is ground upon the mortar of *māyā*, he suffers great misery. However, when the *jīva* gains the association of one of Śrī Kṛṣṇa's devotees by devotional activities that he has performed unknowingly or even accidentally (*ajñāta-sukṛti*), then under the shelter of those elevated souls, he is gradually enabled to comprehend his state of opposition to Bhagavān, whereupon he abandons sensual happiness, and begins to internalize himself. The devotees of Śrī Kṛṣṇa are just like veritable touch-stones, which convert iron into gold, and they can transform the *jīvas* who come in their association into touch-stones as well.

manye bhāgavataḥ sākṣāt
pārṣadān vo madhu-dvisaḥ
viṣṇor bhūtāni lokānāṁ
pāvanāya caranti hi

Śrīmad-Bhāgavatam (11.2.28)

The king of Videha, Śrī Nimi Mahārāja, is saying to Śrī Nārada, the saint among the demigods, "My lord, I understand that you are indeed an eternal associate of Bhagavān Madhusūdana, because such eternal associates travel everywhere in order to purify the materialistic living entities."

ata ātyantikaṁ kṣemaṁ
pṛcchāmo bhāvato 'naghāḥ
saṁsāre 'smin kṣaṇārdho 'pi
sat-saṅgaḥ śevadhir nṛṇām

Śrīmad-Bhāgavatam (11.2.30)

"O great souls, who purify the three worlds! I ask you – what is the *svarūpa*, or nature, of supreme auspiciousness? And what is the *sādhana* to attain that? In this world, even half a moment's association with a devotee is the cause of supreme good fortune for mankind."

Who should the living entity remember at every moment?

8.251

'kāṅhāra smaraṇa jīva karibe anukṣaṇa?'
'kṛṣṇa-nāma-guṇa-līlā—pradhāna smaraṇa'

Śrīman Mahāprabhu asked, "Whom should the *jīva* remember at every moment?" Śrī Rāmānanda Rāya replied, "The principle objects to keep in mind are Śrī Kṛṣṇa's names, forms, qualities, and pastimes."

In the first stage of *sādhana*, remembrance is done forcefully, but as the living being's oppositional stance towards Śrī Kṛṣṇa gradually diminishes, to that extent the natural remembrance of Śrī Kṛṣṇa's names, forms, qualities, and pastimes takes place. Ultimately, the devotee will not desire to discuss mundane topics, even for a second. Dedicated to not wasting even one second of time, he thus considers wasting a mere moment as being equivalent to universal devastation:

tasmāt sarvātmanā rājan
hariḥ sarvatra sarvadā
śrotavyaḥ kīrtitavyaś ca
smartavyo bhagavān nṛṇām

Śrīmad-Bhāgavatam (2.2.36)

"Therefore, O Parīkṣit, human beings, always and in every circumstance, with their complete energy, should remember, glorify, and hear about Bhagavān Śrī Hari."

Śrī Jīva Gosvāmī in *Śrī Bhakti-sandarbha* has described five types of *smaraṇa*, or remembrance. They are:

(1) *smaraṇa* – to initially inquire, just slightly, about Śrī Kṛṣṇa
(2) *dhāraṇā* – to remember Śrī Kṛṣṇa to a limited extent
(3) *dhyāna* – to experience a partial manifestation, or catch a momentary vision, of Śrī Bhagavān in the heart; or to glimpse His form, dress, or ornaments
(4) *dṛḍha-smṛti* – to retain a fixed meditation upon Bhagavān
(5) *samādhi* – to receive *darśana*, or *sphūrti*, of Bhagavān's *līlās*, which are filled with varieties of *rasa*.

Śrī Kṛṣṇa's name, form, and pastimes are all of the same nature as Śrī Kṛṣṇa. Remembrance of Śrī Kṛṣṇa is the most important remembrance, of which the foundation, or root, is the congregational chanting of the holy name:

'kṛṣṇa-nāma', 'kṛṣṇa-guṇa', 'kṛṣṇa-līlā'-vṛnda
kṛṣṇera svarūpa-sama—saba cid-ānanda

Śrī Caitanya-caritāmṛta, Madhya-līlā (17.135)

"The holy name of Śrī Kṛṣṇa, His transcendental qualities and pastimes as well as the very *svarūpa* of Śrī Kṛṣṇa, are all equal. They are all *cidānanda*, or spiritual and full of bliss."

What is the most important meditation?

8.252

'dhyeya-madhye jīvera kartavya kon dhyāna?'
'rādhā-kṛṣṇa-padāmbuja-dhyāna—pradhāna'

Śrī Caitanya Mahāprabhu asked, "Of all types of meditation, which one should the *jīva* engage in as his actual religious duty?" Śrīla Rāmānanda Rāya replied, "The most important meditation is to contemplate the lotus feet of Śrī Rādhā-Kṛṣṇa."

The *samādhi* of the *jñānīs* and *yogīs* is *nirvikalpa*, a state in which the meditator, the object of meditation, and the act of meditation, do not endure. Since everything becomes *śūnya*, or zero, neither the realization nor the perceiver live on. Conversely, in the *samādhi* of the devotees, the the meditator, the object of meditation (Śrī Bhagavān), and the meditation process all continue. Meditating upon the divine pastimes of the Supreme Person, the devotee obtains a *sphūrti*, or a vision within the heart, of them, and he actually sees his object of meditation:

tasmād ekena manasā
bhagavān sātvatāṁ patiḥ
śrotavyaḥ kīrtitavyaś ca
dhyeyaḥ pūjyaś ca nityadā

Śrīmad-Bhāgavatam (1.2.14)

"Therefore, with a one-pointed mind, one should constantly hear about, chant, meditate upon, and worship Bhagavān, who is very affectionate to His devotees."

Where should one reside?

8.253

'sarva tyaji' jīvera kartavya kāṅhā vāsa?'
'śrī-vṛndāvana-bhūmi yāṅhā nitya-līlā-rāsa'

Śrīman Mahāprabhu asked, "Where should the *jīva* reside, abandoning everything?" Śrī Rāmānanda Rāya replied, "One should live in Vraja-bhūmi, Śrī Vṛndāvana, where the *rāsa-līlā* is eternally performed."

Among the diverse pastimes of *akhila-rasāmṛta-sindhu* Śrī Kṛṣṇa, the *rāsa-līlā* festival reigns as the crest jewel of all. Every other pastime is contained within this *rāsa-līlā*, which occurred in the supreme abode Śrī Vṛndāvana. Whoever possesses the single-minded greed to attain *vraja-prema* should reside only in Śrī Vṛndāvana. Śrī Rāmānanda Rāya's precise meaning is that one should live in Vṛndāvana, which is manifest here on earth, and which is special as it provides the setting for the extraordinary *rāsa-līlā*. There are three principle manifestations of Śrī Vṛndāvana-dhāma: *aprakaṭa*, *prakaṭa*, and *dṛśyamāna*.

(1) *aprakaṭa* – the supreme abode, Śrī Goloka-dhāma, which exists eternally and which is entirely beyond the material elements.

(2) *prakaṭa* – everything that accompanies the Lord's appearance in this world. Because Bhagavān performs His manifest pastimes here in this world, the material nature is involved in His pastimes.

(3) *dṛśyamāna* – that which is within the common, sensual jurisdiction of general people.

āsām aho caraṇa-reṇu-juṣām ahaṁ syāṁ
vṛndāvane kim api gulma-latauṣadhīnām
yā dustyajaṁ sva-janam ārya-pathaṁ ca hitvā
bhejur mukunda-padavīṁ śrutibhir vimṛgyām

Śrīmad-Bhāgavatam (10.47.61)

Śrī Uddhava is saying, "The best thing that could possibly happen for me is that I take birth in this Vṛndāvana as a forest bush, creeper, herb, or even a medicinal root. Ah! If I could become one of these then I would continuously be able to serve the foot-dust from the lotus feet of the *vraja-gopīs*. If I could bathe myself in their foot-dust then I would become most fortunate. How blessed are those *gopīs*. Just see! They have abandoned those things that are most difficult to give up – relations with their family members and the restrictions imposed by society and seniors. They have obtained the lotus feet of Bhagavān, complete absorption in those feet, and the topmost love for Him. What more can I say? Even the Śrutis, which are the Vedic instructions that emanate from the breathing of the Supreme Lord, are still searching for that the same super-excellent, love-laden form of Śrī Kṛṣṇa, but they cannot attain it."

What is the best topic to hear?

8.254

'śravaṇa-madhye jīvera kon śreṣṭha śravaṇa?'
'rādhā-kṛṣṇa-prema-keli karṇa-rasāyana'

Śrīman Mahāprabhu asked, "Out of all topics to hear, which topic is the best for the living entity?" Śrī Rāmānanda Rāya replied, "Hearing about the amorous affairs of Śrī Rādhā-Kṛṣṇa, which is like a medicinal tonic for the ears (*karṇa-rasāyana*), is the best of all."

What to speak of the *jīvas*, even *rasika-śekhara* Śrī Kṛṣṇa hears the songs describing His own loving affairs. After taking complete *sannyāsa*, Śrī Bilvamaṅgala Ṭhākura was traveling towards Śrī Vṛndāvana, singing about the sweet amorous pastimes of Śrī Rādhā-Kṛṣṇa. Being unable to withhold Himself, Śrī Kṛṣṇa began following behind him, listening to his singing. Eventually, those songs were compiled into a book by the same Śrī Bilvamaṅgala Ṭhākura, entitled *Śrī Kṛṣṇa-karṇāmṛta* [meaning "that which pours nectar into the ears of Śrī Kṛṣṇa"]. The amorous affairs of Śrī Rādhā-Kṛṣṇa are compared to the most vital *rasāyana*, life-restoring tonic. *Śravaṇa*, or hearing, is of two types: *vicāra-pradhāna* and *ruci-pradhāna*. In *vicāra*[22]*-pradhāna*, the hearer is full of doubts, just like Arjuna. In *ruci-pradhāna*, the hearer has no doubts in the statements of the scriptures, and he hears the descriptions of the qualities of the Lord, with great relish. Śrī Nārada is an example of this. It is also written:

vikrīḍitaṁ vraja-vadhūbhir idaṁ ca viṣṇoḥ
śraddānvito 'nuśṛṇuyād atha varṇayed yaḥ
bhaktiṁ parāṁ bhāgavati pratilabhya kāmaṁ
hṛd-rogam āśv apahinoty acireṇa dhīraḥ

Śrīmad-Bhāgavatam (10.33.40)

"O Parīkṣit, a grave person who faithfully and continuously hears the narrations of the transcendental pastimes that Bhagavān Śrī Kṛṣṇa performed with the young girls of Vraja, and then describes those pastimes accordingly, achieves supreme devotion for the lotus feet of Bhagavān. He very quickly attains freedom from the diseases of the heart, which are the transformations of lust."

What is the most worshipable object?

8.255

'upāsyera madhye kon upāsya pradhāna?'
'śreṣṭha upāsya—yugala 'rādhā-kṛṣṇa' nāma'

Śrīman Mahāprabhu asked, "Among all worshipable objects, which is the best?" Śrī Rāmānanda Rāya replied, "The holy names of Śrī Rādhā-Kṛṣṇa are the chief worshipable object."

Śrīla Raghunātha dāsa Gosvāmī has said:

22 *Vicāra* means "analysis," or "deliberation."

rādheti nāma nava-sundara gīta-mugdhaṁ
kṛṣṇeti nāma madhurādbhuta-gāḍha-rūpam
sarva-kṣaṇaṁ surabhi-rāga-himena ramyaṁ
kṛtvā tad eva piba me rasane kṣudhārte

Abhīṣṭa-sūcana, text 10

"The name 'Rādhā' is just like fresh, pleasing nectar that enchants the mind, and the name 'Kṛṣṇa' is like astonishingly sweet and thick condensed milk. O tongue tortured by thirst, mix the two together, add the fragrant ice of *anurāga* and continuously drink this superb beverage."

Śrī Narottama Ṭhākura also says: "*rādhā-kṛṣṇa nāma gāṇa, ei se parama dhyāna, āra nā kariha paramāṇa* – the chanting of the holy names of Śrī Rādhā-Kṛṣṇa is the supreme meditation. Do not accept any other process as the goal" (*Śrī Prema-bhakti-candrikā*, song 6 text 15).

Śrī Kṛṣṇa is the very source, or root cause, of all incarnations (*bhāgavat-svarūpa*), and His *hlādinī-śakti* is Śrī Rādhā. Among couples such as Śrī Śiva-Pārvatī, Śrī Lakṣmī-Nārāyaṇa, Śrī Sītā-Rāma, and Śrī Rukmiṇī-Kṛṣṇa, the name of the Divine Couple Śrī Rādhā-Kṛṣṇa is indeed the ultimate object of worship for the *jīvas*:

etāvān eva loke 'smin
puṁsāṁ dharmaḥ paraḥ smṛtaḥ
bhakti-yogo bhāgavati
tan-nāma-grahaṇādibhiḥ

Śrīmad-Bhāgavatam (6.3.22)

"The supreme religious activity, or duty, for the *jīvas* of this world is to attain devotional sentiments for the lotus feet of the Lord, by methods such as chanting the holy names."

What is the fate of those desiring liberation and those desiring sense gratification?

8.256

'mukti, bhukti vāñche yei, kāṅhā duṅhāra gati?'
'sthāvara-deha, deva-deha yaiche avasthiti'

Śrīman Mahāprabhu asked, "What is the fate of those who desire liberation and of those who desire sense gratification?" Śrī Rāmānanda Rāya replied, "Those who desire liberation and those who desire sense gratification achieve the bodies of non-moving species and demigods, respectively.

Those who perform pious activities in this world achieve the bodies of Indra (the king of heaven) or other demigods. Alternatively, they are born into a high-class human family. And those who perform inauspicious activities repeatedly take the bodies of non-moving species (such as trees), worms, insects, birds, and beasts. Those desirous of liberation, who do not have any desire to enjoy materially, or in other words, those whose activities are bereft of consciousness and whose consciousness is in a sleep-like state, attain the bodies of non-moving species of life; while those who are dedicated to material enjoyment attain bodies appropriate for their desires by taking birth in the higher planets as demigods.

muktyai yaḥ prastaratvāya śāstramūce mahāmuniḥ
gautamaṁ taṁ vijānītha yathā vittha tathaiva saḥ

"Those who merge in the undifferentiated Brahman (*sāyujya-mukti*) become unconscious like stones, and achieve a state of spiritual inactivity (destruction). And those who follow the theories of Gautama become liberated and achieve a similar state."

The following pertains to those who are possessed of desires for material enjoyment:

iṣṭveha devatā yajñaiḥ
svar-lokaṁ yāti yājñikaḥ
bhuñjīta deva-vat tatra
bhogān divyān nijārjitān

Śrīmad-Bhāgavatam (11.10.23)

"One who worships the demigods, upon receiving the result of his pious activities, goes to the heavenly planets where he enjoys just like a demigod."

kvacit pumān kvacic ca strī
kvacin nobhayam andha-dhīḥ
devo manuṣyas tiryag vā
yathā-karma-guṇaṁ bhāvaḥ

Śrīmad-Bhāgavatam (4.29.29)

"According to the work he has performed and the modes of nature he has acquired, the living entity takes birth sometimes as a human being, sometimes as a demigod, and sometimes as a bird, an animal, and so on. Blinded by ignorance, the *jīva* sometimes becomes a man, a woman, and sometimes a eunuch."

In the *Śrīmad Bhāgavad-gītā* (9.20–21), also, it says:

trai-vidyā māṁ soma-pāḥ pūta-pāpā
yajñair iṣṭvā svar-gatiṁ prārthayante
te puṇyam āsādya surendra-lokam
aśnanti divyān divi deva-bhogān

te taṁ bhuktvā svarga-lokaṁ viśālaṁ
kṣīṇe puṇye martya-lokaṁ viśanti
evaṁ trayī-dharmam anuprapannā
gatāgataṁ kāma-kāmā labhante

"Those who are full of material desires and dedicated to fruitive activities mentioned in the three Vedas, worship Me and drink *soma-rasa*, the remnants of *yajña*, and pray to ascend to heaven. By the result of their pious activities, they achieve the planet of Indra and enjoy the divine paraphernalia suitable for the demigods.

"After having enjoyed the vast expanses of the heavenly planets, when their stock of pious activities is exhausted, then again they fall into this world of birth and death. Thus, persons who practice this *sakāma-karma*, or reward oriented activity as described in the three Vedas, are full of petty material desires, and they repeatedly wander in the cycle of birth and death."

The observation has been made that in some books, the words *mukti-bhukti* have been substituted for the words *mukti-bhakti*. It follows that those who desire *bhakti*, at the time of perfection, achieve the bodies of associates of Śrī Kṛṣṇa that are suitable to their moods, and render loving service to Him in concordance with their respective *bhāvas*, or feelings of servitude. Their attainment of this service to the Lord has been compared to attaining the body of demigods. As a result of gaining service to Śrī Kṛṣṇa and obtaining a body like that of a demigod, the word *bhakti* is sometimes used instead of *bhukti*, for just as the demigods have freedom to enjoy varieties of happiness, so, too, a devotee attaining an associate's body gets to taste an array of the most astonishing *rasa* by participating in Śrī Kṛṣṇa's pastimes.

8.257–260

arasa-jña kāka cuṣe jñāna-nimba-phale
rasa-jña kokila khāya premāmra-mukule

abhāgiyā jñānī āsvādaye śuṣka jñāna
kṛṣṇa-premāmṛta pāna kare bhāgyavān

ei-mata dui jana kṛṣṇa-kathā-rase
nṛtya-gīta-rodane haila rātri-śeṣe

doṅhe nija-nija-kārye calilā vihāne
sandhyā-kāle rāya āsi' mililā āra dine

"Impersonalists (*brahma-jñānīs*) who are devoid of knowledge of transcendental mellows are like the crows that continue to eat the bitter and tasteless fruit of the neem tree, whereas those who enjoy the mellows of *bhakti-rasa* (*rasikas*) are like the cuckoos who taste the soft and fragrant buds of the mango of *prema*. The unfortunate empiric speculators (*jñānīs*) simply experience the happiness of dry and tasteless impersonal knowledge, and consider themselves fortunate. However, those who are truly fortunate constantly drink the nectar of *kṛṣṇa-prema*. The *jñānīs* remain ignorant of the happiness of *bhakti-rasa*, and merely desire to achieve the *sāyujya-mukti* of merging into Brahman, which is dry (*nīrasa*), devoid of attributes, and which has no taste, form, qualities, pastimes, or astonishing varieties of bliss. Thus they remain absorbed in the delusion of the supposed oneness of the *jīva* and Brahman (*brahma-aikya-jñāna*), which has no real existence at all. Being cheated of *bhakti-rasa*, they simply chew the fruits of the neem tree in the form of the four supposed *mahā-vākyas*, or principle statements, of the Vedas, by chanting *aham brahmāsmi* (I am Brahman), etc."

Śrī Kṛṣṇadāsa Kavirāja Gosvāmī has said that this false knowledge is like the bitter fruit of the neem tree, which is very unpalatable and which is enjoyed by crow-like *jīvas* who are quarrelsome and attached to false logic. Thus *prema* is likened to the buds of a mango tree, whose taste is sweet, well liked, and full of flavorful juice. The devotees of Śrī Kṛṣṇa who taste this are compared to cuckoos. They are fortunate, while the *jñānīs* are bereft of good fortune.

In this way, Śrīman Mahāprabhu and Rāmānanda Rāya passed the full night, relishing the *rasa* of *kṛṣṇa-kathā*, or topics of Kṛṣṇa, and thus as they chanted, danced, and wept, the night ended. The next morning they departed to perform their respective duties, but in the evening Śrī Rāmānanda Rāya returned to meet the Lord again and pass the whole night as before.

The Final Evening

8.261–264

iṣṭa-goṣṭhī kṛṣṇa-kathā kahi' katakṣaṇa
prabhu-pada dhari' rāya kare nivedana

"'kṛṣṇa-tattva', 'rādhā-tattva', 'prema-tattva-sāra'
'rasa-tattva', 'līlā-tattva' vividha prakāra

eta tattva mora citte kaile prakāśana
brahmāke veda yena paḍāila nārāyaṇa

antaryāmī īśvarera ei rīti haye
bāhire nā kahe, vastu prakāśe hṛdaye

That evening, when Śrī Rāmānanda Rāya came to meet Śrīman Mahāprabhu, they discussed topics of Śrī Kṛṣṇa for some time. After this, Śrī Rāmānanda Rāya caught hold of the lotus feet of the Lord and prayed with great humility: "You have manifested within my heart the truths about Kṛṣṇa, Rādhā, *prema*, *rasa*, and varieties of pastimes. This is exactly how Śrī Nārāyaṇa imparted the Vedas to Lord Brahmā. The Supersoul, or the supreme controller within everyone's heart, always speaks internally, not externally, thus granting a manifestation of the desired object within. This is His general practice.

As the *Śvetāśvatara Upaniṣad* (6.8) describes, Śrī Bhagavān manifested and compiled the Vedas, which were disclosed within the heart of Brahmā:

yo brahmāṇaṁ vidadhāti pūrvam
yo vai vedāṁś ca prahiṇoti tasmai
taṁ ha devam ātma-buddhi-prakāśaṁ
mumukṣur vai śaraṇam ahaṁ prapadye

"I accept the shelter of that Bhagavān Śrī Kṛṣṇa, who in the beginning of creation inspired, or manifested, the Vedic knowledge within the heart of Brahmā, and who manifests knowledge of the self (*ātma-buddhi*)."

It is also said:

prāha bhāgavataṁ nāma
purāṇaṁ brahma-sammitam
brahmaṇe bhāgavat-proktaṁ
brahma-kalpa upāgate

Śrīmad-Bhāgavatam (2.8.28)

"Śrī Śukadeva Gosvāmī spoke this *Śrīmad-Bhāgavata Mahā Purāṇa*, which is equal to the Vedas, in the same manner that Bhagavān Himself spoke to Lord Brahmā at the beginning of the creation."

kālena naṣṭā pralaye
vāṇīyaṁ veda-saṁjñitā
mayā 'dau brahmaṇe proktā
dharmo yasyāṁ mad-ātmakaḥ

Śrīmad-Bhāgavatam (11.14.3)

"O My dear Uddhava, with the passage of time, this message of Vedic knowledge was lost when the annihilation took place. Thus when the time of creation came again, I took it upon Myself to instruct Brahmā, and in these instructions I indeed described devotional service to Me (*bhāgavata-dharma*)."

līlā-kathās te kathitāḥ samāsataḥ
kārtsnyena nājo 'py abhidhātum īśaḥ

Śrīmad-Bhāgavatam (12.4.39)

"O best of the Kurus, I have given a brief exposition of Śrī Bhagavān's pastimes. Even Lord Brahmā himself would be incapable of describing these pastimes in their entirety."

kasmai yena vibhāsito 'yam atulo jñāna-pradīpaḥ purā

Śrīmad-Bhāgavatam (12.13.19)

"This *Śrīmad-Bhāgavatam* is the best manifestation of knowledge of the truth of the Supreme Lord. Bhagavān Nārāyaṇa had previously manifested it to Lord Brahmā"

Śrī Rāya's purpose here is to show the similarity between the way that the original poet Śrī Brahmā received complete Vedic knowledge within his mind, simply by the will of Śrī Bhagavān, and the way that Śrīman Mahāprabhu manifested all these truths in the heart of Śrī Rāmānanda Rāya and then had him reveal these same truths by speaking them.

The next verse from *Śrīmad-Bhāgavatam* (1.1.1) gives evidence for Śrī Rāmānanda Rāya's statement:

8.265

janmādy asya yato 'nvayād itarataś cārtheṣv abhijñaḥ svarāṭ
tene brahma hṛdā ya ādi-kavaye muhyanti yat sūrayaḥ
tejo-vāri-mṛdāṁ yathā vinimayo yatra tri-sargo 'mṛṣā
dhāmnā svena sadā nirasta-kuhakaṁ satyaṁ paraṁ dhīmahi

"'We meditate on that Paramātma, that form of eternality and truth, by whom this world is created, maintained, and destroyed; He who pervades all spiritual substances. From that transcendental Being come the spiritual world and the individual living being, both of which are similar in nature to Him. The temporary material creation, however, is different from Him: He is not inert matter, He is conscious; He is not dependent, He is self-manifest; He is not Hiraṇyagarbha Brahmā (who appeared from the navel of Garbhodakaśāyī Viṣṇu), rather He bestowed the Vedic knowledge upon Brahmā. He causes even greatly learned scholars to become bewildered, in the way that illusion creates mirages, such as the so-called appearance of water in the effulgent sunrays, land in water, and water on dry land. This material creation consisting of the states of sleep, dreaming, and deep dreamless sleep, is brought about by the three modes of material nature. By His illusionary potency, this material creation appears eternal, although temporary. By His own self-manifest effulgence, He remains always and in every condition liberated from the illusory potency named *māyā*, and her activities.'"

This explanation is based on the commentary by Śrīla Śrīdhara Svāmī. Our Gosvāmī lineage has also presented the following explanation of this verse:

> "All evidence ascertains that it is that Supreme Truth which creates, maintains, and destroys this universe. Upon deliberating on both the apparent and hidden meanings, one sees that only He is to be known, as He is the original form of all existence. It is He alone who is the self-manifest and independent master of this world that we see. It is He who, as the indwelling Supersoul, gave teachings to *ādi-kavi* (the original poet) Lord Brahmā on that all-pervading truth. Contemplating Him, all greatly learned scholars and *paṇḍitas* fall into illusion again and again. The five material elements seem to exist in Him, but this is like a mirage in the desert. In Him the three types of creative potency – *jīva-śakti*, which manifests the *jīvas*, *māyā śakti*, which manifests the temporary universe, and *cit-śakti*, which manifests the spiritual world – are present in a real form. By the potency generated from His own *svarūpa*, not from another agent, or His *ātma-śakti*, He remains eternally beyond ignorance. We meditate upon that Absolute Truth Śrī Kṛṣṇa."

Śrīla Bhaktivinoda Ṭhākura has given another translation of this verse in his book *Śrī Bhāgavat-arka-marīci-mālā*: A minute portion of the internal potency (*svarūpa-śakti*) is the *taṭasthā-*, or *jīva-śakti*, and the shadow portion of that internal potency is called the external potency, or *māyā-śakti*. From the *taṭasthā-*, or *jīva-śakti* of Bhagavān, the individual spirit souls are manifest, and from *māyā-śakti*, the material world has manifested. Due to having a consciousness of separatism, and thus being opposed to the service of Bhagavān since time immemorial, the soul is put into a condition whereby he is illusioned into thinking that he is controlled by material nature. Bewildered by the false ego and mistaking an object for something else altogether, he considers the material body to be the real self. The soul thus remains connected to this material world. The conclusion is that the material world, full of both moving and non-moving entities, is manifested both directly and indirectly from Bhagavān.

Mixing together *puruṣa*, *prakṛti*, and the *maha-tattva*,[23] there are a total of twenty-eight ingredients in the creation. From these twenty-eight *tattvas* all of the other moving and non-moving groups of living entities are said to be manifest; and of all these *tattvas*, the omniscient Supreme Person is the knower and the embodiment of real knowledge. Scholars have described the method by which one may differentiate between two objects, even though their intrinsic natures may be identical. Among the twenty-eight elements of the creation, there are two types of *puruṣas*, or conscious entities. One is *pūrṇa-puruṣa*, the Supreme Controller, He who is the Lord of the illusory potency called *māyā*, and the second is *aṇu-puruṣa*, or the infinitesimal conscious entity, the *jīva*, who can be controlled by *māyā*. Thus Bhagavān (the Complete Consciousness) is He who knows both the created and the uncreated.

That Bhagavān, who is perfectly served by the strength of His own *svarūpa-śakti*, is situated in His own *svarūpa* even before the creation. Thus He is complete and self-manifesting.

After bestowing mercy upon the heart of the original poet, Śrī Brahmā was able to manifest the real meaning of the Vedas, which due to being exceedingly difficult to understand even for vastly learned persons, are the cause of their bewilderment.

There are three types of creation, namely, that pertaining to spirit, that pertaining to the *jīva*, and that pertaining to dull matter. There are some examples of creation pertaining to spirit, such as fire. Just as fire

---

[23] *Puruṣa* – conscious being; *prakṛti* – material nature; *maha-tattva* – the total material elements.

stays unmanifest until forced to appear, upon the rubbing of two sticks, in the same way even though the entire spiritual creation is eternally present, it only manifests according to the desire of Bhagavān.

There are other examples pertaining to the creation of the *jīva*, such as water. Upon becoming excessively cold, water becomes hard like stone, and upon being excessively heated it becomes vaporous. The *jīva* emanates as a tiny particle of spirit (*cit-kaṇa*) from the sun-like Śrī Kṛṣṇa. Upon becoming opposed to the service of Bhagavān, the *jīva* takes shelter of a transformation of his original *dharma* and becomes bound by the deluding potency called *māyā*. When the *jīva* becomes inclined towards Bhagavān and takes shelter of *bhagavat-prema*, his heart melts and becomes exceedingly soft and affectionate. The fruit of this is the inclination to engage in the service of Bhagavān.

Pertaining to the creation of inert matter the example of the element earth is given. By fashioning clay we can make pots and earthen bowls. In the same way, the material creation is simply a transformation of the sum total of the material elements (*pradhāna*). By Bhagavān's inconceivable potency (*acintya-śakti*), the creation is certainly a reality; it is not false, because it has emanated from *satya-svarūpa* Bhagavān (the very form of truth) even though it is temporary and destructible by nature.

Śrī Bhagavān, the object of His devotees' love, mercifully performs all types of activities by His potencies (*jīva-śakti* and *māyā-śakti*), but He always remains separate from these activities. Immutable, He is situated in His supreme abode, in His own *svarūpa*, resplendent with His full potency [Śrī Rādhā].

The moving and non-moving material creation is manifested directly and indirectly from Śrī Bhagāvan, who is endowed with complete potencies, and who is all-knowing, complete, self-manifest, and beyond any transformation. It is by His mercy that the factual meaning of the Vedas was manifested in the heart of Lord Brahmā, and by His inconceivable potency He remains unchanged even though performing the creation of the spiritual world, the *jīvas*, and the material world. I worship that Supreme Lord Śrī Kṛṣṇa, the Lord of Goloka, whose spiritual form is true and eternal. We will worship Him by remembering and chanting His name, form, qualities, and pastimes, which are all spiritual, being composed of *sat*, *cit*, and *ānanda*.

The sublime philosophy of inconceivable simultaneous oneness and difference between Bhagavān and His potencies (*acintya-bhedābheda*) as preached by Śrī Kṛṣṇa Caitanya Mahāprabhu, is established in the explanation of this verse.

Śrī Rāmānanda Rāya, in quoting all of the above mentioned evidence, intentionally attests that Śrī Gaurasundara alone is factually the controller and instigator of intelligence, to which the Gāyatrī *mantra* refers with the word *bhargo*. He reveals that none other than Śrī Gaurasundara has given this *kṛṣṇa-tattva*, *rādhā-tattva*, *prema-tattva*, and *vilāsa-rasa-tattva*, as spoken from his, Rāya's, mouth.

pracoditā yena purā sarasvatī
vitanvatājasya satīṁ smṛtiṁ hṛdi
sva-lakṣaṇā prādurabhūt kilāsyataḥ
sa me ṛṣīṇām ṛṣabhaḥ prasīdatām

Śrīmad-Bhāgavatam (2.4.22)

"At the time of creation, in order to awaken within Brahmā remembrance of the previous *kalpa*, He inspired the presiding goddess of knowledge, who manifested herself through the mouth of Brahmā in the form of the Vedas and as the different limbs of knowledge. May Śrī Bhagavān (Śrī Caitanya Mahāprabhu), who is the root cause of all knowledge, be merciful upon me, and manifest Himself within my heart."

Śrī Jīva Gosvāmī says that the word *satyam* indicates *jñānam-anantaṁ brahma*, or the Supreme Truth. This *para-tattva* is – in terms of His *svarūpa*, His energy, His thinking, feeling strength, and willing – completely independent and eternally all-pervading. The *para-tattva* is *sarva-śaktimān* (omnipotent), *sarva-avatārī* (the source of all incarnations), *sarveśvara* (the Supreme Controller), *param-satya* (the Supreme Truth), and *para-brahma* (the Supreme Soul) – He is Vrajendra-nandana Śrī Kṛṣṇa.

In his commentary, Śrīla Viśvanātha Cakravartī Ṭhākura explains that Śrī Kṛṣṇa is directly and indirectly the *upādāna-kāraṇa*, or the ingredient cause of creation, and also *nimitta-kāraṇa*, the efficient cause. The universe is created, maintained, and destroyed by Him. He has complete knowledge of matter and spirit. He is self-manifest and independent; He does not rely on anyone or anything. By Him, even learned persons are bewildered. Solely by virtue of His desire, He manifested the Vedic knowledge in the heart of Brahmā. One may confuse the three elements of water, fire, and earth, considering any one to be the other – seeing water in earth [a mirage], earth in water [a reflection], or fire in water [the sunrise]. In the same manner, by dint of one's faulty intelligence created from the three modes of material nature, one might consider the body of that Supreme Controller to be false, or knowledge of Him also to be falsehood. Consequently, any object resulting from the mixing together of earth, water, fire, and air is a product of *māyā's* creation, and as such is also false or temporary. He who directs the creative potency of *māyā*, is not false or temporary. He who by His own potency (*svarūpa-śakti*) dispels the influence of *māyā*, or the illusory energy, and is forever present in His eternal abode. I meditate upon that Supreme Controller.

The verse *janmādasya yataḥ* also depicts the pastimes of Śrī Gaurāṅga:

Śrī Gaurāṅga Mahāprabhu, who descended to this world, is Kṛṣṇa covered by His *āśraya-svarūpa* [Śrī Rādhā] in order to taste His [Kṛṣṇa's] own sweetness [*ādasya*]. He manifested His pastimes of birth [*janma*] in the house of Śrī Śacī-devī and Śrī Jagannātha Miśra [*yataḥ*], from Navadvīpa-dhāma [*tataḥ*], and He later traveled [*anvayāt*] to Śrī Nīlācala-dhāma [*itaraśca*]. He is expert [*abhijñaḥ*] in the subject matter of the wealth of *prema* [*artheṣu*], and He [*yaḥ*] expanded [*tene*] the essence of the Vedas, *kṛṣṇa-tattva* [*hṛdā*] before the best of poets Śrī Rāmānanda Rāya [*ya ādi-kavaye*]. In front of Him, even learned scholars [*sūrayaḥ*] are placed into bewilderment [*muhyanti*]. When the five material elements – earth, water, fire, air, and ether [*tejo-vāri-mṛdāṁ*][24] – interact in the right

[24] The five elements represent Mahāprabhu's experiencing *aṣṭa-sāttvika-bhāvas*. For example, when *śuddha-sattva* takes the shelter of water, an incessant flow of tears comes from His eyes, when it takes shelter of fire there is perspiration on His body, when it takes shelter of earth He becomes stunned; air – trembling; ether – pallor. The manifestation of His *sāttvika-vikāras* suffuses *bhakti* into the whole atmosphere.

proportions in the presence of Mahāprabhu, then an astonishing level of *bhakti* arises which allows those proud scholars, the fools, the poor, forest tribes, hunters, aboriginals, bears, trees, creepers, etc., to attain the mercy of *prema-bhakti* and become inclined towards Bhagavān. By the effect of His own [*svena*] internal potency [*dhāmnā*], He dispelled the illusion [*nirasta-kuhakaṁ*] of *jñānī-sādhakas* such as Śrī Vāsudeva Sārvabhauma. He [*yatra*] manifested His opulence and glories in the three blissful *dhāmas* of Navadvīpa, Nīlācala, and Śrī Vṛndāvana [*tri-sargaḥ*]; He is always true and eternal [*amṛṣā*]. I always meditate [*dhīmahi*] upon that *para-tattva* Śrī Gaurāṅga Mahāprabhu, who is *satya-svarūpa*, whose form and nature are eternal and true [*satyaṁ paraṁ*].

8.266–270

eka saṁśaya mora āchaye hṛdaye
kṛpā kari' kaha more tāhāra niścaye

pahile dekhiluṅ tomāra sannyāsi-svarūpa
ebe tomā dekhi muñi śyāma-gopa-rūpa

tomāra sammukhe dekhi kāñcana-pañcālikā
tāṅra gaura-kāntye tomāra sarva aṅga ḍhākā

tāhāte prakaṭa dekhi sa-vaṁśī vadana
nānā bhāve cañcala tāhe kamala-nayana

ei-mata tomā dekhi' haya camatkāra
akapaṭe kaha, prabhu, kāraṇa ihāra"

Śrī Rāmānanda Rāya asked, "O Lord! I have but one more doubt remaining within my heart. Please be merciful upon me and reconcile this. At first I saw Your form as a *sannyāsī*, but now I am seeing Your dark-complexioned form as a cowherd boy (Śrī Śyāmasundara) and also before You I see a golden doll, by whose golden bodily effulgence Your entire body appears now covered. A flute rests upon Your lips, and varieties of ecstatic emotions are causing Your lotus eyes to restlessly rove about. After seeing Your *svarūpa* in this manner, a most astonishing *bhāva* awoke within my heart. O Prabhu, please abandon Your deception and explain the factual cause of this."

Śrī Rāmānanda Rāya is witnessing both the *sannyāsī-svarūpa* of Śrī Caitanya Mahāprabhu, and also His *rasarāja-mahābhāva-svarūpa*. His *sannyāsī* form is Śrī Kṛṣṇa, eternally in separation from Himself, performing austerities; and His *mahābhāva-svarūpa* is a manifestation of the special, eternal mood of *adhirūḍha-mahābhāva*. Being supremely merciful, Śrīman Mahāprabhu now desires to reveal the truth of His identity. Thus, a mood of majesty is manifesting here to some degree. Śrī Rāmānanda Rāya uses the word *sandeha* (doubt), which should be taken to mean "astonishment" in this context. Śrī Kṛṣṇa, standing in His threefold-bending pose, with a flute to His lips, and covered by a golden complexion, is the actual *svarūpa* of Mahāprabhu.

8.271–273

prabhu kahe,—"kṛṣṇe tomāra gāḍha-prema haya
premāra svabhāva ei jāniha niścaya

mahā-bhāgavata dekhe sthāvara-jaṅgama
tāṅhā tāṅhā haya tāṅra śrī-kṛṣṇa-sphuraṇa

sthāvara-jaṅgama dekhe, nā dekhe tāra mūrti
sarvatra haya tāṅra iṣṭa-deva-sphūrti

Keeping His true self concealed, Śrīman Mahāprabhu said to Śrī Rāmānanda Rāya, "You possess an exceedingly deep love for Śrī Kṛṣṇa, and it is the nature of a *mahā-bhāgavata* who has such deep ecstatic love for the Lord to not see everything simply as movable or inert; rather he sees Śrī Kṛṣṇa manifest everywhere. He does not see the moving or non-moving living entities or their forms. He only sees his worshipful Lord everywhere.

The pure devotee possessing unalloyed love for the Lord does not see the forms of the moving and non-moving living entities; rather, everything is a reminder (*uddīpana*) of the sweet pastimes of His worshipful Master. In the same manner, the *jñānīs* see the whole world as the all-pervading Brahman, and the *yogīs* see the presence of the Paramātmā everywhere, and everything within the Paramātmā: "*yo māṁ paśyati sarvatra, sarvaṁ ca mayi paśyati / tasyāhaṁ na praṇaśyāmi, sa ca me na praṇaśyati* – For one who sees Me in all beings and sees all beings in Me, I am never lost, nor is he ever lost to Me" (*Śrīmad Bhagavad-gītā* 6.30).

What, then, will a loving, pure devotee who is expert in tasting the *rasa* of devotional service be capable of perceiving?! His heart melts and he realizes that everything, everywhere, awakens the special ecstasies of remembrance of Śrī Kṛṣṇa's pastimes.

8.274

sarva-bhūteṣu yaḥ paśyed
bhagavad-bhāvam ātmanaḥ
bhūtāni bhāgavaty ātmany
eṣa bhāgavatottamaḥ

Śrīmad-Bhāgavatam (11.2.45)

"The second amongst the nine Yogendras, namely Śrī Havi Mahārāja, said to Nimi Mahārāja, 'O King, he who sees in all living entities and all forms of life, Śrī Kṛṣṇa as the very soul of all souls, and who sees all living entities as parts and parcels of Śrī Kṛṣṇa, is the topmost amongst all devotees, a *mahā-bhāgavata*.'

Essentially, the *parama-bhāgavata* sees his beloved Lord within all living entities, and sees that same *prema* which he has for his worshipful deity present within all living entities. Only those great devotees like

Vyāsa, who know *tattva* fully and who are expert in spiritual attainment, are able to understand Bhagavān. They make the incarnations of Bhagavān, His personal character, form, activities, and His supremely pure ecstatic transformations, their one true goal; consequently, they can genuinely understand His *tattva*. However, it is completely impossible for the demonic *jīvas*, covered by the modes of passion and ignorance, to understand Bhagavān.

The Lord keeps Himself hidden too, just as Śrī Caitanya Mahāprabhu is doing here, but when it comes to the *mahā-bhāgavatas*, the Lord cannot fool them. Every object is limited, or bound, by the three confines of time, place, and circumstance. Yet Bhagavān's nature, which is of unparalleled depth, crosses beyond all of the restrictions presented by these three limits. By His potency known as the *yogamāyā-śakti*, Bhagavān conceals His own form; nevertheless, His exclusive devotees are always able to have His *darśana*.

Śrīla Bhaktisiddhānta Sarasvatī Ṭhākura Prabhupāda describes how Mahārāja Nimi, the king of Videha, inquired from Śrī Havi Mahārāja, one of the nine Yogendras, about the vision, behavior, characteristics, and speech of each of the three levels of devotees, namely, the *uttama* (topmost), *madhyama* (middle class), and the *kaniṣṭha* (neophyte). Śrī Havi Mahārāja replied:

Ātmanaḥ – One who is free from material desires, and transcendentally situated; **bhagavad-bhāvam** – and who has attained a spiritual body (*siddha-deha*) appropriate for the service of Bhagavān, **paśyet** – sees; **ātmany bhāgavaty** – one's own eternal transcendental spiritual body (*siddha-deha*); **bhūtāni paśyed** – in all living entities, [and who sees]; **yaḥ sarva-bhūteṣu** – all conscious entities contained within the moving and non-moving species of life, [within Bhagavān]; **eṣaḥ bhāgavatottamaḥ** – [is] the topmost devotee, the *mahā-bhāgavat*, who always sees the mood of *sevya*, (the one who is to be served, i.e., Śrī Kṛṣṇa), and *sevaka* (the who serves, i.e., the Vrajavāsīs) in everything because he possesses profuse sentiments of devotion and is not subject to external vision.

8.275

vana-latās tarava ātmani viṣṇuṁ
vyañjayantya iva puṣpa-phalāḍhyāḥ
praṇata-bhāra-viṭapā madhu-dhārāḥ
prema-hṛṣṭa-tanavo vavṛṣuḥ sma

Śrīmad-Bhāgavatam (10.35.9)

"The *gopīs*, afflicted by separation and sunk deeply in the remembrance of Śrī Kṛṣṇa, said, 'The trees and creepers, heavily laden with flowers, and fruit, are bowing down with their branches. These creepers are horripilating on the pretext of bringing forth blooming flowers and are revealing that Viṣṇu is present in their hearts. In manifesting this, their happiness is flowing as a stream of honey, and the trees, who are the husbands of those creepers, are showing their happiness in a similar manner.'

This verse is spoken by the lovely maidens of Vraja, who are afflicted by separation from Śrī Kṛṣṇa. Their love and affection for Him is immensely deep. On seeing the trees and creepers of the forest, the *gopīs* think, "These trees and creepers of the forest are supremely attached to Śrī Kṛṣṇa, as we are. Just as the tears flow effortlessly from our eyes when we see Śrī Kṛṣṇa, so these trees and creepers are weeping streams of sweet honey." The *gopīs* are exhibiting the symptom of *mahābhāva*, superimposing their own moods upon others. They are extolling others' good fortune, and out of humility, considering themselves to be worthless and destitute. It is not that Bhagavān's qualities are not revealed in the heart of the *gopīs*; rather, they are attributing their own sweet and most desirable *bhāvas* upon the trees and creepers, and describing that.

8.276–280

rādhā-kṛṣṇe tomāra mahā-prema haya
yāṅhā tāṅhā rādhā-kṛṣṇa tomāre sphuraya"

rāya kahe,—"prabhu tumi chāḍa bhāri-bhūri
mora āge nija-rūpa nā kariha curi

rādhikāra bhāva-kānti kari' aṅgīkāra
nija-rasa āsvādite kariyācha avatāra

nija-gūḍha-kārya tomāra—prema-āsvādana
ānuṣaṅge premamaya kaile tribhuvana

āpane āile more karite uddhāra
ebe kapaṭa kara,—tomāra kona vyavahāra"

Śrīman Mahāprabhu continued, "My dear Rāmānanda, you have great *prema* for Śrī Rādhā-Kṛṣṇa within your heart, and therefore, you see Them manifested everywhere."

Hearing this Śrī Rāmānanda Rāya replied, "My dear Lord, please give up all this cleverness. Do not conceal Your real form from me. In order to taste *rasa*, You have assumed the ecstasy and bodily complexion of Śrī Rādhikā. Savoring *prema* is Your supremely confidential business. Automatically, You have also filled the three worlds with *prema*. You have come here to deliver me. Why, then, are You still acting with cunning? What is this behavior of Yours?"

8.281–284

tabe hāsi' tāṅre prabhu dekhāila svarūpa
'rasarāja', 'mahābhāva'—dui eka rūpa

dekhi' rāmānanda hailā ānande mūrcchite
dharite nā pāre deha, paḍilā bhūmite

prabhu tāṅre hasta sparśi' karāilā cetana
sannyāsīra veṣa dekhi' vismita haila mana

āliṅgana kari' prabhu kaila āśvāsana
"tomā binā ei-rūpa nā dekhe anya-jana

After hearing Śrī Rāmānanda Rāya's statements, Mahāprabhu laughed and revealed His *svarūpa*. What was the nature of that *svarūpa*? It was the combined form of the personification and king of the amorous mellow (*śṛṅgāra-rasarāja*), Śrī Kṛṣṇa, together with the personification of *mahābhāva*, Śrīmatī Rādhikā. Upon seeing this unprecedented form, Śrī Rāmānanda Rāya lost consciousness due to excessive transcendental bliss and fell to the ground. With the touch of His lotus hand, Śrīman Mahāprabhu revived him. Upon regaining consciousness, and again seeing His *sannyāsī* form, Śrī Rāmānanda Rāya became exceedingly astonished. After embracing and pacifying Rāmānanda Rāya, Śrīman Mahāprabhu said, "Rāya, apart from you, no one else can see this form."

8.285–288

mora tattva-līlā-rasa tomāra gocare
ataeva ei-rūpa dekhāiluṅ tomāre

gaura aṅga nahe mora—rādhāṅga-sparśana
gopendra-suta vinā teṅho nā sparśe anya-jana

tāṅra bhāve bhāvita kari' ātma-mana
tabe nija-mādhurya kari āsvādana

tomāra ṭhāñi āmāra kichu gupta nāhi karma
lukāile prema-bale jāna sarva-marma

Śrīman Mahāprabhu again said, "You know everything concerning My internal identity and the truth of My ambrosial activities. Therefore I have shown My special form to you. Actually, My complexion is not golden, but by the touch of the body of Śrīmatī Rādhikā, it has become golden, and apart from the son of the king of Vṛndāvana, Vrajendra-nandana Śrī Kṛṣṇa, She never touches another person. I am able to taste My own sweetness by making My mind and soul one with the mood of Śrīmatī Rādhikā. Before you, I am not able to conceal anything about My true identity. I definitely tried to conceal Myself from you, but because of the extremely powerful nature of your *prema*, I was unable to succeed in this. You have understood My internal form – you know who I am."

Śrī Rāmānanda Rāya could understand very well that Śrīman Mahāprabhu was certainly Vrajendra-nandana Śrī Śyāmasundara. In Vraja, Śrī Kṛṣṇa could not taste the *mādanākhya-bhāva* of Śrīmatī Rādhikā, and for this reason, He became Śrī Gaurāṅga by taking Her *bhāva* and complexion, and came to this world. By Śrī Gaurāṅga's mercy, Śrī Rāmānanda Rāya now remembered his factual position, or his previous birth as Śrī Viśākhā Sakhī, who is qualified for the *darśana* of *rasarāja* Śrī Kṛṣṇa and *mahābhāva* Śrī Rādhā. Bhagavān is the crest jewel of the clever, but the devotee is more clever still. It does not please Bhagavān to defeat His devotee; rather He is very pleased to be defeated by the devotee. Śrī Rāmānanda Rāya detected Mahāprabhu's deception in concealing Himself and defeated Him, thus forcing Him to reveal His form as Gopendra-suta, the son of the king of the cowherds, Śrī Kṛṣṇa.

Śrīman Rāmānanda Rāya did not fall unconscious upon seeing the *sannyāsī* form of Mahāprabhu, or upon seeing His form as Śrī Vrajendra-nandana playing upon the flute. But He did fall into a swoon when he saw the combined form of *rasarāja* Śrī Kṛṣṇa and *mahābhāva* Śrī Rādhā. This is as it should be; Śrī Viśākhā becomes exceedingly blissful upon seeing the form of Śrī Kṛṣṇa, as well as the form of Śrī Rādhā. However, seeing Their combined form caused her to be so overwhelmed with *bhāva* that it became extremely difficult for her to maintain her equanimity, and she lost consciousness. In fact, this form as *rasarāja-mahābhāva* is the essence of all the qualities of all the incarnations of the Supreme Personality of Godhead.

It is said that both Vrajendra-nandana Śrī Kṛṣṇa and Śrī Gaurāṅga Mahāprabhu are the very essence of Godhead, but how has this duality come about in the Supreme Lord? Śrī Kṛṣṇa and Śrī Gaura are not separate *tattvas*, rather they are one. Externally Śrī Gaura is golden due to accepting Śrī Rādhā's sentiments and complexion, but internally He is Kṛṣṇa. In much the same way that in His manifest pastimes, Śrī Kṛṣṇa assumed various disguises such as a lady florist, a doctor, and a lady bangle peddler, thus performing His pastimes of disguised identity, likewise, He has assumed the form of Śrī Gaurasundara, concealing His internal form in order to taste *mahābhāva*. He covered His opulence and displayed His *sannyāsī* form. The mood of the *viṣaya* (the enjoyer, the object of the devotees' *prema*) is prominent in Śrī Kṛṣṇa, the king of the transcendental amorous mellow; whereas in Śrīman Mahāprabhu, where the blackish body of Śrī Kṛṣṇa is covered by the golden complexion of Śrī Rādhā, whose very nature consists of the highest ecstasy of *mādanākhya-mahābhāva*, the prominent mood is of the *āśraya* (the enjoyed, the receptacle of *prema* for Bhagavān).

Without *mādanākhya-mahābhāva*, it is not possible to taste Śrī Kṛṣṇa's unparalleled sweetness. Each and every one of Śrī Kṛṣṇa's limbs is covered by the limbs of Śrī Rādhā. Factually, the complexion of Śrī Kṛṣṇa's body is not golden; it is simply because each one of His limbs is covered by the golden limbs of Śrī Rādhā that He is seen as having a fair complexion. Both Śrī Gaura and Śrī Kṛṣṇa are the self-same Kṛṣṇa, and both are the enjoyers of *sambhoga-rasa* (the happiness of meeting), which means that both are the enjoyers, or *viṣaya-vigraha*. Furthermore, taking shelter of the golden complexion and sentiments of the *āśraya-vigraha* Śrī Rādhā, in the mood of separation, or *vipralambha-rasa*, then Śrī Kṛṣṇa is Śrī Kṛṣṇa Caitanya.

Dhīra-lalita-nāyaka[25] Śrī Nanda-nandana, the original Godhead, is the only form of Śrī Viṣṇu able to enjoy Śrī Kṛṣṇa's *svarūpa-śakti*, Śrī Rādhā, who is the complete *cit-śakti*. No other form of Viṣṇu, only Gopendra-suta Śrī Kṛṣṇa, the son of the king of the cowherd community, partakes of *śṛṅgāra-rasa* (the mellow of amorous love) and is *dhīra-lalita-nāyaka*. All others have strong feelings of *aiśvarya*.

Therefore, Śrī Rādhā alone is described thus:

govindānandinī, rādhā, govinda-mohinī
govinda-sarvasva, sarva-kāntā-śiromaṇi

Śrī Caitanya-caritāmṛta, Ādi-līlā (4.82)

[25] Śrī Kṛṣṇa is portrayed as *dhīra-lalita-nāyaka*. This hero is characterized by skill in amorous pastimes, fresh youthfulness, expertise in humour, the absence of anxiety, and submission to his beloveds.

"Śrī Rādhā gives pleasure to Govinda. She is His enchantress, His all-in-all, and the crown jewel of all His sweethearts."

8.289–290

gupte rākhiha, kāṅhā nā kariha prakāśa
āmāra bātula-ceṣṭā loke upahāsa

āmi—eka bātula, tumi—dvitīya bātula
ataeva tomāya-āmāya ha-i sama-tula"

Śrīman Mahāprabhu said, "O Rāmānanda Rāya, please keep My actual identity, the axiomatic truths, and what I have shown you, secret. Do not reveal them to anyone. People may laugh, since I always act like a madman. Actually, I am a madman, and you are also. Therefore both of us are on the same platform."

Full of humility, Sri Caitanya Mahāprabhu is explaining that in this world of mundane logic and dry speculative knowledge, one should not present these talks before the unqualified non-devotees. Such persons, who are subject to mundane material intelligence, and addicted to logic, argument, and word jugglery, cannot understand the value of such topics, and by laughing at such topics, they will become offenders. We should properly understand the word *pāgala*, or madman, to mean *premonmāda*, or one maddened by the influence of *prema*.

One whose every endeavor is performed under the influence of *prema*, for the happiness of Śrī Kṛṣṇa, and who is intoxicated by the nectar of the path of *rāgānuga-bhakti*, cannot be understood by persons absorbed in the *rasa* of material enjoyment. The materialists will consider the *prema*-filled endeavors of the devotees to be a form of madness. When someone is attracted by *kṛṣṇa-prema*, he abandons all material endeavors and is said to be divinely intoxicated, or transcendentally maddened.

Śrīman Mahāprabhu declared, "O Rāmānanda, you are seeing Me as a separate golden person, but I am not. I am Vrajendra-nandana Śrī Kṛṣṇa. My mood as Gaura has come about by the touch of the body of Śrīmatī Rādhikā, and it is eternal. Whoever is able to understand the basic truth of Śrī Kṛṣṇa Caitanya and of Śrī Rādhā-Kṛṣṇa can, by the mercy of Śrī Svarūpa Gosvāmī, be enabled to obtain eternal service, according to his actual eternal form."

8.291–294

ei-rūpa daśa-rātri rāmānanda-saṅge
sukhe goṅāilā prabhu kṛṣṇa-kathā-raṅge

nigūḍha vrajera rasa-līlāra vicāra
aneka kahila, tāra nā pāila pāra

tāmā, kāṅsā, rūpā, sonā, ratna-cintāmaṇi
keha yadi kāṅhā potā pāya eka-khāni

krame uṭhāite seha uttama vastu pāya
aiche praśnottara kaila prabhu-rāmarāya

Śrīman Mahāprabhu spent ten nights like this with Śrī Rāmānanda Rāya, happily discussing topics of Śrī Kṛṣṇa. The pastimes in Vṛndāvana are very confidential. They described these pastimes at great length, but still they could not exhaust the subject matter. Consider a person who digs and extracts from a mine many varieties of valuable substances such as copper, bell-metal, silver, gold, jewels, and wish-fulfilling jewels, and in the process he extracts items of increasing value one after the other. Exactly thus, by the method of questions and answers, Śrī Rāmānanda Rāya and Śrī Caitanya Mahāprabhu extracted higher and higher axiomatic truths.

In the current verses, Śrī Kavirāja Gosvāmī has given copper, bell-metal, silver, etc., as examples to describe a variety of *sādhyas*, each one superior to the previous. The descriptions begin with *varṇāśrama-dharma* and conclude by revealing the topmost limit of *sādhya*, which is *mādanākhya-mahābhāva*. All of this is accomplished by the stratagem of questions and answers.

Śānta, *dāsya*, *sakhya*, *vātsalya*, and *mādhurya rasas* are compared to copper, bell-metal, silver, gold, and *cintāmaṇi* jewels, respectively. In Vṛndāvana, the water of Yamunā, the sand of the riverbanks, the *kadamba* trees, cows, sticks, and flutes are all manifestations of *śānta-rasa*. Citraka, Patraka, Raktaka, and others are embodiments of *dāsya-rasa*. Dāma, Śrīdāma, Subala, and others are embodiments of *sakhya-rasa*, and Śrī Nanda and Yaśodā are the embodiments of *vātsalya-rasa*. Lastly, Śrī Rādhā, Lalitā, and the other *gopīs* of Vraja are wealthy in their own respective *bhāvas* in *mādhurya-rasa*. Starting from copper, the succeeding metals increase in value through bell-metal and silver to gold, etc. In the same way, from the initial *sādhya* of *varṇāśrama-dharma* there is an incremental scale of *bhakti*, in terms of superiority.

There is a gradation in the examples given. Copper is like following *varṇāśrama-dharma*. As copper is common, of little value, and considered not worth keeping, it is thus rejectable. This *varṇāśrama-dharma* is within the category of *āropa-siddhā-bhakti* (an activity which is not in itself composed of *bhakti*, but is termed *bhakti*). Bell-metal (bronze) is a mixture of the two metals: copper and tin, and is equivalent to *jñāna-miśrā-bhakti*, which is not the topmost *sādhya*. Pure silver is like *svarūpa-siddhā-bhakti*, which is superior to an alloy (a mixed metal). Gold is compared with *prema-bhakti* in the mood of *dāsya*; it is better and more developed than *svarūpa-siddhā-bhakti*.

Jewels correspond to *sakhya-* and *vātsalya-prema-bhakti*, by which Śrī Kṛṣṇa is controlled. The ultimate jewel is the *cintāmaṇi*, or the wish-fulfilling jewel, representing the *mādanākhya-mahābhāva* of Śrīmatī Rādhikā. This is extremely rare and fulfills each and every one of Śrī Kṛṣṇa's desires.

8.295–302

āra dina rāya-pāśe vidāya māgilā
vidāyera kāle tāṅre ei ājñā dilā

"viṣaya chāḍiyā tumi yāha nīlācale
āmi tīrtha kari' tāṅhā āsiba alpa-kāle

dui-jane nīlācale rahiba eka-saṅge
sukhe goṅāiba kāla kṛṣṇa-kathā-raṅge"

eta bali' rāmānande kari' āliṅgana
tāṅre ghare pāṭhāiyā karila śayana

prātaḥ-kāle uṭhi' prabhu dekhi' hanumān
tāṅre namaskari' prabhu dakṣiṇe karilā prayāṇa

'vidyāpūre' nānā-mata loka vaise yata
prabhu-darśane 'vaiṣṇava' haila chāḍi' nija-mata

rāmānanda hailā prabhura virahe vihvala
prabhura dhyāne rahe viṣaya chāḍiyā sakala

saṅkṣepe kahiluṅ rāmānandera milana
vistāri varṇite nāre sahasra-vadana

The next day, Śrīman Mahāprabhu begged Śrī Rāmānanda Rāya to permit Him to leave. When departing the Lord ordered him, "Give up all material business and go to Nīlācala (Śrī Jagannātha Purī). I will quickly finish touring the holy places and return there. The two of us shall remain together at Nīlācala and happily pass our time discussing topics of Śrī Kṛṣṇa."

Saying this Śrīman Mahāprabhu then embraced Śrī Rāmānanda Rāya, and after sending him back to his home, the Lord also left there in order to take rest. After rising from bed the next morning, Mahāprabhu had *darśana* of Hanumān, and after offering him obeisances, the Lord departed for South India to continue His tour of the holy places.

After this He arrived in Vidyāpura, where all the residents followed different religious persuasions, but after seeing Śrīman Mahāprabhu, they gave up their own philosophies and became Vaiṣṇavas. On the other hand, Śrī Rāmānanda Rāya was so overwhelmed in separation from the Lord that he gave up all his material affairs, and became completely immersed in meditation upon Him. Śrīla Kavirāja Gosvāmī explains here, "I have briefly described the meeting between Śrī Caitanya Mahāprabhu and Rāmānanda Rāya. No one can actually describe this meeting completely. It is even impossible for Bhagavān Śrī Śeṣa Nāga, who has thousands of mouths."

Śrīla Bhaktivinoda Ṭhākura describes that the worship of Hanumān is performed in Vidyānagara. He is the deity of that village, and after offering His respects to him, Śrīman Mahāprabhu continued on His tour of the holy places in South India.

8.303–307

sahaje caitanya-caritra—ghana-dugdha-pūra
rāmānanda-caritra tāhe khaṇḍa pracura

rādhā-kṛṣṇa-līlā—tāte karpūra-milana
bhāgyavān yei, sei kare āsvādana

ye ihā eka-bāra piye karṇa-dvāre
tāra karṇa lobhe ihā chāḍite nā pāre

'rasa-tattva-jñāna' haya ihāra śravaṇe
'prema-bhakti' haya rādhā-kṛṣṇera caraṇe

caitanyera gūḍha-tattva jāni ihā haite
viśvāsa kari' śuna, tarka nā kariha citte

The character and activities of Śrī Caitanya Mahāprabhu are just like condensed milk, and the character of Śrī Rāmānanda Rāya is like sweet sugar candy. Mixing them together produces a supremely sweet substance. The pastimes of Śrī Rādhā-Kṛṣṇa are like adding camphor. One who is able to taste this substance is most fortunate. Anyone who even once receives this through the doorway of the ears becomes greedy to relish it further still, and His ears will never want to stop hearing it. By hearing the talks between Rāmānanda Rāya and Śrī Caitanya Mahāprabhu one becomes enlightened with the complete transcendental knowledge of *rasa-tattva* (the mellows of Śrī Rādhā-Kṛṣṇa's pastimes), and he can achieve *prema-bhakti* for the Divine Couple's lotus feet. The activities of Śrī Caitanya Mahāprabhu are supremely confidential, and this confidential knowledge is received only by submissive hearing. Do not allow your mind to make any type of speculation in this regard, and hear these talks with full faith.

8.308–312

alaukika līlā ei parama nigūḍha
viśvāse pāiye, tarke haya bahu-dūra

śrī-caitanya-nityānanda-advaita-caraṇa
yāṅhāra sarvasva, tāṅre mile ei dhana

rāmānanda rāye mora koṭī namaskāra
yāṅra mukhe kaila prabhu rasera vistāra

dāmodara-svarūpera kaḍacā-anusāre
rāmānanda-milana-līlā karila pracāre

śrī-rūpa-raghunātha-pade yāra āśa
caitanya-caritāmṛta kahe kṛṣṇadāsa

This part of Śrīman Mahāprabhu's pastimes is most deep and confidential. One who has faith can achieve this, while it remains very far from those subject to faulty mundane logic. He who has accepted the lotus feet of Śrī Caitanya Mahāprabhu, Śrī Nityānanda Prabhu and Śrī Advaita Ācārya Prabhu as his all-in-all can attain this transcendental treasure of *rasa*.

I (Śrīla Kṛṣṇadāsa Kavirāja Gosvāmī) am offering millions of obeisances to the lotus feet of Śrī Rāmānanda Rāya, from whose lotus mouth Śrī Caitanya Mahāprabhu has spread the wealth of *prema-rasa*. This pastime of Śrī Caitanya Mahāprabhu's meeting with Śrī Rāmānanda Rāya has been described in accordance with the notebooks of Śrī Svarūpa Dāmodara. Desiring the mercy of the lotus feet of Śrī Rūpa and Śrī Raghunātha Gosvāmīs, I, Kṛṣṇadāsa, narrate this *Śrī Caitanya-caritāmṛta*.